York St John

LIBRARY OF NEW TESTAMENT STUDIES

432

formerly the Journal for the Study of the New Testament Supplement series

Editor

Mark Goodacre

PSYCHOLOGICAL ANALYSES AND THE HISTORICAL JESUS

New Ways to Explore Christian Origins

BAS VAN OS

t&t clark

Published by T&T Clark International
A Continuum imprint
The Tower Building, 11 York Road, London SE1 7NX
80 Maiden Lane, Suite 704, New York, NY 10038

www.continuumbooks.com

British Library Cataloguing-in-Publication Data
A catalogue record for this book is available from the British Library

ISBN: HB: 978-0-567-12028-1

Typeset by Free Range Book Design & Production Limited
Printed and bound in Great Britain

CONTENTS

Preface by J. Harold Ellens

For nearly two millennia after his life story began, Jesus of Nazareth definitively shaped almost everything of significance in Western society and culture. However, for nearly two centuries now, since the rise of modern historical and literary criticism, his life story has been severely critiqued. Its truths and warrants have been challenged. The gospels have been peeled apart and their central figure emasculated by scholarly analysis. Indeed, the Jesus of the biblical narratives has survived that critique 'by the skin of his teeth', as it were. Exactly 100 years ago, Albert Schweitzer published *The Quest of the Historical Jesus* in English (1910; German original 1906/1913). Schweitzer considered the question whether Jesus was delusional and then concluded that he was sane but imbued with an otherworldly vision of reality few of us today can really enter into or affirm.

Many biblical scholars and psychologists in the late nineteenth and early twentieth centuries thought the Jesus story in the gospels sounded very much like a progressive psychosis. Few of them were willing to draw that conclusion without some ambivalence. There was that other, admirable side of the person and work of that fellow from Nazareth that urged thoughtful persons to examine carefully how one is to understand the strange side of Jesus while preserving the admirable Jesus of the gospel narratives. Schweitzer solved the problem for himself personally by declaring that Jesus was imbued with a 'thoroughgoing eschatology'. Schweitzer also gave a sidelong glance toward Jesus' apparent apocalyptic view of history. This meant that for Schweitzer it seemed perfectly sane to live life as though one's existence is all about the issues of the heavenly world rather than about this world, and that this world will ultimately be eclipsed by the heavenly world descending upon it and cataclysmically ending history as we know it.

Many scholars were not that kind or imaginative and had largely ruled out any serious interest in the literal character or narrative of the Jesus story. Karl Barth, however, largely agreed with Schweitzer on the point of Jesus' otherworldly or transcendental outlook. Barth declared in his commentary on Paul's Epistle to the Romans that any Christianity detached from eschatology had 'wholly and without exception' nothing to do with the Jesus of the gospels. Barth took issue with his predecessor, Friedrich Schleiermacher, who wished to interpret Jesus as a person uniquely imbued with the universal divine spirit, 'a man with a life full of God', as the modern scholar, Marcus Borg is inclined to declare. Barth indicated that he thought Schleiermacher was too subjective and had lost the historical figure in the Jesus story. Barth also severely criticized his contemporary, Rudolf Bultmann, for cutting and patching the gospel stories to separate the authentic Jesus traditions from editorial additions and manipulations perpetrated by the disciples after the first Easter.

It is into this historical and critical maelstrom that Bas van Os has boldly stepped with his definitive new assessment of the Jesus matter in *Psychological Analyses and the Historical Jesus, New Ways to Explore Christian Origins*. Van Os takes Jesus seriously! Van Os is a rigorously honest and skilful scholar. He has brought to bear upon the question of Jesus' person and work the fruits of deep and careful investigation into psychology, biblical interpretation, sociology, historical analysis, literary criticism and the cryptic mathematics of demography. This book will force a significant change in the way scholars and laypersons, alike, must view that life-and-culture-shaping figure in the gospel stories of 2,000 years ago.

The noted Princeton New Testament scholar, James H. Charlesworth, endorses this important book.

> Impressively interacting with advanced biblical scholarship, and cognizant of the dangers in moving too easily from psychobiography to historical studies (David Stannard in *Shrinking History: On Freud & the Failure of Psychohistory*, 1980), Bas van Os presents a major contribution to Jesus Research (which as I have emphasized is not driven by theology). He agrees with Albert Schweitzer who rightly protested any psychiatric study of the historical Jesus; yet, he demonstrates how recent psychological theory helps in Jesus Research. Employing psychobiology, Bas van Os demonstrates how psychological insights can make plausible what seemed impossible. Using modern research in conversion patterns, new religious movements, and social memory he demonstrates that, within the Jesus Movement, there is continuity between Jesus and his followers. This study is well informed and will be welcome to all who realize that all methodologies can help us avoid subjectivity as we advance Jesus Research.

Similarly, sociologist Rodney Stark (author of *The Rise of Christianity*) underlines the remarkable synthesis of historical and psychological analysis achieved in this new volume:

> I am amazed by this wonderful book. I did not expect to like it, being strongly biased against all forms of psychobiography. But Bas van Os rises far above that field's limitations and achieves a cautious and sensible study.

Wayne Rollins, founder of the Psychology and Biblical Studies section of the Society for Biblical Literature comments:

> This book is a prodigious achievement, breaking ground simultaneously in three fields: historical Jesus research, psychological biblical criticism, and early church studies. With an impressive command of European and American scholarship, Bas van Os initiates us into the world between the historical Jesus and earliest Christianity with an intriguing thesis: that the effect of the former on the latter provides compelling psychological, anthropological, demographic, and sociological insight into the historical Jesus. The reader will not be able to put the book down

as van Os initiates us into five disciplines new to most biblical scholars: attachment theory, rational choice theory, anthropological psychology, the psychology of coping with loss, and role theory, all of which open unexpected doors to a past that is constantly at work in the conscious and unconscious life of church and scholar.

The appearance of this manuscript is exciting news for those of us in the field of psychological biblical criticism and will throw down the gauntlet for historical Jesus scholars to expand their understanding of their subject.

Bas van Os has given us a highly readable volume that defines the battle and picks the terrain for Jesus studies for the next century. It provides a framework for studying historical religious leaders and followers, new ways of assessing how Christianity arose and Jesus' self-consciousness developed, historical findings that illumine Paul's epistles and the gospels, and substantive information for faith and doctrine. He has taken what many of us have laboured with for decades, and cast it in a new perspective that makes it all make greater sense.

J. Harold Ellens
Farmington Hills
Autumn 2010

J. Harold Ellens is an Independent Scholar, having completed his work as a Research Scholar at the University of Michigan, Department of Near Eastern Studies, and as Visiting Lecturer at Princeton Theological Seminary. He is a retired Presbyterian theologian, an ordained minister, a retired US Army Colonel, an international lecturer, a retired Professor of Philosophy, Theology and Psychology, and a psychotherapist in private practice. He has authored, co-authored and edited 185 books, including *Understanding Religious Experience* and (with W.G. Rollins) *Psychology and the Bible: A New Way to Read the Scriptures* (4 vols). He has written 170 professional journal articles, is the Founding Editor and Editor Emeritus of the *Journal for Psychology and Christianity* and Executive Director Emeritus of the Christian Association for Psychological Studies.

FOREWORD

This is not a theological study, although it may yield some insights that theologians can use. Neither is it a historical-critical analysis of the Gospels, although some findings may be of importance to the methodology employed in such analyses. I am not looking for absolute truths or relatively certain facts behind the Gospels, although my findings could be relevant for that enterprise as well.

Rather, this is an attempt to reintegrate psychology in the search for the historical Jesus and his earliest followers from an interdisciplinary and social-scientific point of view. For the past hundred years, since Albert Schweitzer's 1910 dissertation on the psychiatric study of Jesus, most New Testament scholars have tried to avoid the charge of 'psychologizing', even when they wrote about the beliefs and motives of their particular construct of the historical Jesus. The present study is interdisciplinary as it integrates a historical-critical reading of the New Testament with demography, anthropology, sociology and psychology. It does not use the social sciences in a historical-critical approach, but rather uses each discipline in a more general social-scientific approach, with a clear distinction between the observed facts and the theories to explain those facts. The only facts that can be observed are the literary remains of early Christianity. In this approach, any construct of the historical Jesus is a competing theory, and part of a larger theoretical framework, to explain these remains as plausibly and efficiently as possible.

Given the scope of this study, it is impossible to master all disciplines and be fully informed of all relevant research. I immediately apologize to specialists in each field that I touch upon, for the many omissions and mistakes. But the publication of my attempts at understanding Jesus and his impact will hopefully provoke criticisms that will help to verify whether there is value in the reintegration of psychology in our historical analyses of Jesus and the origins of Christianity.

This study could not have been written without the gracious encouragement and help of various scholars, such as Andries van Aarde who printed my first article on the psycho-biographical study of Jesus, even though it was critical of his own work. Edmondo Lupieri and Mauro Pesche gave me the opportunity to present my demographical model of early Christianity at the 2006 Annual Meeting of the Society of Biblical Literature (SBL), and Philip Jenkins was kind enough to offer a stimulating response. Rodney Stark kindly commented on my 2006 paper on the demography of early Christianity as well as on the first draft of this study. Mark Allan Powell and Robert L. Webb offered to include the study in T & T Clark's Library of New Testament Studies. I would also like to thank the members of the SBL sections for Psychology and Biblical Studies and the Psychological Hermeneutics of Biblical Texts, where I could share the progress of my research over the past four years. At the *Vrije Universiteit* in Amsterdam, Kees van der Kooi helped me to see the relevance of this study for contemporary thinking about Jesus, whereas Bert-Jan Lietaert Peerbolte invited me to present my work at the 2010 annual meeting of Dutch and Flemish New Testament scholars. A special word of thanks is due to J. Harold Ellens. After I presented my critique of three psycho-biographical studies of Jesus at the SBL International Meeting in 2006, Harold encouraged me to go on and investigate what psychology can contribute to the study of the historical Jesus. To my objection that this should probably be a multi-disciplinary study by various experts, he countered that someone should make the case first and then see how others react.

Finally, I would like to apologize publicly to my wife Inge and our children, that I used this study as a sorry excuse for not spending more time with them during the last months of writing.

Bas van Os
Leusden
3 July 2010

PART ONE

THE LIMITS AND POTENTIAL
OF PSYCHOBIOGRAPHY

INTRODUCTION TO PART ONE

This study is set up in three parts. In Part One, I will present a theoretical framework in which psychology can make a positive contribution in the search for the historical Jesus and his earliest followers. In Part Two, I will use ancient demographics and modern research in conversion patterns, new religious movements and social memory to assess whether there is sufficient continuity between Jesus and those followers who left us their written traditions about him. In Part Three, I will use various psychological theories to explore the impact that Jesus may have had on his followers.

Part One consists of three chapters. In Chapter 1, the problematic relationship between historical Jesus research and psychology of the past hundred years is explored. Although I agree that Albert Schweitzer was right to protest against the psychiatric study of the historical Jesus, I believe that psychology has served her term in exile and deserves to come back.

In Chapter 2, I analyse three authoritative – but incompatible – psychological portraits of Jesus to demonstrate that it is impossible to write a definitive psychobiography of Jesus from the perspective of his childhood experiences. We cannot observe the historical Jesus and he left us no diaries, letters or other direct records. All that we have are statements made by some of his earliest followers – and they are virtually silent about Jesus' childhood. That does not mean that psychological studies cannot contribute to the process of historical enquiry. But they need a methodological framework in which they take their proper place, neither overreaching nor underachieving.

In Chapter 3, using the methodology developed for psychobiography, I propose the outlines of such a framework, in which the quest for the historical Jesus generates theories to explain the surviving remains of what his earliest followers wrote about him. In generating such theories as well as in sorting out which theories are more plausible than others, we can and should use psychological and sociological insights. A theory that is sociologically or psychologically implausible is just as deficient as a theory that is implausible from a natural, medical or cultural point of view. Sometimes a psychological insight can make plausible what seemed impossible.

Chapter 1

THE EXILE OF THE PSYCHOLOGICAL JESUS

In a sense, psychology follows history. While hearing stories about Jesus, an appreciation of the main character is unavoidable. Some will be able and willing to believe that Jesus was a god, clothed with a real or seemingly real human body. Others will want to see him as an enlightened soul, far ahead of most of his fellow humans. Yet others can only diagnose him as misled or even delusional. In turn, our appreciation of his character feeds into our appropriation of the story: what we believe to be possible or impossible, what we judge to be false, true or exaggerated, inspirational or annoying. When we pass on the story, we will select, adapt and even invent words, deeds and events that will bring out more clearly the type of character we believe Jesus was, or should be in the story that we want to see told. Thus our own psychology and social setting come into play as well, as Hal Childs showed so perceptively for the work of John Dominic Crossan in *The Myth of the Historical Jesus and the Evolution of Consciousness* (Childs 2000). We take the time to read and think about Jesus, because the stories about him have an impact on our life and society. And, consciously or unconsciously, we like to think that 'our' Jesus is somehow more real than 'their' Jesus. This is as true for us as it was for previous generations of writers about Jesus, all the way back to Jesus' earliest followers who passed on and shaped the traditions that we study today. In a way, it is even true for Jesus himself.

Some Early Psychological Analyses of Jesus

As early as 1898, T & T Clark published Thomas Adamson's *Studies of the Mind in Christ*. This Scottish theologian accepted the canonical Gospels, and all of the canonical Gospels, as 'the only authority' on the subject. But he did stress Jesus' humanity (1–2):

> It is possible that many who believe in His actual manhood would recoil from the thought that He had been a real child, helpless on His mother's breast, subject to growth of body and of mind. Many who do believe that He died, never thought weariness or sleep were genuine and regular in Him as in us. Many who know that he answered innumerable and varied questions, as no other could have done, are

horrified at what seems to be the impiety of ascribing to Him any real questions – questions asked because of ignorance, and from a desire for information.

Yet on reflection one sees that if Christ is to be anything at all, even real God, to us, He must be real man. Now that means, of course, much more than the possession of a mere human body; His mind must have been as truly human. Nay, true humanity must have been His at every stage of growth, for His manhood could not be more genuine than His childhood was.

Of course, it is easy for us to believe that His body was real like ours; but we find it more difficult to grasp the fact that He had a true human mind, a mind which worked by the same faculties and the same limits as ours; for we look on Him as the Son of God become man. We instinctively ascribe to Him, even incarnate, the same fullness of knowledge we believe Him to have possessed when pre-incarnate. Or rather, we imagine that He possessed the same knowledge in His humanity as in His Divine nature, because these both belonged to Him. That were, however, to destroy His manhood, both as to completeness and reality. It, and so its significance – His work, – would become a mere show, a pretence, an imposition, a failure.

Whereas Adamson took the humanity of Jesus as the only possible starting point for his analyses of Jesus' mind, he uncritically accepted the Gospel traditions. He had little regard for the historical-critical method that was prevalent in Germany, where numerous scholars sifted through the Gospel accounts in search of the ideal human Jesus. They included aspects of psychology in their discussion of the question whether and how Jesus saw himself as the *Messiah*. Their debate was inaugurated by Heinrich Holtzman (*Die Synoptische Evangelien. Ihr Ursprung und geschichtlicher Charakter*, 1863), who read the development of Jesus' self-consciousness in the Gospel of Mark as the story of an unfolding development. He argued that Jesus claimed to be the Messiah after the events in Caesarea Philippi (Mk 8.27f). Wilhelm Baldensperger in his *Das Selbstbewußtsein Jesu im Lichte der messianischen Hoffnungen seiner Zeit* (1888), argued for a better understanding of the concept of 'Messiah' in Jesus' days, and concluded that Jesus did not so much claim this title, but could not escape his growing understanding of God's will. Wilhelm Bousset (*Jesu Predigt in ihrem Gegensatz zum Judentum*, 1892) countered that Jesus struggled with the Messianic idea, as it was inadequate to express what he felt to be his life's mission. William Wrede, however, argued that psychologizing over Jesus was unwarranted; he placed the Messianic idea in the minds of Jesus' followers, as a response to their resurrection experiences (see *Das Messiasgeheimnis in den Evangelien. Zugleich ein Beitrag zum Verständnis des Markusevangeliums*, 1901). The odd man out was Friedrich Nietzsche who judged the sources as inadequate and developed his 'psychology of the redeemer' from a typological perspective (*Der Antichrist*, 1895); he called Jesus both 'the noblest human being' and 'an idiot'.

Prompted by Baldensperger's work, the American pastor Albert Hitchcock produced his 1906 dissertation entitled *The Psychology of Jesus: A Study of the Development of His Self-Consciousness*. It was published posthumously with a warm recommendation by his doctoral supervisor G. Stanley Hall in 1908. Hitchcock set out to uncover Jesus as 'perfectly human', as the perfect human is the perfect image of God. He thought that he could reach that person, by removing the miraculous accretions of his devout followers. He granted Wrede his 'Messianic secret', but believed Jesus employed it as 'a factor in his training of his disciples'. Although Hitchcock believed in the immortality of the soul, he suggested that the resurrection experiences reflect psychic rather than material facts. I should also mention Scott Fletcher's *The Psychology of the New Testament* (1912), which sought to combine modern biblical scholarship and modern psychology; it has a chapter on Jesus and the psychological impact he had on his disciples.

Meanwhile, however, the historical-critical work of more than a century of European scholarship was meticulously dissected by the young Albert Schweitzer in his *Geschichte der Leben-Jesu-Forschung* (1906/1913). In his *Schlußbetrachtung* in the 1913 edition, he concludes that their image of Jesus was thoroughly unhistorical: 'Sie ist eine Gestalt, die vom Rationalismus, vom Liberalismus belebt und von der modernen Theologie in ein geschichtliches Gewand gekleidet wurde.' Schweitzer unmasked the quest for the historical Jesus as an attempt by scholars to use 'history' as a means to bypass the Jesus of dogma and to reconstruct a new story about Jesus that better served the liberal and romantic notions of their age. He believed they created a Jesus that would fit into the mould of human measure and human psychology (ch. 19): 'Um ihre Leben-Jesu in Markus zu finden, muß die moderne Theologie bei diesem Evangelisten eine Menge von Dingen, und zwar immer die Hauptsachen, zwischen den Zeilen lesen und sie durch psychologische Vermutungen zum Text hinzuerfinden.' Instead, Schweitzer emphasized Jesus' otherness and offensiveness with respect to modern culture. He painted a picture of an intensely religious Jew who died as he expected to inaugurate God's *eschaton* through his own crucifixion.

But the radical otherness of Jesus served a purpose in Schweitzer's own life as well. Schweitzer followed the call of Jesus, to become 'fishers of men', when he left behind his modern and civilized world and became a doctor in Africa. Schweitzer, too, told a story that he thought inspiring:

> Als ein Unbekannter und Namenloser kommt er zu uns, wie er am Gestade des Sees an jene Männer, die nicht wußten, wer er war, herantrat. Er sagt dasselbe Wort: Du aber folge mir nach! und stellt uns vor die Aufgaben, die er in unserer Zeit lösen muß. Er gebietet. Und denjenigen, welche ihm gehorchen, Weisen und Unweisen, werd er sich offenbaren in dem, was sie in seiner Gemeinschaft an Frieden, Wirken, Kämpfen und Leiden erleben dürfen, und als ein unaussprechliches Geheimnis werden sie erfahren, wer er ist … .

Having released Jesus from German Idealists and French Romanticists, Schweitzer had to fight on another ground as well. In order to preserve the sanity of the eschatological Jesus he followed, Schweitzer made an extensive study of the psychopathology of his days to critique *The Psychiatric Study of Jesus* (1913/ET 1948). On historical-critical as well as psychological grounds he dismissed the works of the German George de Loosten (1905), the American William Hirsch (1912), the Frenchman Charles Binet-Sanglé (1910 and 1912), and the Dane Emil Rasmussen (German translation, 1905). Accepting the idea that Jesus saw himself as the Messiah who would bring about the *eschaton* and return on the clouds, they diagnosed him as mentally ill and delusional. According to Schweitzer's summary, De Loosten believed that Jesus' delusion, depression and psychosis were caused by a degenerated ancestry, 'an extremely exaggerated self-consciousness combined with a high intelligence and a very slightly developed sense of family and sex'. Hirsch attributed Jesus' delusion, paranoia, psychosis and megalomania to his unusual mental talents and preoccupation with the Holy Scriptures. Binet-Sanglé diagnosed Jesus as a 'religious paranoid', brought about 'through the suggestive power of various incidents, through John the Baptist, through his own miraculous cures, through the marvelling of those who were healed of their diseases and through the enthusiasm of the disciples'. All three authors thought that Jesus had hallucinations. Schweitzer argued that these psychiatrists have not familiarized themselves with the historical-critical analyses of the Gospels, use sources such as the infancy Gospels and the Talmud that have nothing to contribute to the study of the historical Jesus, and generally read Jesus from the perspective of modern culture. What today is a delusional belief in New York or Berlin may have been the norm in first-century Palestine. Finally, he discussed the theologian Rasmussen, who used the ideal type of the prophet to analyse Jesus. He claimed that Jesus had the same symptoms of 'epilepsy, but also paranoia, *dementia paralytica*, and possibly hysteria' as for example Buddha, Mohammed, Luther, Sabbatai Zvi and Kierkegaard. In Rasmussen's case, Schweitzer criticized his medical knowledge and diagnostic ability.

At the same time that Schweitzer revolutionized the understanding of the historical Jesus, psychology itself was renewed by the work of Sigmund Freud in Vienna, whose *Traumdeutung* (1900) is often cited as the recognition of the unconscious and the start of the psychoanalytical movement, which in its early years included his colleague Alfred Adler and the Swiss Carl Gustav Jung. In 1909, Freud and Jung were invited to Clark University in the United States by its president G. Stanley Hall. The conference there marks the beginning of the acceptance of psychoanalysis in North America. In 1917, Hall published his *Jesus the Christ in the Light of Psychology*. Reviewing the new historical insights, as well as the progress in the field of psychology, he set out to uncover the psychological Jesus Christ, not in a strict historical sense but as 'the true and living Christ of the present and of the future'. In his opinion, the psychology of Jesus and his followers, including modern artists and authors, produced what is essentially a good and beautiful idea that is worthy of being believed in (xviii):

> As a result of all this, I believe I can now repeat almost every clause of the Apostles' Creed with a fervent sentiment of conviction. My intellectual interpretation of the meaning of each item of it probably differs *toto caelo* from that of the average orthodox believer. To me not a clause of it is true in a crass, literal, material sense, but all of it is true in a sense far higher, which is only symbolized on the literal plane.

It is interesting to note that Hall does not even lend a footnote to the work of his student Hitchcock. It was simply overtaken by the new developments in historical criticism and psychology. In his own analyses, Hall made extensive use of the work of Albert Schweitzer. But he had difficulty in understanding how Schweitzer's disappointed Jesus could give rise to early Christianity (400):

> The Jewish apocalyptists felt that God had failed, and the world as it was was lost, and so he must intervene and make it over. With the Jewish history and temper this was a natural, if not inevitable, result of centuries of thwarted hopes. It was obsession with this idea that drove Jesus to his death and despair. The problem how Christianity evolved from this, which, despite Schweitzer's protest, is a purely psychological one, he does very little to solve, so that it still challenges us. Until this is explained his whole conception, original and stimulating as it is, must remain in suspense with doubt predominant.

In other words, as a psychologist, Hall found Schweitzer's reconstruction stimulating but not yet plausible. Hall would rather posit the myth of the dying and rising God as the framework for understanding both Jesus' final days as well as the rise of early Christianity. In psychodynamic terms, the degraded and worn out 'Ur-Father' had died; his empire of fear was over. 'God and man were each atoned and the God-idea as well as Jesus was resurrected from the dead in transfigured form.'

Hall stated in his introduction that he regarded himself 'as a pioneer in a new domain in which he is certain to be followed by many others'. But he was wrong. It is only in retrospect that we can see how devastatingly effective the work of Albert Schweitzer has been. The quest for the historical Jesus had lost its appeal to many theologians, accused as they stood of creating Christ in their own image, and of unwarranted psychologizing. Henceforth, New Testament scholars, especially in Germany, would focus on the Jesus of faith, not the Jesus of history. These scholars would concentrate on the theology of the New Testament authors, and the *Sitz im Leben* of the stories and sayings they used – the study of how such fragments functioned and developed in the early communities of Jesus followers. The great New Testament scholar Bultmann in a sense continued the work of the scholars that preceded Schweitzer, not, however, to find the historical Jesus, but to distil a relevant faith out of the mythical cocktail brewed by early Christians. His mission was the 'Entmythologisierung' of the New Testament.

Without a life story to work with – indeed, with even the myths thrown out – psychologists were left empty-handed. Those who did try to make a psychological analysis did so without significant interaction with biblical scholarship. A chapter on Jesus' inner struggle in a major psychological study like *Exploration of the Inner World* by Anton Boisen (1936), in part inspired by the author's own psycho-religious crisis (*Out of the Depths* 1960, 210), or its follow-up article in a biblical journal (1952), would not influence biblical scholarship (1960, 194).

The Return of the Historical Jesus

The old quest for the historical Jesus was dominated by the negative application of the criterion of dissimilarity (Theissen and Winter 1997/ET 2002): Christ needed to be stripped of the dogmas of his followers in order to arrive at the ideal Jesus. A report that brought his early followers 'distress, damage, or anything undesirable to the witness himself or to those to whom he intends good', or 'honour, advantage, or anything desirable to those he opposes', is likely to be 'an honest report' (Reimarus 1766). Although stated here in positive terms, it has proven to be a *negative* criterion, as it has been used to denounce many 'reports' as later Christian accretions and unhistorical. Schweitzer demonstrated that if you think through this project to its logical end, the result would not only be dissimilar to the Church, but also to modern culture. In fact, you would end up with a very Jewish Jesus and leave everything else to the creativity of his first-century followers.

But the story of a Jesus who blends completely with first-century Judaism and who is very dissimilar to the Jesus of faith proclaimed by the early Church, 'cannot be taken seriously as the means of our forgiveness', said Ernst Käsemann, a student of Bultmann, in 1952 (Theissen and Winter, 113ff.). He inaugurated the so-called 'New Quest', in which the uniqueness of Jesus was sought. He pleaded the positive use of the dual criterion of dissimilarity. A core of trustworthy Jesus traditions consists of those that cannot be attributed to his Jewish environment nor to the early Church. It is a *positive* application, as it only yields snippets that are deemed historical; it says nothing definite about the remainder that does not pass the test. But again, the very nature of the criterion can only yield a partial and skewed image: a fragmentary Jesus detached from both his Jewish context and subsequent Christian dogma.

Understandably, this theologically motivated endeavour could hardly satisfy Jewish or Christian historians, or any historian for that matter. Historical research is aimed at plausible, if tentative, reconstructions of the past. It consciously combines the unique and incidental with what is general and likely to be true. In the English title of Theissen and Winter this is translated as *The Quest for the Plausible Jesus*. The present wave of historical Jesus studies, which took off in the 1980s as the 'Third Quest' or as 'Jesus Research', is just that: historical studies. It does not have a unified theological programme, or absolute criteria (criteria such as dissimilarity or embarrassment, multiple attestation, coherence, contextual plausibility, plausibility in light of the consequences, are used as soft criteria). It professes a secular-historical approach. Moreover, it is open to social sciences and social history; in the last decades a handbook (Blasi, Duhaine and Turcotte, editors, 2002; see also Horsley 1989 and Malina 2001), social histories (Stegemann and Stegemann 1995/ET 1999; Stegemann, Malina and Theissen, editors, 2002), and social science commentaries on the Gospels have been published (Malina and Rohrbaugh 1992 and 1998). The Third Quest locates Jesus the Jew in first-century Palestine, and it takes non-canonical sources into consideration to account for the impact Jesus had in terms of his crucifixion by Pilate and his followers in the first century (Theissen and Winter, 142–3). It involves scholars with various sympathies, Jews, liberals, conservatives, Catholics, evangelicals, agnostics and atheists. It also produces various outcomes, that are often in line with those sympathies, as William Arnal argues in *The Symbolic Jesus: Historical Scholarship, Judaism and the Construction of Contemporary Identity* (2005). Whereas scholars such as Robert Funk and John Dominic Crossan have been accused of a liberal agenda, Arnal notes that scholars who emphasize the Jewishness of Jesus, may (also) have an agenda: some may wish to emancipate Anglo-American scholarship from German (Lutheran) theologians, others may wish to overcome the *aporia* of the Holocaust, again others may favour a conservative Jesus as a role model for their own brand of Christianity. This inherent subjectivity of any historian is perhaps best acknowledged, as it is inevitable. The great advantage of the Third Quest, as I see it, is that it has provided scholars with a platform to exchange ideas, and to debate evidence, methodologies and conclusions from different viewpoints.

By and large, there has grown a consensus among these scholars that Jesus lived in Galilee, was baptized by John, travelled with a group of disciples, enjoyed a reputation as a prophet and a healer, shared meals with people who were sinners or ritually impure, was involved in a temple incident in Jerusalem, was crucified by the Romans, and was believed by some of his followers to have been resurrected from the dead. These 'facts' are attested to in various Christian and non-Christian sources (often as a source of some embarrassment to the witness), they form a coherent framework for his life's story and they fit within a first-century Palestinian context. The way that each scholar works out the details gives various explanations for his crucifixion and the rise of early groups of Jesus followers (who were not yet called Christians). What is notably absent from most reconstructions, however, is the acknowledgement that any plausible story must also be psychologically plausible. Even though each reconstruction assumes much about the intentions and emotions of Jesus and his followers, this is seldom approached methodically. Klaus Berger's excellent book on New Testament psychology (1995/ET 2003) is presented with the explicit intent 'allen Psychologen oder denen, die sich dafür halten, einen direkten und ungenierten Zugriff auf das Neue Testament unmöglich zu machen'. Paul Barnett (2005, 8) believes 'christological conviction' was the engine behind early Christianity and explicitly rejects psychological and sociological explanations as 'doomed to failure', as if they have nothing to do with conviction. This is unfortunate. Both psychobiography and the psychology of religion have made significant progress in the last decades. Its findings are now slowly being taken into account, a delay probably due to Schweitzer's condemnation of psychologizing. An in-depth conversation between psychologists and biblical scholars is necessary to progress in a responsible way. This was recognized at an early stage by such a biblical scholar as Gerd Theissen, who includes sociology and psychology in his historical work on Jesus and early Christianity. The discussion continues within the *Psychology and Biblical Studies* section of the Society of Biblical Literature, whose participants have published such volumes as *Soul and*

Psyche: The Bible in Psychological Perspective (Rollins 1999), *Psychological Biblical Criticism* (Kille 2001), *Psychology and the Bible: A New Way to Read the Scriptures* (4 vols ed. Ellens and Rollins 2004), and *Psychological Insight into the Bible* (ed. Rollins and Kille 2007). In the United Kingdom, a collection of essays with the title *Jesus & Psychology* was published (ed. Fraser Watts 2007). In this collection Justin Meggitt ('Psychology and the Historical Jesus') notes that biblical scholars can denounce psychological analysis of Jesus and at the same time offer their own (non-expert) insights into his motives and self-understanding. The first psycho-biographical studies of Jesus (*inter alia* by Capps, Miller and Van Aarde) have been published and debated. In response, Jesus researcher James Charlesworth called psychobiography 'a new and challenging methodology in Jesus Research' (in Ellens and Rollins 2004, 21–57). He acknowledges that 'historical research leads us to ask questions that have been charted by the psychologists of religion', and concludes: 'It is becoming apparent that as New Testament exegetes need philology and archaeology, those devoted to Jesus Research need not only sociology – a given for decades – but also psychobiography.'

The Need for a Psychologically Plausible Scenario for the Crucifixion and the Early Veneration of Jesus

With regard to the death of Jesus, there are three options: Jesus was killed to his surprise, Jesus willingly took the risk of dying because of some higher purpose, or Jesus sought his death. Only in the first option, one could argue that the psychology of Jesus is not an essential part of the historical reconstruction. In the other options, the decision of Jesus to go to Jerusalem in the face of danger needs to be explained. Most humans would act to avoid danger and death. If Jesus acted differently, we need a psychologically plausible explanation. No reconstruction is plausible or sufficient without a strong psychological component.

With regard to the original followers of Jesus, there may have been various responses to his death. The response that requires a sociologically and psychologically plausible explanation is the veneration of the crucified Jesus. Most humans would have moved on after the death of their charismatic leader, as suggested by Gamaliel in Acts 5.34-39. Why then did some people continue to follow him, and why did some of them come to venerate him as a divine being? A century ago, this question could be kept away from the historical Jesus by seeing the Gospels as second-century products far removed from the historical Jesus, or as the result of a perversion of the Jesus story by a Paul who had neither known nor understood Jesus. But those explanations are no longer tenable. Indeed, Paul had a high Christology, to the point that he arguably can be called a 'proto-Trinitarian' (Fee 2007), even if that term is a bit provocative. But Paul did not act in isolation. He seems to have assumed that his audience appreciated his theology. Furthermore, this was not a 'Pauline' audience. Paul worked together with a large number of people who had become followers of Jesus before, or independently from him. In fact, all major first-century Christian communities in large Graeco-Roman cities were established before or without Paul (see ch. 5).

A growing number of scholars argue that the veneration of Jesus, who became somehow included in the divine identity of God, was both earlier and more 'Jewish' than previously thought (see Hengel 1995; Newman, Davila and Lewis [eds] 1999; Hurtado 2003; Stuckenbruck and North [eds] 2004; Bauckham 2008). Regardless of the hypothesis that there are older layers in the synoptic Gospels with a lower and earlier Christology than Paul's (Casey 1991), we have to explain why many of his earliest followers and even members of Jesus' own family identified the crucified Jesus as God's promised Messiah 'within two decades' after his death (Frederiksen 1988/2000, 136). If it is argued that the resurrection experience was 'the decisive impulse' for the development of a high Christology (Pokorny 1985; see also Hurtado 2005), we still need to explain how it is possible that these experiences caused this specific theological development, for the Christian veneration of Jesus goes well beyond the existing patterns of Jewish Messianic beliefs at the time (Fitzmyer 2007, 183; Zetterholm 2007, xxiv), even if we take into account that the suffering and resurrection of a Jewish Messiah was a concept that some Jews may have entertained (Knohl 2000 and 2009). This is where psychological and sociological theories come into play, for there are only two *loci* where this development may have taken place: in the mind of Jesus and in the community of the earliest followers of Jesus.

With some exaggeration, one can argue that there are two dominant reconstructions of the historical Jesus. Since Albert Schweitzer destroyed the dream of French Romanticism and German Idealism, the eschatological Jesus has been dominant. His apocalyptic worldview and prophetic understanding provided his earliest followers with the necessary inputs to identify him as their Messiah and to experience him as one who was resurrected. With the Jewish Seminar, some say, we have seen the re-emergence of the liberal Jesus: a teacher of wisdom with few apocalyptic expectations, let alone Messianic pretensions (Funk 1999; see also Crossan 1991, Borg 1987). Both portraits are psychologically challenging. How, in the first alternative, did Jesus develop his apocalyptic convictions and understanding of his own role in the *eschaton*? Or, in the second, how did so many of his earliest followers come to ascribe these claims to him, if he was only a teacher of wisdom? Both portraits also suffer from time limitations: could Jesus have developed his prophetic awareness between his baptism and the start of his ministry, or are we supposed to think he came to John thinking he was to inaugurate the *eschaton*? In the second alternative: could his followers, with his own brothers in their midst, have developed a relatively high Christology – or any Christology connected to a crucified man – within one or two decades after his death, if there was little input for this in the life of Jesus himself?

In the concluding chapter, I will come back to this question.

Chapter 2

The Problem of Writing a Psychobiography of Jesus

The genre of psychobiography has had an unfortunate start. In 1910, Freud seized upon a dream about a vulture and its tail that Leonardo Da Vinci had as a little child. Using Egyptian mythology in which the vulture represents the mother-god Mut, and identifying the tail as a penis, Freud translated the message of the dream as follows: 'It was through this erotic relation with my mother that I became a homosexual.' The only problem was that the word 'vulture' was based upon a mistranslation of the Italian *ni(b)bio* – in reality, Leonardo had dreamt about a kite. Why did Freud make this mistake, when he explicitly notes the pitfalls of psychoanalysis on the basis of a single clue and uncertain and fragmentary historical material? Freud also said that the psychobiographer should avoid either pathographizing or idealizing his subject. But Elms (1988) has shown that Freud, at this point in his life, compared himself to Leonardo and believed that they wrestled with similar things, including homosexuality.

In 1980, David Stannard wrote a damning critique of the genre: *Shrinking History: On Freud and the Failure of Psychohistory*. He argues that the psychoanalytical experience of psychiatrists is no basis for historical reconstruction. A story that works in therapy is not yet history, let alone fit for generalizations across cultures and centuries. The 'logical status of psychoanalytic theory, and its offspring psychohistory, is clearly problematic at best', and lacks empirical confirmation.

More fortunate attempts at psychobiography – although each with their share of criticism – can be found in the work of Erik Erikson, especially his book-length *Young Man Luther* (1958) and *Ghandi's Truth* (1969), perhaps because Erikson (who coined the term *identity crisis* for adolescents) pioneered a more balanced type of psychobiography with attention to all phases of an individual's life (see *Encounter with Erikson: Historical Interpretation and Religious Biography*, edited by Capps, Capps and Bradford 1977; see also Szaluta 1999, ch. 4). By the 1980s, it became clear the psychobiography had to become more robust if it was to deal effectively with the justified criticisms of historians. This is not yet visible in *Foundations of Psychohistory* by Demause (1982). But Runyan (1982), Szaluta (1999) and the handbook edited by Schultz (2005) all engage constructively with the concerns of historians and offer methodologies to improve the historical value of psychobiographies.

An interesting collection of essays, responses and rebuttals is *The Historian's Lincoln: Pseudohistory, Psychohistory and History* edited by Boritt (1988; see also the collections of essays edited by Coltrera in 1981, and McAdams and Ochberg in 1988).

I found Runyan's methodological work to be very useful in the case of the historical Jesus, as he also discusses the limits of psychobiography when the availability and quality of historical material is simply insufficient, and includes non-psychoanalytical theories in his methodology. Recent psychobiographies of religious personalities include *Ignatius of Loyola: The Psychology of a Saint* (Meissner 1992), *Inside the Mind of Joseph Smith: Psychobiography and the Book of Mormon* (Anderson 1999), *Augustine: The Scattered and Gathered Self* (Dixon 1999) and *The Reluctant Prophet: A Psychobiography of Archbishop Oscar Romero* (Torres 2008). Psychobiography touches biblical studies in David Halperin's *Seeking Ezekiel: Texts and Psychology* (1993) and Aryeh Kasher's *King Herod: A Persecuted Persecutor. A Case Study in Psychohistory and Psychobiography* (2007).

The Issue: Is It Possible to Write a Psychobiography of the Historical Jesus?

In this chapter I will assess the potential and limitations of psychobiography in the case of the historical Jesus. I will discuss three different studies that have caught the attention of biblical scholars (Ellens and Rollins 2004, volume 4): *Jesus at Thirty: A Psychological and Historical Portrait* by John Miller (1997), *Jesus: A Psychological Biography* by Donald Capps (2000) and *Fatherless in Galilee: Jesus as Child of God* by Andries van Aarde (2001). Miller is a theologian and a psychiatrist. Capps is specialized in the psychology of religion. Van Aarde is a biblical scholar and fellow of the Jesus Seminar. All three of them study the historical Jesus. But in order to evaluate their contributions, I must first discuss the methodology behind writing a psychobiography of a historical figure. The following points are taken from *Life Histories and Psychobiography: Explorations in Theory and Method* (1982) by William McKinley Runyan. Runyan distinguishes between life histories as, on the one hand, a method for interaction with a respondent, and, on the other hand, as a subject matter itself: the 'sequence of events and experiences in a life from birth until death'. According to Runyan, 'the field of psychology is concerned with making true, descriptive, explanatory, and predictive statements' on three levels:

1. What is true of all human beings; here he is thinking of psychodynamic theories, social learning principles, phenomenological processes and cognitive development stages.
2. What is true of groups, for example people of a certain sex, race, social class, culture or historical period.
3. What is true of particular individuals, such as a clinical patient or a historical figure.

I have combined Runyan's observations in the diagram below. Note that over time someone can come to belong to a different social class or age group, etc.

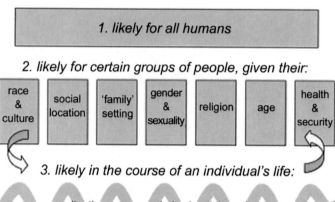

a three-tier model for psychobiography

1. likely for all humans

2. likely for certain groups of people, given their:

| race & culture | social location | 'family' setting | gender & sexuality | religion | age | health & security |

3. likely in the course of an individual's life:

situation x person x behaviour interactions

In the study of an individual life history, psychology is an important field as it can help us understand how history impacted the person, how the subject processed these experiences, and how he or she responded to them. General psychological theories and specific insights in certain groups inform the biographer in the interpretation of this subject. In turn, the study of lives can help the psychologist to develop more general psychological theories. According to Runyan, more general methodological development can take place in two ways. First, the life course of the subject can be described as a series of interactions between the person, the situation and his or her behaviour. Depending on the context, one can apply behavioural, psychodynamic, phenomenological or trait-factor approaches. Second, stage-state and state-sequential analyses can be used to analyse 'aspects of the probabilistic and causal structure of groups of lives, and these analyses can in turn be of use in thinking about the course of individual life histories'. With regard to the case studies of individual lives themselves, Runyan describes criticisms levelled at them. He deplores the lack of good criteria to discern between good and bad psychobiography. Nevertheless, he gives some observations and conclusions that I believe are relevant to our topic:

- In judicial cases, it was found that case studies on the basis of psychometrics, and psychopathology yield relatively poor results. There is some benefit in analyses of long-term patterns of behaviour and typical anecdotes, whereas relatively good predictors of future behaviour come from case studies on the basis of the current traits, attitudes and ambitions of the subject, and the community and family standards in which he or she currently lives.

- In the study of historical lives, a key issue is the availability and nature of the data. 'In the absence of sufficient historical evidence, it is just not possible to develop credible psychological interpretations of the lives of historical figures … . Also, in the absence of evidence about childhood experiences, some types of early developmental explanations are best avoided, as psychological theory is often not sufficiently determinate to permit accurate retrodictions or reconstructions.' Especially psychoanalytical approaches seem to suffer from lack of data, as the subject is, so to speak, 'not on the couch'. In some cases, however, the psychobiographer has advantages over the therapist, for instance when he can observe the entire lifespan of the person, when there is a wealth of ego-documents, and when he can consult a variety of external testimonies and data about the subject. But even so, 'biographical reconstruction is extremely risky and in most cases unjustified'.

- Runyan also observes that 'too many psychobiographies have suffered from flaws such as overemphasizing the psychological, the pathological, or the influence of childhood conflicts. A number of contemporary psychobiographers … are, however, aware of such dangers, and are avoiding them by integrating the psychological with the social and historical, by analyzing not just pathology but also strengths and adaptive capacities, and by studying formative influences not just in childhood but throughout the life span'. On the other hand, 'understandings derived from similar groups to which the subject belongs', socially, culturally and historically, 'are not likely to be sufficient either, because we are often most interested in those individuals who stand out significantly from other Renaissance painters, other nineteenth-century writers, or other twentieth-century American politicians'.

- Finally, Runyan sees that 'errors have sometimes been made in naively assuming that psychoanalytic or other psychological theories could automatically be applied to an individual in any cultural or historical setting', but this does not at all mean that psychohistory does not work or cannot work. Rather, psycho-biographical interpretation is 'a complex three tiered intellectual enterprise which needs to draw not just on those theories which hold universally, but also on group and context-specific generalizations and on idiographic studies of the particular individual'. He argues against Freudian psycho-analytical theory as the main theoretical basis: 'a belief in the paramount importance of early psychosexual experience, should in my opinion probably be revised or abandoned, other aspects of the theory, such as the concept of unconscious motives and conflicts, the notion of identification, and the operation of defense mechanisms may prove of enduring utility for psycho-biographers … . The challenge is to use psychoanalytic theory "selectively", and to also draw on personality psychology, social and cognitive psychology, and developmental psychology.'

Dominian and Drewermann

Two relatively recent works which I do not regard as psychobiographies of the *historical* Jesus need to be mentioned, as they nevertheless illustrate the psycho-analytical concepts that can be applied. The first is Jack Dominian's *One Like Us: A Psychological Interpretation of Jesus* (1998). Although Dominian is aware of historical-critical approaches and even summarizes the work of the Jesus Seminar, he does not write about the historical Jesus. As a believing Catholic he consciously chooses to discuss the humanity of the 'Jesus of Faith, the Son of God, the second person of the Trinity', in other words the *canonical* Jesus. Or, to be more precise: Dominian analyses the Gospels from the viewpoint of 'modern dynamic psychology', to reconstruct an ideal childhood that led to the high self-awareness of the Johannine Jesus, the Word Incarnate. The reason why his work is useful for the subject of this monograph is his summary of the psycho-analytical concepts developed by Freud and his successors read alongside the canonical Gospels:

- Sigmund Freud (1856–1939) postulated that human personality was built on the sexual and aggressive drives developed in early childhood. The unconscious, therefore, is an important factor in human behaviour and wellbeing.
- Melanie Klein (1882–1960), a student of Freud, studied the origin of aggression in babies as part of the dynamics between hunger and gratification. The mother – more precisely, the breast – is the first object of love and hate. Security at this tender age lays the foundation for a secure inner self.
- Donald Winnicott (1896–1971) focused on the mother holding the infant in both a physical and emphatic way. To provide good maternal care, the woman needs a supportive and sensitive husband.
- John Bowlby (1907–90) is the founder of Attachment Theory (see ch. 7). When a young child does not have a secure parental basis from which to explore the world, this may create attachment problems in later life.
- Erik Erikson (1902–94) developed Freud's theory of libido for all stages of life in order to develop such things as basic trust, self-control, conscience and self-esteem. He saw trust, developed in childhood, as the capacity for faith in a later stage.

Dominian notes that 'Freud was a declared atheist, whereas Jung believed in God and the role that the spiritual played in the human personality'. But as he has not been trained in Jungian theory, he leaves Jungian analyses of Jesus to others.

Jung developed the concept of the collective unconscious of humanity, and recognized certain archetypes that appear in (religious) myths from various civilizations. According to Edward Edinger (1996, 9), Jung's book *Aion* (1951) laid the foundation of a new discipline: 'archetypal psychohistory'. In *Aion*, Christ is described as 'a symbol of the self' (ch. 5). A good example is Eugen Drewermann's *Discovering the God Child Within: A Spiritual Psychology of the Infancy of Jesus* (1986/ET 1994). Again, this is not an analysis of the *historical* Jesus. It is rather a depth-psychological reading of the infancy stories in Luke, as a more universal story of religious experience. Historicity is not the issue. Jesus himself has become an archetype, and his story has become a myth that can lead others to discover the divine in their self (see also *Journey out of the Garden: St. Francis of Assisi and the Process of Individuation* by Susan McMichaels, 1997).

John Miller

In 1997, John Miller gave us his *Jesus at Thirty: A Psychological and Historical Portrait*. He approaches Jesus from two angles: his family background as his starting point, and his baptism when he was about 30 years old as his 'turning point'. Miller reconstructs that Jesus grew up in a loving and deeply religious family. Miller believes Jesus had healthy sexual feelings towards women, but remained celibate because of his father's premature death, in his early teenage years. Apart from the emotional loss, the loss was also economic. As the eldest son, he assumed the role of surrogate-father towards his siblings and surrogate-husband towards Mary. Having no wife and children of his own, Jesus went through an identity crisis or the *Age Thirty Transition*, in the sense of the psychologies of Erik Erikson (1968) and Daniel Levinson (1978). 'Without denying Freud's insight that we are heirs as adults to the repercussions of the emotional transitions and crises of our childhood (those of the oral, anal and oedipal stages especially), Erikson insists that these by no means exhaust what can be said about human development.' Each successful transition brings certain 'virtues': the transition from puberty into marriage can produce fidelity and love; having children brings 'generativity'. Levinson discovered that most normal American males experience turbulence in their late twenties and early thirties, forming a Dream and forming mentor relationships. He notes that there is evidence of a similar development in other cultures as well, for example in the early rabbinic *Sayings of the Fathers* (5.24).

In Miller's reconstruction, much of Jesus' suffering was caused by the death of Joseph when Jesus was still young, causing a decisive crisis around his thirtieth year. Jesus' baptism gave him back a father in heaven, and helped him to overcome his pseudolife and seek his own dream. Miller sees this transition as successful in the sense that Jesus emerged as a man capable of 'generativity' – that is a fatherly role – to others, despite the fact that he had not fathered a family of his own. In this, Miller notes, Jesus resembles Erikson's Ghandi (1969, 399): 'The true saints are those who transfer the state of householdership to the house of God, becoming father and mother, brother and sister, son and daughter, to all creation, rather than of their own issue.'

Donald Capps

In 2000, Donald Capps published his *Jesus: A Psychological Biography*. Before presenting his biography, however, Capps discusses four major topics:

1. The critical study of the historical Jesus. In this section, he engages with E.P. Sanders, John Meier, John Dominic Crossan and Marcus Borg.
2. The theory of psychobiography. Here, Capps presents the work of Runyan, which I discussed above.
3. The psychohistory of groups, or to be more precise: the case of the Puritan Plymouth Colony in New England, which he uses as a proxy for 'the emotional ethos of first-century Palestinian family and village life'.
4. The social world of Jesus, summarized in the key-words 'Mediterranean', 'peasant' and 'Galilean'.

In his biographical part, Capps discusses the question of Jesus' relationship with his father, his role as a village healer and his disturbance of the temple. Capps shows that Miller's reconstruction of a loving relationship between Joseph and Jesus is an example of retrodiction, something that Runyan does not favour in psychobiography. The question is, however, to what extent Capps can escape the same charge. Capps disagrees with Meier's assessment that Jesus' youth was insufferably normal, and sides with those who believe that Jesus' birth was illegitimate, that his father was unknown, and that he and his mother were victims of social ostracism. That is the reason why he could not marry. Capps also believes that Joseph did not accept Jesus as his son, and that Jesus' legitimate brothers and sisters looked down on him. The status of first-born would have fallen to his younger half-brother James. This created in Jesus a longing for adoption, which he found with his heavenly father. Because of his illegitimacy, Jesus never married. He did not become a carpenter because his father was one – Capps believes Joseph's occupation was unknown – but because this was a trade that was open to the dispossessed. As such, Jesus was the perfect candidate for John's movement in the desert, where young men formed an alternative religion to that of the temple religion from which the illegitimate Jesus would have been excluded. John's baptism cleansed him of the original sin of his illegitimate conception and enabled his adoption by his heavenly 'Abba'. Thus Jesus took on a 'fictive identity' as the Son of God.

Capps discusses the healing of psychosomatic illnesses from a Freudian perspective. Jesus directed his anger with his biological father and with Joseph, who would not adopt him as a father, towards the demons of his age. But other people, living in a society plagued by 'disabling anxiety', Jesus touched, looked at and spoke to with grace. He transferred unto them his experience of a trustworthy heavenly 'Abba' and thus effected their healing. Capps diagnoses Jesus as a peasant with a utopian-melancholic personality. Jesus' Utopia is the coming kingdom of God. Jesus' melancholy, on a deeper level, contains reproach and rage for his illegitimacy and Joseph's failure to adopt him. In a melancholic personality, this rage is self-directed, and can lead to suicide. But Jesus could overcome his melancholy through two symbolic actions: his baptism cleansed him of the sexual pollution in which he was conceived, and his 'impulsive' (as Capps argues) disruption of the temple stands for a cleansing of his mother's body. Finally, the resurrection appearances are most likely 'reparative dreams', in which his traumatized followers found reassurance.

Andries van Aarde

Around the same time, in 2001, Andries van Aarde published his *Fatherless in Galilee: Jesus as a Child of God*. As a biblical scholar and a reader of Stannard's *Shrinking History* (1980), Van Aarde is 'suspicious of some recent psychoanalytical studies of Jesus, such as John Miller's book, *Jesus at Thirty*'. Instead, Van Aarde uses a different approach; rather than reading the Gospels with the categories of modern psychology in mind, he begins with a hypothetical 'Ideal Type', that of a fatherless child in a Mediterranean and Palestinian setting, and then tests whether Jesus fits the image.

He finds Miller's acceptance of the Joseph tradition uncritical and doubts whether Miller can say that Jesus had an 'emotionally secure' childhood on account of Jesus' love of the word 'Abba', a term for addressing God and Jesus' positive sayings on children, as well as his use of the father-son relationship as image in his parables. Miller's 'deductionistic inference that Jesus performed duties as a surrogate father is dubious', and Van Aarde finds his use of New Testament evidence methodologically debatable. According to Van Aarde, a historical-critical investigation of Jesus' childhood cannot confirm that Joseph was the biological father of Jesus, or that Joseph was of royal descent. The birth narratives of Luke and Matthew postdate the destruction of Jerusalem in 70 CE and the end of the early Christian community in that city. Rather, Jesus emerges as 'a "sinner," away from his home village, trapped in strained relationship with his relatives, but experiencing a fantasy homecoming in God's Kingdom' (2004, 228). According to Van Aarde, 'there are indications that opponents alleged that he was born out of wedlock', a father figure was absent in his life, and Jesus remained a bachelor. As an illegitimate child, a *mamzer*, Jesus was not considered to be a child of Abraham, could not marry a legitimately Jewish woman, and he would have had no access to the temple. Van Aarde postulates the ideal type of Jesus as a fatherless figure, not as 'the real Jesus', but as potentially a way of understanding the evidence before us. In order to develop and, to an extent, test this hypothesis, it should fit with the canonical and non-canonical textual evidence (read with a chronological stratification in mind), it would have to be congruent with the social stratification of first-century Herodian Palestine, and it should be plausible from a social-psychological and a cultural-anthropological point of view.

In his 2004 essay 'Social Identity, Status Envy and Jesus as a Fatherless Child', Van Aarde uses the concept of 'status envy and social identity' in the context of Mediterranean societies. In Western society, the son envies the status of the father, which turns the father into the desired figure of identification. Van Aarde places Jesus in a society where the infant son sleeps with his mother. She manages the household and teaches the young children. This produces a cross-identification with the mother, which such societies resolve through 'elaborate teenage initiation ceremonies with genital operations', hazing, deprivation of sleep and tests of manliness. Thus the mother's child becomes a man with the male characteristics of those societies. Without a father and without such initiation, boys continue to display female behaviour, including 'taking the last place at the table, serving others, forgiving wrongs, having compassion, and attempting to heal wounds' (2004, 237). Without a father, Jesus' status as a male was never 'clarified' in puberty. Whereas the father figure in patriarchal society normally represents God, Jesus learned to approach God directly as a child. As a fatherless figure he saw himself as the protector of other fatherless children in Galilee and of women without a husband. God became their father and he became their brother.

Analysis

James Charlesworth evaluated the contributions of Miller, Capps and Van Aarde positively and concluded that 'with the new methods developed by psychologists of religion, we can explore the psychobiographical possibilities as we imagine Jesus, the man, in his earthly context' (2004, 48). He does not criticize Capps or Van Aarde, other than calling them 'challenging' or 'controversial', but he notes that Miller misses the 'tendencies of the evangelists', and is not current with the scholarly understanding of the word 'Abba'. Miller 'places too much historical validity on Luke's portrayal of Jesus', who is the only one who reported that Jesus began his ministry at age 30. These criticisms do not necessarily invalidate Miller's analysis, but make it less convincing.

From a psychobiographical point of view, Capps criticizes Miller for 'retrodicting', that is for reconstructing the childhood of Jesus on the basis of too little evidence. But if we compare Van Aarde's analysis with Capps's, also Capps's reconstruction of the relationship between Joseph and Jesus cannot be based on current historical-critical assessments. If so, Capps's endeavour to use Freudian concepts to explain Jesus' adult behaviour may be too ambitious. This is particularly clear in Capps's treatment of the temple incident, which must be an *impulsive* act in his reconstruction. But many scholars believe it was a premeditated symbolic act, in which case other explanations need to be explored. In the cases of Miller and Capps, we see the process of the psychiatrist at work who starts his enquiry open-minded with a host of possible characters in mind. As he engages with his subject, he formulates a working hypothesis, which he will refine or reject dependent on the information he can take into account. With the lack of consensus between biblical scholars and historians, however, he risks favouring those opinions that fit with the working hypothesis and ignoring dissonant opinions (the risk of cognitive bias). Van Aarde believes he can avoid the pitfalls of deduction and induction by applying a different method. But employing an ideal type, too, is 'investing' in a working hypothesis, which invites cognitive bias. This is perhaps best illustrated by the following quote: 'I did ... become existentially impelled by Jesus' fatherlessness because it addressed my own situation.' I wonder, for instance, whether Van Aarde should not have read the Rabbinic material about marriage more critically. Furthermore, there is ample evidence that customs between various Palestinian groups and regions differed. The Talmudic writings are as partisan and idealized as the New Testament and far more removed from the days of Jesus (see Jacob Neusner's 1994 *Introduction to Rabbinic Literature*). I also wonder why Van Aarde believes the initiation model works for Galilean youths, noting for instance that Jewish boys are customarily circumcised as a baby, not as a teenager.

All three psychological portraits emphasize the family background of Jesus as an important element for analysis. All three reconstructions go a long way to explain Jesus' adult behaviour. But Miller says that Jesus had a good relationship with his father, Capps says that they had a bad relationship, and Van Aarde argues that there was no relationship at all. These are not complementary portraits, but mutually exclusive portraits. The situation reminds me of Christopher Pelling's warning in *Literary Texts and the Greek Historian* (2000, 34):

> Here we face one classic methodological danger. Everyone is familiar with the type of detective story where the evidence is bewildering, till in the last chapter the detective summons to the library those most involved – all of them probably by now suspects – and gives a brilliant reconstruction of what really happened. We applaud the brilliance, and immediately see that, if the reconstruction is right, then the evidence would look exactly the way it does ... . The fallacy is that the detective needs to show, not just that this story could explain the evidence, but that this is the only story that could ... . If a logical causal chain goes forward from the reconstructed crime to the evidence, it need not follow that we can follow the chain backwards from the evidence to the crime: for any number of alternative chains might explain precisely the same evidence. No wonder that the brilliance of the detective is invariably followed by the breakdown of the criminal, for without the confession we would not, or at least should not, be wholly convinced.

So what went wrong? Here we have three highly skilled scholars who are knowledgeable about psychological method in general and psychobiography in particular, who are familiar with the historical-critical analysis of the Gospels, and sensitive towards the culture and time of their subject. If good science means that competent practitioners should be able to come up with similar or at least compatible results when using the same evidence and methods, we must ask the question whether there is enough basis for a good psychobiography of Jesus.

If we evaluate the work of Miller, Capps and Van Aarde from the perspective of Runyan's methodological discussion, we can make the following observations:

- Each analysis focuses on only a part of Runyan's three-tiered model. In terms of the group level, Miller's focus is on Jesus' family setting and age; the focus of Capps and Van Aarde is on Jesus' family setting, his culture and his social location. On the individual level, Miller's focus is on Jesus' teenage years and his baptism, Capps's on Jesus' childhood, his work as a healer and his disturbance of the temple. Van Aarde only discusses the individual level to test whether Jesus fits the group level.
- All three psychological portraits emphasize the family background of Jesus as the most important element for analysis, or more specifically, his childhood (Capps and Van Aarde). Knowing his family background should help us to understand Jesus. All three retrodict or hypothesize Jesus' childhood experience. But Runyan explicitly advised against this approach if the data are insufficient. A psychobiographer who wishes to explain adult behaviour from unknown childhood experiences is immediately caught up in a circular argument, for he needs to reconstruct or validate childhood experiences by the adult life that he wishes to explain. It should come as no big surprise, therefore, that Miller, Capps and Van Aarde reached incompatible conclusions about the role of Joseph.
- A comparison with psychobiographical studies of people like Augustine, Luther, Ignatius of Loyola, Joseph Smith and Ghandi, shows that the data available for a study of Jesus are extremely limited. All we have are the canonical Gospels and some snippets of information from other sources. There are no ego-documents, such as personal letters or a diary; there are no writings by Jesus. The information about his childhood is even more limited and its historicity heavily disputed. Runyan already noted that this is the case for many historical figures. In such cases we have to check whether there are other perspectives that can enhance our understanding of the subject, before speculating about the subject's childhood.

Conclusion

The studies of Miller, Capps and Van Aarde are excellent examples of integrating biblical scholarship with psychology. But their psychological reconstructions can only be regarded as challenging and stimulating hypotheses, as there is simply not enough data to write a good psychobiography of Jesus on the basis of his childhood experiences. If Jesus' adult self-awareness and behaviour were largely driven by his *specific* childhood experiences, this lack of data would be insurmountable for any psychobiographer. But there are more ways in which psychology can be useful in the historical enterprise, as will be discussed in the next chapter. Furthermore, if Meier (1991, 352) is correct and Jesus' youth in Nazareth was 'insufferably normal', we may be less dependent on his childhood experiences after all.

Annex: A Word on the Concept of 'mamzer'

All three psychobiographical portraits discussed in this chapter engage with the question why Jesus was unmarried at age 30. All three assume that it was a father's task to find his son a wife and all quote the tractate *Qiddushin* from the (Babylonian) Talmud. According to Miller (1997), Joseph died too early to find Jesus a wife. This argument is not very convincing, as Miller believes that Jesus had younger brothers, but fails to discuss how they got married (1 Corinthians 9:5). From a demographic perspective, the idea that only a father could arrange a marriage is nonsensical. As will be shown in Chapter 4, a third of the children had already lost their father by the age of 10.

Other scholars attribute Jesus' unmarried status to his illegitimate birth. They again point to tractates such as *b.Qiddushin* and *b.Ketubot*, or to the discussion of these texts in Joachim Jeremias (1969/German original 1962, ch. 15). Capps (2000) believes Joseph never recognized Jesus and thus left him with the stain of illegitimacy. His reconstruction of Jesus' problematic childhood is based on Jane Schaberg's *The Illegitimacy of Jesus* (1987). She identifies Jesus as a *mamzer*, who would not have been able to enter the assembly or to marry. The argument of Van Aarde (2001, ch. 5) is also based on the concept of a *mamzer*: as a fatherless child, Jesus was 'not allowed to enter the temple (cf. Deut 23.3) or to marry a full-blooded fellow Israelite' (133, the reference should be to Deut. 23.2). In his discussion of these three psychobiographies, Charlesworth (2004) notes, 'Why and how did Jesus' failures to prove his parentage to those who claimed he was a *mamzer* (not a bastard, but one who could not prove convincingly to authorities who his parents were) affect his psychological personality?' Bruce Chilton's *Rabbi Jesus* (2000) opens with the chapter 'A *Mamzer* from Nazareth', concentrating on the idea that Jesus' birth had been illegitimate. He defines a *mamzer* as 'an Israelite of suspect paternity' (12). According to Chilton, 'scholars have overlooked the fact that the conditions of Jesus' conception as Matthew refers to them made him a *mamzer*, no matter what his actual paternity was' (13). It would imply that Jesus was ostracized and could not enter the Sabbath assembly (the synagogue), nor visit the temple. Unlike his brother James he could not learn to read the Holy Scriptures. Furthermore, he could not marry a 'normal' Jewish girl.

The problem with all these contributions is not just that it requires us to disbelieve the traditions in which Jesus is intimate with Scripture, speaks and reads in synagogues, visits the temple, and is addressed as 'rabbi'. And yes, it can be granted that there was a debate about Jesus' birthrights, precisely because he was claimed to be the Davidic Messiah (Rom. 1.3). Whether the Gospels react to gossip, or the gossip to the Gospels, or both, can be debated, but that is not my point. The point at stake is not even the uncritical acceptance of later Rabbinic writings for a reconstruction of first-century reality (although I wonder whether these scholars really do believe that the thousands of Israelites, whose paternity could be suspect, were actively kept away from marriage, synagogue and temple). The point is that, starting with Jeremias, the Rabbinic literature that is referred to is read rather selectively, so that the social picture of first-century Judaism is painted in the darkest possible colours. Whoever reads the discussion in *Ketubot* and *Qiddushin* in full can see how the rabbis tried to apply the letter of the law in a way that would cause as little social disruption as possible. The Talmudic authorities clearly wanted to restrict the application of Deut. 23.2 when they write: 'one who is beyond doubt a *mamzer* is the one who may not enter, but one who may or may not be a *mamzer* may enter' (*Qiddushin* 73a, translation Neusner 2005). Everyone has the benefit of doubt. If a girl was raped by an unknown man, or if the child was a foundling, the child was not to be declared unfit even for marrying the daughter of a priest (73a), except under specific circumstances. After some debate, it was decided that if an unmarried woman had a child and merely claimed it was from a valid man, she was to be believed as well (75a). Finally, the rabbis stressed that even those with the status of *mamzer* would be purified in the world to come, quoting Ezek. 36.25: 'I will sprinkle clean water upon you, and you shall be clean' (72b).

The discussion described in *Ketubot* and *Qiddushin* is actually quite clear. After some debate, it was decided that if a betrothed Israelite woman gives birth to a child, the child receives the status of her husband, unless he has the mother condemned for adultery. In that case, the child will have the status of the Israelite woman, unless it is proven beyond doubt that the biological father was one for whom a marriage with an Israelite woman was forbidden. If the father remained unknown, the child was not made 'invalid'. The very fact that the rabbis gave so much attention to this issue, indicates that such births were not uncommon in their day – nor, one would think, in the day of Mary.

If we apply these later Rabbinic rules to the narratives in Matthew and Luke, then Jesus would have received the status of Joseph, not because Joseph recognizes the child, but because of the bare fact that Mary is betrothed to him. That would still have been the case if he had divorced her in silence (Mt. 1.19). If it were proven that Mary had committed adultery (which would have required a court case and at least two witnesses), the child would have received Mary's status, but still not the status of a *mamzer*. The same applies if Mary had not yet been betrothed. Only if it were proven beyond doubt that the biological father would have been forbidden for Mary to marry, then Jesus could have been declared a *mamzer*.

In other words, there may or may not have been gossip about Jesus' early birth, but such births were not uncommon. Such gossip may have hurt Jesus, his mother and perhaps his family. But it is highly unlikely that such gossip alone would have led to exclusion from the synagogue, the temple or a Jewish marriage.

Chapter 3

A THEORETICAL JESUS AND EARLY CHRISTIANITY

Psychology is not only an art, but also a science. One could view the intuition of psychiatrists as an art, based on interacting with a limited and oddly selected group of patients. The brilliance of their art is not measured by its historical correctness with respect to the lives of their patients, but by its power to heal or strengthen their souls. Erikson practised psychobiography with a view to the impact that 'selected portions of the past' have on 'our renewed awareness' and 'our contemporary commitments' (Szaluta 1999, 98). In fairness, this is probably true of most historians, although they hate to admit it. But psychology is also a science. From the work of brilliant artists, such as Freud and Erikson, new ideas are generated. These are formulated as hypotheses and tested empirically with large and various groups of individuals. Statistical analysis is employed to find out the influences of various factors in various combinations. This, in turn, provides a framework for new artists to work in, and generate new interpretations and ideas.

In the previous chapter, I discussed the problem of writing a psychobiography of Jesus. We cannot observe the historical Jesus and he left us no diaries, letters or other direct records. All that we have is secondary. Every scholarly reconstruction of the historical Jesus is a hypothesis amidst other hypotheses. Every reconstruction of the psychology of Jesus on the basis of the work of biblical scholars is a hypothesis about a hypothesis, or worse, a hypothesis about an eclectic mixture of hypotheses.

At the same time, however, secondary evidence about Jesus is primary data about some of his earliest followers. The evangelists, Paul and other early Christian writers (even if they did not yet call themselves Christians) wrote to communicate what they believed to be worth communicating about Jesus. As Dunn puts it, it is about *Jesus remembered* (2003).

If we accept that a historical Jesus is a theoretical construct, we may actually come to terms with the lack of evidence. Let me unpack that idea a little. A theory is normally used to explain phenomena that can be observed. A theory can be subjected to further tests and observations, and then confirmed, adapted or rejected. A good theory is open to falsification by experiment or additional research. There can be competing theories, awaiting falsification. But while they exist together, some theories are 'better' – as a theory – than others, as they strike a better balance between plausibility and explanatory power, or because they require fewer assumptions.

Methodological Considerations

If we apply such methodological considerations to the study of the historical Jesus and early Christianity, and consider the possible contribution of psychological methods, the following can be said:

- Jesus of Nazareth can no longer be observed. Jesus has not meaningfully entered the historical record, other than through the writings of some of his followers. There are non-Christian sources about Jesus, but Josephus, Tacitus, Celsus and the Talmud primarily react to the claims made by his followers. From a theoretical point of view, the historical study of these remains, and the people who produced, used and transmitted them, takes precedence over the study of the historical Jesus. Quite correctly, then, N.T. Wright's three-volume study (1992, 1997, 2003) starts with *The New Testament and the People of God.* Crossan (1992; 1998) and Dunn (2003; 2008; forthcoming), too, study both the historical Jesus and the early Church, but they present their findings in a chronological order: first Jesus, then the movement that we now call Christianity.
- A good theory about the origins of these canonical and non-canonical writings should involve all relevant aspects. In the case of religious writings that deeply affected the souls of authors and audiences, the psychological aspect is indeed a very relevant part of such a theory.
- In this context, psychological analyses of the historical Jesus are a means to an end, but a psychology of Jesus is not the objective. Inasmuch as it is theorized that a historical Jesus – as opposed to a purely imagined, proclaimed or literary Jesus – had an influence on the ideas and work of the authors and primary audiences, it makes sense to include the historical Jesus in our framework. Note that this can apply only to early followers. As time passes by, new followers will have been affected more by the proclaimed Jesus than by the historical Jesus. Inasmuch as understanding Jesus' motives and self-awareness helps to reconstruct how he impacted his early followers, who had known him or who knew people that had known him, it should even include a theory about the psychology of Jesus. In that case a primary theory about the literary remains of early followers of Jesus includes a secondary theory about the historical Jesus, and both would need to include the psychological aspect.
- The most important test criterion of a psychological analysis of the historical Jesus is whether it helps us to understand the impact he had on his followers and, through them, on the observable literary remains of these followers.
- Psychological analysis can also be used to evaluate scholarly reconstructions of the historical Jesus as one of the tests to assess the likelihood of the

scholarly or literary construct. The question then simply is: is it likely that a Jesus as reconstructed by, say, Dominic Crossan (1992) behaved as he did, that other actors in the reconstruction behaved as they did, and that this led to the 'birth of Christianity' (1998)? Or do psychological insights suggest alternative explanations that should also be considered?

Evaluating Competing Theories

If we ask the right questions and apply the appropriate methods we will come up with sensible hypotheses. The next question is whether there is enough evidence to test these hypotheses. If not, are all hypotheses of equal worth, or are there criteria to decide that one hypothesis is more useful than another?

A good psychological theory explains the personality of a person or a group in such a way that it predicts the behaviour of the subject(s) and thus allows for falsification. Such a theory should be as economical as possible. When competing theories have equal predictive powers, the theory that introduces the fewest assumptions and postulates the fewest hypothetical entities should be preferred ('Occam's razor').

In psychobiography and other historical research, the element of prediction is not present. Instead, we have to balance the concepts of explanatory power and plausibility. If a theory does not explain the behaviour of Jesus or that of his followers, it is not a good theory, however plausible it may be. If there are several good explanations, then the most plausible is to be preferred. Here, of course, we cannot escape our subjectivity: the concept of resurrection, for example, has no plausibility to secular scholars, however well it may explain the data to a religious scholar. Historical research since Lucian accepts the belief in divine intervention as an object of study, not as an explanation of historical events. The criterion of economy implies that when several theories provide equally good and plausible explanations, we should favour the theory that introduces the fewest assumptions or entities. The more we are able to explain the preserved records on the basis of the actors and events already known and present in these records, the more economical our theory will be. The most economical theory will take into account all the undisputed data, explaining efficiently as much as possible of the data that cannot be proven to go back to Jesus, and avoiding as much as possible the use of 'missing data'.

Thus we have three filters to rank comprehensive and support theories. The three filters are:

1. **Explanatory power.** A theory that can explain more of the data takes preference over a theory that explains less.
2. **Plausibility.** If there are two competing explanations of the same data, the most plausible theory is to be preferred.

3. **Economy.** If the two explanations are both plausible, the most economical theory is to be preferred.

A comprehensive theory provides an explanation for all the observable data (in our case the literary remains of first-century followers of Jesus), whereas a supporting theory (e.g. a construction of the historical Jesus) provides an explanation for part of the observable data. A supporting theory can be ranked only within the framework of a comprehensive theory (in other words: it is not meaningful to rank two constructions of the historical Jesus against each other if the underlying assumptions about the early movement are fundamentally different).

The aim of the present study is not to develop a comprehensive theory of the historical Jesus and his early followers, but to discuss what kind of contribution certain psychological methods can make to the development of such a theoretical framework, however, I will outline a theory for what I believe to be the core of such a comprehensive theory, namely the distinctive Christological convictions of the movement, which I will sketch in the concluding chapter of this study.

Psychobiographical Analyses of Jesus

Chapters 7 through 11 are essays in psychobiographical analyses of Jesus and the impact he had on his disciples during his lifetime. Together they form not an attempt to write a full psychobiography, but each is a discussion within a specific area where I believe such analyses are already possible and can be fruitful for understanding his earliest followers. Runyan's three-tier model can be used to check which psychological questions can be asked about the historical Jesus. For each question, we can then decide what the available evidence is, and what kind of strategy helps us to make maximum use of the available evidence.

The key question to answer on level 1 is whether things that are true for all humans are also true for Jesus. This is a matter of theology and philosophy, but it would be impossible to apply psychological methods, if one does not approach Jesus as fully human. On the second level, we need to discuss which groups or categories give us a meaningful perspective on Jesus. We must, on the one hand, categorize Jesus correctly, and, on the other hand, acquire a good understanding of each category. On the individual level, we need to reconstruct Jesus' history and psychological development.

In the diagram below, I indicate some of the points of consensus and contention regarding Jesus' background and development (levels 2 and 3).

psychobiography of Jesus

1. point of view: human

2. background

1st cent. Galilean Jew, Naz/Sep/ Capem	peasant artisan or entre- preneur	father siblings first-born	male sexual?	mystic charism. apocal.	until around 30?	health but insecure

3. development:

Formative events: loss of father, baptism, arrest of John, healings, various reactions (followers, John, family, scribes, authorities), death of John ...

Responses: follow John, start preaching, denounce family, start traveling, 'dramatic' entry into Jerusalem, temple confrontation, ...

Background

With regard to Jesus' culture, there is a high degree of consensus. For some decades now, scholars have approached Jesus as a first-century Galilean Jew. Social scientists have written perceptive commentaries from the perspective of late antique Mediterranean thinking. Our knowledge of Galilee in the first half of the first century and its inhabitants is increasing, although there are still debates as to the degree of Hellenization and Judaization of Galilee. Archaeologists and other specialists are piecing together the life and interaction of people living and working in villages and cities such as Nazareth, Sepphoris, Tiberias, Capernaum and nearby Bethsaida. But the extent to which Jesus has participated in these places is unknown.

There is a debate regarding his social location. Was Jesus raised as a peasant from Nazareth without education or adequate income, as Crossan believes? Or was he a skilled worker, earning his money in construction, perhaps on building projects in Sepphoris and Tiberias, which attracted many workers in his youth and early adult years? One could even argue that his family belonged to the entrepreneurial class, with a workshop and employees, like his followers Peter, Andrew, John and James, whose families owned fishing boats, and employed workers.

With regard to his family, opinions vary widely as well. Was he the oldest son among brothers and sisters, or the youngest son of Joseph by his second wife Mary? Did people believe he was the legitimate son of Joseph, or an illegitimate *mamzer* as Bruce Chilton (2000) has it? Did he have a loving relationship with his father, a resentful relationship or was he raised fatherless? If Joseph was his father, when did Joseph die?

Whereas Jesus' gender is beyond discussion, his sexuality and sexual status are not. Was he sexually active? It has been claimed that he was a homosexual (but note that homosexuality in late antiquity was no obstacle to marriage). Morton Smith (1973) 'discovered' a letter with quotations from a secret Gospel of Mark that could support this idea – but many now regard *Secret Mark* as a forgery (Carlson 2005 and Jeffery 2006). Others claim he was married or had a sexual relationship with Mary Magdalene. Traditionally he has been viewed as celibate. These questions are hard to answer, and even if we could answer them, it is difficult to reconstruct reliably what this meant psychologically in Jesus' time and culture.

In terms of religion, we come on to firmer ground. Jesus was a Jew, closer to Pharisaic or Chassidic beliefs than to Sadducean thinking. He seems to have combined a close mystical relationship with God (his 'Abba'), with some sort of apocalyptic awareness. Fortunately we have some ego-documents of other Jews, or Jewish Christians like Paul, which help us to understand what these concepts may have meant in the first century.

As to his age, it is often stated that Jesus was born in 6 BCE and died around 30 CE. But the year of birth is derived from Matthew, whereas Luke suggests it happened 12 years later, in 6 CE. No Gospel informs us about the year of his death, and only Luke dates the year when John became active: 28/9 CE. So how old was Jesus during his ministry: nearing 30 (Luke), in his mid-thirties (if we harmonize the accounts of Matthew and Luke) or even in his forties, as the Gospel of John seems to suggest?

Physical discomfort and insecurity can have a profound influence on people's minds, even if their psychological impact is dependent on other factors as well. Whereas Jesus seems to have been a healthy man who could walk long distances, it also seems that after John's arrest and execution, he experienced an increased level of insecurity.

To conclude this section: yes, there are group perspectives that can illuminate parts of Jesus' life. But it is not always clear to which group Jesus belonged and what effects such groups had on the psychology of people in his time and place. The three least disputed group perspectives seem to be those of his culture, religion and security. It seems that it would be a good strategy to investigate these aspects for a psychological analysis, before focusing on his potential age, social location, family background or sexuality. In other words, in order to rein in one's personal imagination, the psychobiographer should first analyse the undisputed categories, before exploring the disputed categories.

Development

Virtually all the preserved evidence about Jesus relates to the period between his baptism and his death. It is, however, unclear how long this period, and more specifically the period of his public ministry lasted. The only point in time is Luke's dating of the start of the ministry of John the Baptist, which we cannot verify from another source. None of the Gospel narratives sets out how long the period was between Jesus' baptism and the start of his ministry. In general, however, there is a consensus that the time from John's arrest to his crucifixion did not last longer than one or two years.

Furthermore, there is agreement only about a limited number of events, actions and sayings of Jesus. In the table below, I have listed some events and actions that are supported by a large degree of scholarly consensus. These should be our starting point before we include other events in Jesus' life that are less certain. In terms of Runyan's model, there are two questions to be asked of a psychobiography that concerns itself with the personal development of Jesus (taking into account Jesus' humanity and background):

- What kind of person would behave in such situations as Jesus did?
- What kind of effects can such situations and behaviour have had on his further development?

Situation	Jesus' behaviour	see Chapter
Absence or death of father	He seeks God as his Father	7
John proclaims God's reign and baptizes	He has himself baptized	8
John is arrested	He proclaims God's reign and forms a group with twelve friends	8
People are healed by him	He first withdraws, then starts to address 'demons' with authority	9
He experiences conflicts with John, his family and authorities	He first withdraws with his friends, then goes to Jerusalem for *Pesach*	10
His last *Pesach* in Jerusalem	Enters the city on a donkey Creates a disturbance in the temple Celebrates a final meal Agonizes in Gethsemane	11

If one looks at these events and Jesus' behaviour, it is fortunate that there is a good correlation between the key events in Jesus' last year(s) and the categories that are least disputed: Jesus was a religious Jew in first-century Galilee who had to cope with loss and insecurity and took up his own role in his perception of God's reign.

Sources

As discussed earlier in this chapter, the sources for psychological analyses of Jesus are the literary remains of some of his early followers. Before progressing with such analyses, we will first need a more comprehensive theory about the origins of these literary remains. Here, too, the methodological framework of psychobiography, or psychohistory when speaking of groups, can be of assistance.

Towards a Psychohistory of Early Followers of Jesus

Szaluta (1999) includes the study of groups in his methodology of psychohistory and psychobiography: 'It encompasses the interactions of leader and led, collective acts, institutions, events, and nations.' He quotes Erikson who says that 'in solving their own problems great men were also solving the problems of the group'. In his book on Jesus, Donald Capps employs a different strategy: he uses psychohistorical analyses of families in a pre-industrial religious society, the Plymouth Colony, to understand better the psychological state of mind of first-century Galilee. Capps concurs with Mazlish ('What is Psycho-history?', 1971), that such an analysis needs to balance sociology and psychology. But where Capps and Mazlish are focused on childhood experiences in those groups, I would like to expand the potential for investigation to include all levels and aspects Runyan identified for psychobiography. Thus I arrive at the following model:

a three-tier model for psychohistory

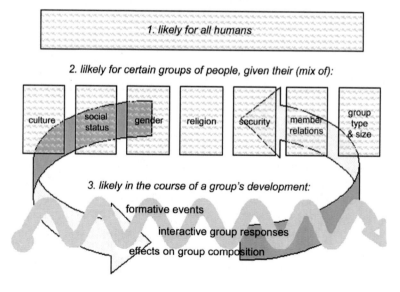

1. likely for all humans

2. lilkey for certain groups of people, given their (mix of):

culture | social status | gender | religion | security | member relations | group type & size

3. likely in the course of a group's development:

formative events

interactive group responses

effects on group composition

The model is nearly identical to that of psychobiography, but focuses on the dynamics and the development of a group, which is not the primary focus of psychology. In *Psychology and Historical Interpretation* (1988, 269), Runyan acknowledges that the psychology of history may be mediated through other disciplines that make use of psychology. In particular, he is thinking of sociology, anthropology, political science, economics, demography and linguistics. An important factor in new religious movements is the fact that the composition of the group changes over time. In our case, a marginal Jewish movement of Jesus followers spread across the Mediterranean and became a Gentile church. In this study, therefore, I will start with demographic analysis to trace this development in detail. Informed by an understanding of the changing composition of the group, we can apply other social scientific insights with more precision. At the same time, Runyan notes that a *historically* sensitive psychological approach must take into account the psychological differences between people in different historical and cultural contexts. Historical and psychological analysis, therefore, need to interact in order to prevent a misapplication of either discipline.

Furthermore, we can identify a number of formative events that help us to understand the development of doctrines within the group, especially since there is a considerable corpus of writings by these followers themselves. Some of these events concern all Jews (including first-century Christians), whereas others regard early Christians in particular. Fortunately, several writings from a significant part of the group, albeit not from all subgroups, have been preserved to work with.

Looking at the model, the available methods and the available data, it seems to me that a psychohistory of this group could make a significant contribution to our understanding of the New Testament. Such a psychohistory should start with the perspective of a new religious movement, coping with formative events and strong growth, in interaction with its social environment, the Hebrew Scriptures and the memories of Jesus. Again the order is backwards: we will have to start with the period when this group enters the historical record (second half of the first century) and work our way back to the earliest followers of Jesus in the 30s CE.

From the outset, I should note that the situation for psychohistorical analyses of early Christianity is better than it is for the historical Jesus. There is information available about a significant number of leaders, and we have an interesting set of letters written by one of them, Paul of Tarsus, that take us right into the action of an important and formative conflict. Furthermore, an enormous amount of scholarly work has been done to discern when, by and for whom, and why early Christian documents were written.

Group Backgrounds

With respect to the second level of the model for psychohistory, there is more secondary literature available than any scholar could read in his lifetime. Social scientific work of early Christianity – especially in its Graeco-Roman context – has really grown in volume and depth in the last decades (though not that much for its early growth outside the Roman Empire). Good overviews are given in *The Jesus Movement: A Social History of Its First*

Century (Stegemann and Stegemann 1999; German original, 1995) and in the *Handbook of Early Christianity: Social Science Approaches*, edited by Blasi, Duhaime and Turcotte (2002); note, however, that Schwartz (2010) urges caution against viewing the Jews as a typical Mediterranean society – and to be a little sceptical about the very concept of Mediterraneanism. From a methodological point of view, scholars can now benefit from the maturing disciplines of the sociology of religion (e.g. Davie 2007), anthropology of religion (e.g. Bowie 2000/2006) and psychology of religion (see below).

Several scholars have now presented studies from a multi-disciplinary point of view. Klaus Berger (1995/ET 2003) tries to save his subject from the uninformed and anachronistic application by psychologists by producing a 'historical psychology of the New Testament' (the translation of the original German title) himself. Luke Timothy Johnson was a pioneer with his *Religious Experience in Earliest Christianity: A Missing Dimension in New Testament Studies* (1998). Malina and Neyrey (1996) have demonstrated that ancient sources need to be understood first from their ancient perspective in *Portraits of Paul: An Archaeology of Ancient Personality*. Gerd Theissen, who discussed the *religion* of the earliest Christians in 2000, produced an impressive psychological study in 2007: *Erleben und Verhalten der ersten Christen: Eine Psychologie des Urchristentums*. Drawing from the fields of psychohistory and the psychology of religion, Theissen discusses the limits and potential of a psychology of earliest Christianity. He deals with several objections: lack of data, naive reading of textual evidence, anachronisms, reductionism and triviality ('good psychology often discovers what common sense already knows'). Despite all this, Theissen believes that psychology helps to clarify what happens when a new religion is born. More particularly he focuses on four factors of religion: experience, myth (and teaching), ritual and ethos. His analyses are based on insights from behavioural psychology (he is most impressed with Sundén's Role Theory), depth psychology (he mentions the British child psychiatrist Winnicott, in particular), and cognitive psychology (especially attribution theory and the concept of cognitive dissonance). But all of this together is not yet a psychohistory of early Christianity in terms of our model. For this, there would have to be more attention to the composition of the group and changes therein, as well as to the historical development of the movement. The demographic development is still missing (see Chapters 4 and 5).

Group Developments

With respect to level three, there is not yet a major psychohistorical study that covers the formative events of what we now call first-century Christianity. I would suggest that such a study would cover at least the following events set out in the table below.

30s CE
- The crucifixion and the resurrection experiences
- Hellenistic Jews and proselytes join the movement
- The lynching of Stephen and dispersion of the Hellenists
- The pogrom in Alexandria and the statue of Caligula in Palestine

40s CE
- The admission of Gentile converts
- The persecution by Herod Agrippa and the absence of Peter
- The rise of James
- The missionary success among the god-fearing Gentiles
- The 'chrestus' incident in Rome

50s CE
- The conflict between Paul and James (and the Antioch incident involving Peter)
- The conflict about the resurrection
- The Gentile collect for Jerusalem
- Paul's arrest

60s CE
- The lynching of James
- The Neronian persecution (first distinction between Jews and Christians) in which Paul and Peter died
- The Jewish War and the dispersion of Palestinian Jews

70s CE
- The destruction of Jerusalem without the return of Jesus
- The loss of Jerusalem as the centre of authority
- The reorganization of Judaism

80s CE
- The Domitian pressure on Jews
- The Domitian pressure on Christians
- Jewish-Christian tensions

90s/100s CE
- The emergence of a non-Jewish majority in Christianity (see Chapter 5)
- The split of Palestinian Jewish Christians (Ebionites/Nazarenes)
- The rise of docetism

James Dunn has written a comprehensive historical study of the formative first decades, the second volume of his trilogy *Christianity in the Making*. Although this volume is called *Beginning from Jerusalem* (2009), it could also have been called *From Jesus to Paul*, as Dunn identifies Paul as the second founder of Christianity (519). Dunn organizes his work in three phases: the beginnings in Jerusalem, the mission of Paul, and the end of the beginning – the deaths of

Paul, Peter and James and the destruction of Jerusalem. Dunn identifies these three men as representing the spectrum of early Christianity at the end of the first generation. At the end of this volume, Dunn asks himself whether he has answered his key questions: 'what degree of continuity did the first Christians maintain with the mission and message of Jesus?' and 'how did a Jewish sect become a Gentile religion?' Dunn answers the first question essentially as a theologian: he concludes that there is a significant level of continuity between the message of the historical Jesus and that of his early followers. The only problem is that he reconstructs the message of the historical Jesus from the writings of his followers in volume 1 (*Jesus Remembered*, 2003). Dunn does not answer it from a sociological perspective, such as: how many of Jesus' early followers at the time that the Gospels were written have known him directly or have known others who had? With respect to the second question, Dunn concludes that the parting of the ways between Judaism and emerging Christianity was only beginning to take place before 70 CE. In his third volume (forthcoming) he will continue this enquiry.

Conclusions

Although the psychobiographical study of Jesus suffers from a lack of data, psychologically informed theories about Jesus can form part of a larger theoretical framework that seeks to explain the observable remains of some of his early followers.

A psychologically informed history of early Christianity will combine the socio-psychological work of scholars such as Johnson, Berger and Theissen, with the historical work of scholars such as Dunn. But it needs to do so with an appreciation for the changing composition of the movement. Even if much is to remain hypothetical, scholars will need to make their assumptions clear (which I will do in Part Two) before we can proceed with using these literary remains in analyses of Jesus (Part Three).

Annex: A Theoretical Jesus and Meier's Historical Jesus

It is perhaps useful to compare the concept of Jesus as part of a theory to explain Early Christianity with the term 'The Historical Jesus' as used by, for instance, John P. Meier. For Meier, 'The Historical Jesus' is not the real Jesus, but 'only a fragmentary hypothetical reconstruction' (1991, ch. 1). In the Introduction, he describes this as the Jesus 'whom we can recover, recapture, or reconstruct by using the scientific tools of modern historical research'. It is 'a scientific construct' and 'a theoretical abstraction'. The words that Meier uses are similar to those used in the present study, but the concepts are very different. I see the following differences:

- Meier's 'Historical Jesus' is the object of his theoretical work, whereas the 'theoretical Jesus' is part of a theory to explain a different object: the literary remains of early followers of Jesus.
- Meier's 'theoretical abstraction' describes the mostly reductionistic nature of 'the historical Jesus': it tries to extract from the sources what is likely to be true. The words 'hypothetical' and 'theoretical' merely express lower levels of reliability. For the 'theoretical Jesus', on the other hand, these words are used functionally: it is the aim of this study to construct and test hypotheses as part of a theory that explains these sources.
- It is difficult to test the value of various scholarly versions of the 'Historical Jesus' as its only stated function is the reconstruction of something that is unknown (the real Jesus). Scholars can discuss only the relative value that each assigns to the sources and criteria. By contrast, competing versions of the 'theoretical Jesus' can and should be ranked in function of the stated purpose of the larger theoretical framework, first in terms of explanatory power, then plausibility and finally economy.

PART TWO

FOLLOWERS OF JESUS AND
THEIR MEMORIES OF HIM

INTRODUCTION TO PART TWO

Part Two is not a psychohistory of Jesus' followers, but a necessary analytical step before we can turn to the impact of Jesus in Part Three. Furthermore, it is not necessarily about all Jesus' followers, but rather those of whom we have sufficient first-century literary remains. We need firmer ground as to who these people were who formed the groups in which Jesus traditions were preserved, shaped and used: what were their social and ethnic backgrounds, their ages, their relationships with one another? How much social continuity was there between them and Jesus: how many of them had known Jesus, or knew people who had? What is the value of the traditions about Jesus that were used by the authors of the first-century Gospels? Again, this is a theoretical approach. I am not looking for what can be said with certainty about Jesus' followers, but rather what a plausible theory would look like that explains the literary remains from the first century CE, most notably the letters of Paul and the Gospels.

Just as I believe that psychology has been missing from historical Jesus studies, so I believe that familiarity with numbers and statistical probabilities has been missing in studies of the earliest followers of Jesus. I suggest that more can be said about the social continuity between Jesus and his followers, if we apply insights from demographical studies of late antiquity and growth factors of new religious movements. This part is therefore organized as follows:

- In Chapter 4, I will apply demographical statistics to the list of 'resurrection witnesses' in I Cor. 15.3-12. This list excludes the women at the grave, but includes the Twelve, James the brother of Jesus and a group of '500 brothers (and sisters?)'. These are the 'first generation' believers and the use of demographics can help us to make reasoned assumptions about their presence in the days of Paul and later in the first century.
- In Chapter 5, I will apply insights into conversion patterns and new religious movements to explore the growth dynamics of the movement. I will combine Rodney Stark's work on the rise of Christianity with spreadsheet modelling, that allows us to test scenarios and make sensitivity analyses of various assumptions. The objective of this exercise is to explore the numerical importance of first-generation witnesses and their descendants as well as that of Gentile converts. This is of particular importance for the last decades of the first century, when the New Testament Gospels were put into writing.

- Finally, in Chapter 6, the result of these quantitative analyses will be combined with insights into literacy and memory to design a method of extracting relatively reliable historical data from Jesus traditions in both the letters of Paul and the first-century Gospels.

Chapter 4

DEMOGRAPHICS AND FIRST-GENERATION FOLLOWERS OF JESUS

Our knowledge of the demography of the Roman Empire has recently been summarized by Bruce Frier (2000) and Walter Scheidel (2008). Their findings are to a large extent based on two sources: the detailed census returns from Roman Egypt (Bagnall and Frier, *The Demography of Roman Egypt*, 1994) and general demographic research with respect to pre-industrial societies (notably Coale and Demeny, *Regional Model Life Tables and Stable Populations*, 1966/1983). The census returns are more reliable than the epigraphic data (Tim Parkin 1992), although the latter give more perspective on the situation in the crowded city of Rome with its huge differences in wealth and health. Richard Saller's *Patriarchy, Property and Death in the Roman Family* (1995), and *Growing Up and Growing Old in Ancient Rome: A Life Course Approach* by Mary Harlow and Ray Laurence (2002) show how such data can be used to reconstruct life courses and marriage patterns, as well as their impact on social structures and politics.

The life expectancy of anyone born in the Roman Empire was roughly around 25 years – a few years more if one was very wealthy, a few less for certain groups of slaves and the urban poor. Without soap and refrigerators, cities were magnets for disease and death. Infant mortality was very high. About one-third of infants died in their first year; only half of them would celebrate their fifth birthday. Once past that crucial period, life expectancy rose to about 50 to 60 years. About 5 per cent of the population was older than 65 years, roughly a third younger than 15 years. Males could expect a slightly longer life than females, especially because of the health risks associated with sexuality and childbirth. Coupled with nature's tendency to produce about 5 per cent more boys than girls (even more so for younger mothers), this means that there was a shortage of women.

High mortality is offset by high birth rates. In antiquity, procreation was often seen as the aim of marriage (sex was rather freely available for males), and only freeborn women were eligible for marriage. As a consequence, the burden and risks of childbirth fell heavily upon married women. 'In Roman Egypt, for example, some 85 per cent of all births were within wedlock, but only around 55 per cent of all Egyptian women aged 15 to 50 were married at any one time; this implies marital fertility rates about four times higher than non-marital rates' (Frier 2000, 798). A freeborn Egyptian woman married from 15 to 40 would on average give birth to about eight children, of whom only four would live beyond the age of 5. The number of children in a family was controlled in various ways. Through prolonged breastfeeding (and less intercourse during periods of breastfeeding), there was a level of natural prevention against pregnancy, so that children would be born two or three years apart if the previously born child did not die too soon. Apart from means to induce abortions, children were sometimes killed or exposed to the elements. Exposed children would die or be found (often to be raised as a slave). Poverty, too, exerted its influence, as poor housing conditions and an insufficient diet reduced fertility, increased the health risks of pregnant women and increased infant mortality.

Freeborn women typically married in their late teens with men who were 5 to 50 years older. They were often widowed, but would mostly remarry if widowed before age 35. About half of the women at age 40 were unmarried widows. Freeborn men typically married for the first time between 25 and 50, and would remarry quite often with a young woman. It is not unlikely that in Roman society, the average age at paternity was 36 (Saller 2007, 91), with the average age of a man's first marriage, therefore, a little before 35. As a result there were considerable differences in age (and power) between the spouses. It also aggravated the existing shortage of women, such that males with limited economic means had less opportunity to marry at a younger age. A significant number of young unmarried males migrated from the countryside to economic centres, often sending home some of the money they earned.

The *Pax Romana*, established under Augustus, inaugurated a period of political stability and economic development, such that in the first two centuries CE there was a relatively stable growth of the population. Famines, wars and epidemics were often regional affairs and could be handled within the empire through internal migration. In the first centuries CE there was a net migration from east to west, both in the form of slaves who were 'gained' in Rome's military campaigns in the east, as well as through voluntary migration.

In the case of the Jewish population, equalling about 5–10 per cent of the total population of the Roman Empire, some peculiarities need to be noticed. Sergio DellaPergola (1992) estimates the development of the number of Jews in antiquity to be from about 0.5 million in 200 BCE to about 3 to 6 million around the start of the first century CE and down again to 1 to 2 million in 200 CE. At the start of this time period, the Jews were spread from Egypt to Mesopotamia, with a small Jewish centre around the city of Jerusalem. In Hasmonaean times the population grew in part through the expansion of the Hasmonaean state, leading to the inclusion of Gentile and mixed populations. There must have been a significant birth surplus among Jews. For Galilee specifically, Reed (2000, 84) concludes with regard to the Early Roman Period:

> The entire Galilee, both Upper and Lower Galilee, experienced demographic growth at this time. The causes of this measurable population growth in Galilee were likely the relative stable political situation under the Herodians and increased agricultural

production fostered under centralized Herodian authority, which allowed birth rates to spiral higher.

In a subsequent study, Reed provides a demographic perspective on 'Instability in Jesus' Galilee' (2010). With a growing population, new cities and villages were located in valleys and around the Sea of Galilee with increased risk of malaria and diseases associated with crowded living conditions. We should also expect a constant migration, especially of young males and elderly widows, from the more healthy hilltops with low infant mortality to the more productive and hazardous valleys and cities.

In the age of the Roman emperors, there were considerable migration streams of both Jewish slaves and freeborn Jews to the major centres of the eastern Mediterranean and to Rome itself. Because of the religious ties with the temple in Jerusalem and the policies pursued by both the temple and secular authorities, Jewish consciousness was maintained in the Diaspora, and even attracted converts from the local population. In combination with Jewish attitudes with respect to marriage, abortion, infanticide, sanitation and communal care, this produced a steady growth of the Jewish population of roughly 10–13 per cent per decade for a period of about 250 years.

All of this changed with the Jewish-Roman wars of 66–70 CE, 115–17 CE and 132–5 CE, all three initiated by Jewish revolts. The Jewish population of Palestine was greatly reduced through casualties of war, famine, deportation and slavery. The large Jewish presence in Alexandria was virtually eradicated in the war of 115–17 CE. Elsewhere in the Diaspora, however, the numbers of Jews increased through the influx of refugees, their social cohesion and the continued high birth rates (Tacitus, *Histories*, V.5). This is not so much visible in the Jewish presence in the individual cities where there were already Jews, but rather in the ever-expanding geographical footprint of Judaism, reaching Armenia, Arabia, Galatia, the northern Adriatic Sea and the western Mediterranean – possibly even the delta of Rhine, Scheldt and Meuse, and both sides of the English Channel. As migrants, the Jews spread along the transport networks and into the commercial centres of the ancient world, while maintaining a recognizable identity. It is not unlikely that this migration was spearheaded by slaves and freeborn unmarried males, with others following through marriage or economic need.

Jesus' First-Generation Followers

A key text for demographic examination is 1 Cor. 15.3-12, where Paul makes claims about groups of Jesus followers at the time of the crucifixion and in his own day. It is part of an undisputed Pauline letter. Unlike the Gospels or the book of Acts, the letter is a contemporary document, making a claim about its own time. Furthermore, the audience is not captive to Paul. Given the discussion about his leadership in Corinth, Paul could expect that his opponents would check his facts if they disagreed with him. Some preferred the leadership of Peter or Apollos. It is quite possible that 'men of James', who were sent to groups in Antioch, Galatia and beyond, visited Corinth as well. The group exchanged members with Jesus' followers in Ephesus and Rome, two other groups that were established before Paul came to those cities. Quite likely, the persons mentioned as travelling around in 9.5 – other apostles, Cephas/Peter, the brothers of the Lord, Barnabas and Paul – were all known to at least some members in his audience. Paul's claim in his letter (a durable form) is therefore subject to 'peer review'. Paul states his claim as follows:

> For among the first things I handed on to you is what I in turn had received:
> 'Christ died for our sins
> – in accordance with the scriptures.
>
> He was buried and he was raised on the third day
> – in accordance with the scriptures ...
>
> And he appeared to Cephas, then to the Twelve.
> Then he appeared to more than five hundred brothers (and sisters?) at once.'

> (Most of them are still alive, though some have died.)

> 'Then he appeared to James, then to all the apostles.'

> Last of all, as to one untimely born, he appeared also to me.

Paul seems to pass on an oral account that he received when he was converted and passed on to those whom he had witnessed (even though some of them were followers of Jesus before Paul met them). Indeed, he claims that it is one of the most important traditions that is passed on to new believers, by all the players already mentioned. According to Paul, it is the foundational tradition of the movement and the basis of the authority of the principal witnesses. The tradition is slightly adjusted here. Paul makes a remark about the five hundred and adds himself to the list. This addition is clearly made in attempt to claim likewise authority (see 9.1-2), albeit in different matters, such as food and marriage, for it was in such matters that those who claimed Paul as an authority differed from those who said other leaders should be followed (see Chapters 3–8 of the same letter). Rhetorically, this only works if it is indeed recognized by the audience that Paul, Peter and Apollos all proclaim the same crucified and risen Messiah that the Twelve, James and all the apostles were proclaiming. Note that the dispute in Corinth did not concern the resurrection of Jesus, but the bodily resurrection of the believers (15.12, 35). Presumably, some people would rather speak about the afterlife of the soul. Paul appeals to common tradition to the effect that a bodily resurrection is implied when the Christ who was raised is the same as the one who died and who was buried.

The Five Hundred

The first point for analysis is the group of five hundred *adelphois*, a plural that Paul uses in various instances to refer to both the male (brother) and the female (sister). It may be that Paul speaks of about 500 male witnesses, not counting women and children (as in Matthew 14.21), or that he speaks of 500 witnesses including the women. It may be that he reports an accurate but rounded number, or that tradition overstated the number. But the claim that most of them are still alive mitigates the level of exaggeration possible. We should therefore assume that Paul believed he was speaking of a group of 300 to 700 people. In the remainder of this chapter I will assume a round figure of 500 for all resurrection witnesses, including the women, the Twelve, James and all the apostles.

Paul's claim that only 'some have died' is demographically challenging: the chances of dying within 20 or 25 years for a randomly selected group are respectively 42 per cent and 50 per cent. If, however, the ages of the witnesses are lower than average, the situation is different. In the table below, I give the *survival* rates per age group (derived from Bagnall and Frier, 1994):

Ages	After 20 years	After 25 years
0–4	62%	57%
5–9	78%	71%
10–19	74%	66%
20–9	66%	57%
30–9	58%	47%
40–9	45%	30%
50–9	24%	11%
60+	5%	1%
Avg population	58%	50%

If there were approximately 25 years between the death of Jesus and the writing of 1 Cor. (30–55 CE), Paul's statement can be true only if the vast majority of witnesses were less than 20 years old at the time of Jesus' death. If there were about 20 years in between (e.g. from 33 to 54 CE), the group between ages 20 and 29 can be included as well. It is likely, therefore, that the vast majority of resurrection witnesses were in the same age group as people who today convert or join new religious movements: teenagers and young adults between 15 and 25 years.

The Twelve

Scholars have noted that Paul mentions the Twelve as a traditional name for the group of men whom Jesus symbolically had chosen, even though the group probably was incomplete at the time of the resurrection experience that they shared (assuming Judas did indeed fall out with the group). Paul mentions them as witnesses, but does not specify how many of them were still around. Later tradition has it that one of them (John, the son of Zebedee) survived until the late 80s or early 90s CE, which on first sight seems unlikely, given the low life expectancy in late antiquity. But although the life expectancy of young adults between 15 and 30 years old would range from 50 to 55 years, these are only averages. In reality, some died younger and others died older and the decline is rather evenly spread over a far longer period. If we assume that most of the 12 apostles (I now take the number as if Judas has been replaced) were around 20 to 25 years old in the year 30 CE, and apply Model West level 4 for males (with a life expectancy of 25 years at birth), we obtain the following result:

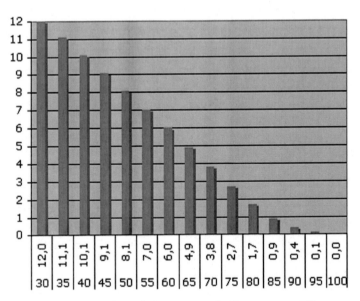

Expected number of survivors in the first century CE.

In this model, we would expect that every five years, one of the Twelve would die. Thus, when Paul wrote 1 Cor., the group of Twelve still existed, but they were likely reduced to some seven or eight members. Three or four may have lived beyond 70 CE, one or two beyond 80 CE. It is not too unlikely that one of these even made it to around 90 CE.

All the Apostles

This group is considerably larger than the Twelve. The synoptic Gospels assign the symbolic numbers of 70 or 72 to this group and place its origins within the mission of Jesus. For Paul, anyone who has seen the Lord and who has been sent out to another place to be witness to the Lord, is called 'apostle', or envoy of Jesus. The term likely included the Twelve, Peter, James and possibly even the other brothers of Jesus referred to in 9.5. In Paul's day it also included people such as Andronicus and Junia(s), mentioned in Rom. 16.7 – in a list that includes people who were well known to Paul's Corinthian audience. Whether the term includes women is uncertain, but not unlikely. Many scholars claim Junia(s) was a female apostle (Bauckham 2002; Epp 2005), but Wolters (2008) argues on linguistic grounds that the name Junia(s) more likely refers to a Jewish man by the name of *Yehunni.*

The Women at the Grave

Several theories have been put forward as to why Paul does not report the women at the grave as witnesses in 1 Cor. 15. Some argue that Paul did not recognize the witness of a woman (even though his Jewish background would tell him that the witness of two women equals that of a man, let alone the witness of three women). Others believe that the position of a woman in the Roman world was such that the audience would not accept the testimony of a woman (which is, however, at odds with the prominent contribution of women such as Paul's friend Priscilla to the community in Corinth). Again others believe that the church was embarrassed by the fact that the first reports of the risen one were from gullible women, and that therefore the tradition that Paul quotes already omitted the women (which does not explain why they then re-emerged in all four canonical Gospels, as well as in several apocryphal works). If we accept that the group of 500 – and possibly also the term apostles – included women, none of these arguments seem particularly compelling.

Demographical analysis points to an additional possibility. There may have been three or four women at the grave: three Marys and a Salomé are mentioned. The one about whose age we are best informed is Mary the mother of Jesus. Jesus was her firstborn when she was between 15 and 20 years old. Jesus was crucified some 30 to 36 years later, when Mary was roughly about 50 years old. At that age, she could be expected to live some 15 years more. The odds are that she died well before Paul wrote his letter around 55 CE. Mary the wife of Kleopas may have been Mary's sister-in-law and Salomé may have been Mary's sister, and they may have had sons who were friends of Jesus (see Chapter 7). If so, they may well have been of about the same age as Mary.

Mary of Magdalene is mentioned in Luke 8.4 as one of the rather independent and well-off women who could afford to sponsor Jesus' mission:

Mary of Magdalene, Susannah and Johanna, the wife of Herod's steward. They could travel with Jesus, which is better understood if they were past a certain age. Their position may have been like that of the noble women in Acts 13.50 and 17.4. Typically, these were older women, often widows (about half the women above age 40 were widowed) who were financially independent when their husbands had died (the difference between bride and bridegroom could be up to 50 years). If Mary Magdalene may be compared to this group, her age may have been comparable to that of the mother of Jesus. If we assume that the ages of these four women were 50, 55, 55 and 60 in the year 30 CE, then the expected number of surviving women over time would be 2.2 in 40 CE and 0.7 in 50 CE. In that case, the chances that all four women had died before 55 CE are more than 50 per cent.

Whereas Peter, indeed most of the 12 apostles, most of the 500 brethren, and also James, were still alive when Paul wrote this letter, it is quite possible that the women had already died. If so, only Peter/Cephas, James and the survivors of the groups of 500, the Twelve and the apostles were still available as witnesses. Perhaps, then, Paul omitted the women, simply because they had died and were no longer witnesses.

Apostates

One group whom Paul does not mention at all is the apostates. How many were there among the primary witnesses? Note that Paul can refer only to those witnesses who are still alive and still part of the movement. They are still witnessing the fact that their resurrection experience was 'real'. If indeed the majority of the Twelve, of the apostles and of the 500 were still witnessing, whereas 40–50 per cent of them had already died, then very few of them had broken with their faith (note that this observation regards only the primary witnesses, nothing is said here about later converts). This means that the group behaved differently from what would be expected if the resurrection experiences were somehow conversions (as one could argue in the cases of Paul and perhaps James, who previously did not follow Jesus). Modern research finds that those who are likely to convert to a new religious movement are also likely to 'deconvert' or 'reconvert' to another movement (see Chapter 5). Furthermore, the low level of apostasy of the first witnesses may testify to the strength of the resurrection experiences as well as to the social cohesion within the group who had shared these experiences.

Geography

One of the striking features of early Christianity is the fact that the number of communities spread so quickly. If natural growth is to a large part responsible for the growth of Christianity (see Chapter 5), then it is likely that a significant number of first-generation believers, their children and grandchildren were moving away from Palestine. Jesus had led an itinerant missionary movement. After his death this mission came to include Diaspora Jews and Gentiles. Not only the Twelve and the brothers of Jesus are reported to have travelled (1 Cor. 9.5), but also other 'apostles', by virtue of their title (e.g. Rom. 16.7). The followers of Jesus therefore had an ideological motif to migrate. But this motif only added to four existing important demographic developments:

- There was a general migration from eastern to western provinces in the Roman Empire. Frier estimates that a net number of some 200,000 persons migrated from east to west every decade.
- There was a specific migration of Jews to Diaspora communities resulting from birth surplus in Palestine.
- Prior to 70 CE, Jerusalem was the city to which significant numbers of Diaspora Jews came for a religious holiday, or for a few years of education. Many then returned to the Diaspora cities.
- Around 70 CE, the Jewish Wars drove large numbers of Jews, as refugees and slaves, out of their traditional homelands of Palestine and Egypt, both to the west and to the east.

The Generations of Jesus' Followers

Scholars often speak of generations of Jesus followers, such as Michael White: *From Jesus to Christianity: How Four Generations of Visionaries and Storytellers Created the New Testament and Christian Faith* (2004). He divides the generations in time periods: 30 CE until the First Jewish Revolt, 70–100 CE, and 100 CE until the middle of the second century. But how correct is it to use a demographic term like 'generations'? If we take the resurrection witnesses as an example, we can analyse the time periods in which they, their spouses, their children and their grandchildren were active:

- The primary witnesses: in 60 CE, half of them were still alive, aged 45–55. Few if any had left the movement. In 80 CE, we would expect that only one out of seven was still alive (70–5 people), aged 65–75; but if we take into account the Jewish War, more will have died among those who stayed in Palestine. We may assume that they did not escape the fate of the other Jews in Palestine, who were killed (directly or indirectly), sold off as slaves, or fled to other countries. But a significant number were called 'apostles' or envoys by Paul, which may indicate that they had already left Palestine when Paul wrote to the Corinthians (compare the use of 'apostles' in Rom. 16.7). All in all, it is not unlikely that some 50–60 people were still alive after the fall of Jerusalem in 80 CE, predominantly in the Diaspora. Such a number would rapidly decrease to about 10–15 in 90 CE and 0–2 in 100 CE.
- Their spouses: Paul states in 1 Cor. 9.5 that the other apostles and the brothers of the Lord were married in the 50s CE. It is likely that most of the 500 married as well. The situation for male and female spouses is

different as a result of the difference in the age of marriage for the genders. Most females at age 15–25 were married to older men; most males were still single. There were therefore very few couples among the witnesses in the same age bracket. Most of them would marry or remarry someone from outside the group, which leads to another group of several hundred spouses. It is difficult to say how many women were present in the original group. It is hard to imagine that they could have been part of such a group without the consent of either a father, a guardian brother or a husband. Given the probability that relatively few elder people (including elder spouses) were part of the group, it may have been that married young women were under-represented in the group. The description of the group in Acts 1 seems to assume the presence of young males, some elder women and their family members. The male spouses of the group of 500 may therefore have been relatively few. Furthermore, not all of them would have joined the movement. Given their more advanced age, they would have died out sooner than the 500 as a whole. Likewise, slaves were more restricted and would have been under-represented in the original group (but not necessarily among later converts). This is relevant to our discussion, as slaves were less likely to marry and have children. In other words, the majority of the 500 were young freeborn males who would marry even younger wives. Their numerous spouses were children or even unborn in 30 CE. It is likely that many of them joined the religious movement of their husbands. Overall, it is likely that a significant number of female spouses outlived the 500 witnesses well into the second century.

- Their children and grandchildren: already in 30 CE there must have been some children born to the young women among the primary witnesses. This increased over time, as the young Jewish males married and continued to father children until an advanced age. The children were therefore born between 20 CE and 80 CE, with a peak around 50 CE. Given the high birth rate among married Jewish couples, and if there were, say, 400 couples, the primary witnesses may have conceived well over 3,000 children (although half of them would die before the age of five). Over time, the daughters would give birth to grandchildren from about 40 CE until the end of the first century. The sons would reproduce from about 55 CE until 140 CE. Depending on the number of marriages inside or outside the group of descendants, the total number of couples would have been between 1,000 and 2,000, having somewhere in the order of 10,000 grandchildren (half of which again would die before the age of five). It may be expected that a significant number of children and grandchildren raised in the movement would never deconvert. Furthermore, many of them migrated out of Palestine, which reduced the number of casualties in the Jewish Wars.

To sum up, the generations show considerable overlap. The first generation consisted of primary witnesses and spouses. The primary witnesses were active until the end of the first century (the dotted line in the graph below), their (female) spouses until the first decades of the second century. The second generation was present from the start and ended around the middle of the second century. The third generation started from the middle of the first century and ended around the start of the third.

generations of Jesus followers

Demographic analysis (indicative)

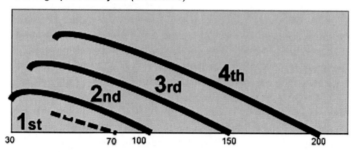

Periodization into four 'Generations' (White, 2005)

1st	2nd	3rd	4th

The Family of Jesus

Was Jesus the Youngest Brother?

There has been some debate about the question whether Jesus was the oldest or the youngest child in the family of Mary and Joseph. The later infancy-narratives claim that Joseph was an old man with older children when he married Mary and respected her virginity until the day he died. This is certainly possible as young women had a higher risk of dying because of the dangers of giving birth, and adult men often married twice or thrice. Hieronymus argued that his brothers were his cousins, but that would conflict with the evidence that some of the cousins of Jesus among the Twelve (see Chapter 7) followed Jesus, while the brothers of Jesus did not follow him, as the Gospel of John has to admit (7.5). Richard Bauckham (1990), in his monograph on *Jude and the Relatives of Jesus in the Early Church*, believes that only the first two options are credible from a historical point of view. So Jesus was either the first-born son in the family, or the last-born.

The first information to consider is found in Paul's letters to the Galatians and the Corinthians and Josephus. Historians generally accept that Jesus' brother James was the leader of the Jerusalem group of Jesus followers in the late 30s CE, that the brothers of Jesus visited Diaspora communities in the 50s CE, and that James was lynched around 62 CE:

- The death of James: if we assume that James was the oldest brother in a previous marriage, that several brothers (and sisters) were born (probably more than six, given the high infant mortality rate in those years), that James's father was widowed and then remarried, then we should assume that James was some 20 to 30 years older than Jesus. This would mean that James was around 50 to 60 years old during Jesus' ministry and between 80 and 90 years of age at the time of his own death. This is possible, but quite unlikely, as less than 2 per cent of 55-year-old men would live to their 85th year. If, on the other hand, James had been the younger brother of Jesus, he would have been around 25 at the time of the crucifixion and roughly 55 when he was lynched. The chance of a 25-year-old male reaching 55 is approximately 45 per cent. Statistically, this is a far more likely scenario.
- The presence of the brothers in the 50s CE: if, say, four brothers were already 45–55 years old in 30 CE, demographics predict that only 0.6 brother would still be alive in 55 CE. This is hard to reconcile with Paul's language in 1 Cor. 9.5 ('The brothers of the Lord' travelling around with their wives at ages 70–80). If, however, we assume four brothers aged 15–25 in 30 CE, we would expect that three would still be alive in 50 CE, two in 60 CE and one in 70 CE. This is in line with the idea that the majority of Jesus' brothers (aged 40–50) were still alive in the 50s CE, that James died in 62 CE and that Jude was remembered as James's brother who could have continued his work (Jude 1).

These findings relate well with two stories (Mk 3.19b-35 and 6.1-6) that I discuss in Chapter 7. The author seems to assume that several of Jesus' sisters were married in Nazareth, whereas his brothers still lived with their mother. As the sisters typically married between 15 and 25, and the brothers between 25 and 35, the most likely explanation is that when Jesus was about 30, his younger sisters were already married, but not his younger brothers.

The story about his cousin Symeon/Simon (the son of his father's brother), who is said to have succeeded James as 'bishop' of Jerusalem until Trajan's reign, is less firm from a chronological perspective (see Bauckham 1990, ch. 2), but it is likely that he was younger than Jesus. Also the remark of Hegesippus that the majority of his relatives (presumably counting his brothers and cousins) were still alive to discuss the succession of James with the surviving apostles and disciples, can only have been plausible to a first-century audience if most of them were younger than Jesus.

How Many Children Did Mary Have and When Did Her Husband Die?

In Roman Egypt, married woman were far more fertile than unmarried women. The likelihood of giving birth for a married woman rose from about 20 per cent per year in her teens to over 35 per cent in her twenties, going down to 30 per cent in her thirties and 15 per cent in her early forties. After a marriage from age 15 to 41, the average number of children would be around eight. As roughly 50 per cent of children died by age five, such a woman would have only four surviving children.

In Mary's case, then, it seems that when Jesus was about 30, she had five sons and several daughters who were married in Nazareth. If this information from Mk 6.3 is correct, Mary had at least seven surviving children and the married daughters must have been born within fifteen years of the birth of Jesus. Given the possibility that there were more than two daughters and given the high infant mortality rate, we should assume that Mary had given birth significantly more times than seven. This means that she probably had a husband for a considerable period of time and that the couple was relatively fertile.

In the table below I have modelled the number of births for a widow who had her firstborn at age 17 (using the average for married women and the maximum fertility socially sustainable – Bagnall and Frier, 143):

Widow at age	Age of firstborn	Average births	Maximum births
35	18	7.0	9.5
36	19	7.2	9.9
37	20	7.5	10.3
38	21	7.8	10.7
39	22	8.1	11.1

As can be seen in the table, a fertile couple under these circumstances can be expected to have had up to about eleven births if the marriage lasted until the woman's late thirties. If Mary had seven or more surviving children, then the family's infant mortality must have been lower than it was on average. It is likely, therefore, that the family generated enough income to provide sufficient food and shelter for this large number of children. It is also probable that the husband was still alive in the teenage years of the first-born son.

By means of illustration, I give a plausible but purely imaginative example of how the family of Jesus could have looked when Jesus was about 30 years old. I do not suggest that this example is accurate in any of its details, but I do believe that such an example can help the reader appreciate the general reality of such a family in late antiquity:

(Husband, died 9 years ago at age 50, would have been 59)
Mary, 47, a widow for 9 years
1. Jesus, 30, unmarried
2. Sister, 27, married, 2 living children (and one deceased)
3. (Brother, deceased at age 0, would have been 25)
4. James, 24, unmarried
5. Joses, 21, unmarried
6. (Sister, deceased at age 4, would have been 19)
7. Sister, 17, married, 1 living child
8. Jude, 15, unmarried

9. (Sister, deceased at age 0, would have been 12)
10. Simon, 10, unmarried
11. (Brother, deceased at age 1, would have been 8)

Before we dramatize the psychological trauma of so many family deaths, I should note that the experience of Jesus was not abnormal. In this particular scenario, infant mortality in this family was 36 per cent, whereas the average was about 50 per cent. Furthermore, given the age differences between spouses, the early death of the father was very common. Typically, children were born to fathers aged 25 to 55. Although fewer men lived to be 50 or 55, the percentage of married men grew with age, such that the total number of married men between ages 25 and 55 was relatively constant, and their first or second wives would all still be in their fertile years. In the table below, I have shown the percentages of fatherless children at ages 10, 20 and 30.

		Age of the father when the child was born		
		30	40	50
Percentage of children that were fatherless at ages 10, 20 and 30	10	19%	26%	36%
	20	40%	53%	72%
	30	62%	79%	94%

The table clearly shows the normality of Jesus' loss of his father. About half the children at age 20 were fatherless. About three-quarters of them were fatherless at age 30. By that age, more than half of them would have lost their mother, so that only one in ten would still have both parents at age 30. About four out of ten had lost both parents at that age. From that perspective, Jesus was not unlucky.

The phenomenon of fatherlessness has received specific attention in an edited volume, *Growing Up Fatherless in Antiquity* (ed. Hübner and Ratzan, 2009). In his contribution, Walter Scheidel (2009, 40) describes the demographic background of the phenomenon and concludes that there were three ideal-typical categories of fatherless children: (1) Children of relatively young men, who grew up with a father and cared for their younger siblings after their father had finally died. (2) Children of relatively young fathers who lost their father at an early age and grew up under the tutelage of their father's male relatives. (3) Children of older men who lost their father early and were more likely to grow up under guardians who were not close paternal relatives. Although I disagree with Van Aarde in terms of Jesus' place in the family (I would include him in the first category), Van Aarde's study (see Chapter 2 above) remains a remarkable psychologically informed analysis of the situation of many of the young men who followed Jesus.

Jesus' Family in the Second Century

Demographic analysis works well with larger numbers (such as the 500). The problem with smaller numbers is their variability. Children are born male and female, but some families have only boys or girls. Infant mortality was about 50 per cent, but some families lost none, others lost all their children. Furthermore, daughters were 'married off' into other families, which means that their offspring seldom counted. With only four men to work with, it is even harder. The average age of reaching paternity was in the mid-thirties, but men produced offspring from their twenties until their sixties. Some men father impressive (male) bloodlines, other lines die out quickly. Richard Bauckham studied both James (1999) and Jude (*Jude and the Relatives of Jesus in the Early Church*, 1990). He concludes that after James and Jude, their cousin Symeon and the descendants of Jude were the most influential leaders in the movement of Jesus followers in Palestine (both Jerusalem and the Galilee) and the Aramaic-speaking Diaspora until the Bar Kokhba revolt. Bauckham argues that their status as *Davidids* and leaders of a Messianic movement may have made them the target of both Roman authorities and Jewish supporters of alternative Messiahs, such as Bar Kokhba. I would add that the disastrous effects of the revolts on the Jewish population of Palestine must have reduced significantly the chances of survival for their family lines. Furthermore, the numerically successful part of the movement in the second century was located in the Graeco-Roman Diaspora. The Aramaic-speaking Jewish followers of Jesus, and especially those who wished to remain Thora-observant, would become an ever smaller and more isolated minority in the Christian movement. They died out, or assimilated with other groups (such as Jews, Syriac Christians or alternative 'sects'), by the end of the sixth century CE.

Conclusion

Demographic analysis of Paul's letter to the Corinthians demonstrates that there was a core of Jesus followers, including his own brothers, who remained in the movement throughout its formative years. As such, we can speak of a significant level of social continuity between the historical Jesus and the early Jesus followers who proclaimed him as the crucified and risen Messiah. If we include their children and grandchildren in our analysis, it seems likely that their presence in the movement lasted well into the second century.

Annex: The Age and Marital Status of Jesus.

The following two demographical insights do not concern the followers of Jesus, but Jesus himself.

Could Jesus Have Expected to Live beyond 30?

In his review of Miller's *Jesus at Thirty*, Justin Meggitt (2007, 23) says, 'given that the average life expectancy ... at this time was probably in the mid-twenties, it seems odd for Miller to argue for the helpfulness of Levinson's insights about the importance of the age-thirty transition ... for understanding Jesus'. Regardless of the merits of Miller's analysis, Meggit makes a classic mistake. The life expectancy *at birth* in pre-industrial societies is dramatically reduced because of the mortality rate of infants. Many died in their first year and about half of them would not live beyond the age of five. Very few people, on the other hand, died around the age of 25. Children who made it past the age of 5 could be expected to live beyond their 45th year. In the demographic model that Bagnall and Frier (1994, 100) use for males in Roman Egypt, with a life expectancy at birth of 25 years, the expected remaining years and total life expectancy develop as follows:

At age	average years left	total life expectancy
0	25	25
5	41	46
10	38	48
20	31	51
30	24	54
40	20	60
50	15	65
60	10	70
70	6	76
80	3	83
90	2	92

A teenager or adolescent could expect to become about 50 years old, if he had a knack for statistics. Most people, however, are optimistic with respect to their own life and would rather use an ideal life expectancy, assuming they were to live in good health and die of old age. Thus, Psalm 90.10 speaks of 70 to 80 years, and Augustine says that a newborn baby has a life expectancy of 80 years (*Sermo* 84, on Mt. 19.16-17).

Was a 30-Year Old Unmarried Man an Exception?

Ideally, a freeborn girl married in her teens and a male in his twenties (the situation for slaves was different). From that perspective, it seems odd if Jesus had been unmarried at the age of 30. But again, these are ideal values.

In Roman Egypt, 95 per cent of freeborn females had married at least once at age 30. But this number grew over time: at age 20, 35 per cent had not yet married. Although almost all females above their thirties were married, the same cannot have been true for freeborn males. Females had a somewhat higher death rate in their fertile years because of the risks of childbirth. As a result, older males remarried, thus reducing the chances for younger males to marry. The injunction in the Talmud that a father can do no better than find his son a wife (*b.Qiddushin* 29a, 30b), is therefore not proof that all Jewish fathers provided wives for all their sons except for Jesus, but rather that women were scarce and fathers died early. In the discussion it is clear the father's power to do so lies in paying the dowry for his son. Males in economically less favourable circumstances would have to postpone marriage plans until their thirties or even forties. In Roman Egypt, only two-thirds of the men around 35 years old had ever married. Only at an age of 50 years, the vast majority of surviving free men are reported to have married at least once.

Age	Females	Males
12	15%	0%
16	30%	0%
20	65%	25%
24	85%	55%
28	90%	60%
32	95%	65%
36	95%	70%
40	95%	70%

Percentage of freeborn Egyptians married or widowed.

Chapter 5

MODELLING A NEW RELIGIOUS MOVEMENT

In the previous chapter we saw that there was a significant number of first-generation witnesses and their descendants in the first century. The question is whether they were of much influence on the Diaspora communities in which the letters of Paul and the surviving first-century Gospels were written. It seems that the influence of new converts, some of whom were more educated and wealthy, must have been growing over time. Thus the weight of the movement shifted from Galilean peasants and artisans, via Jerusalem, to Greek-speaking Jews and Gentiles around the Mediterranean. Many scholars over the past 150 years have stressed the Gentile nature of Christianity outside Palestine. In this chapter, I will use sociological insights in the dynamics of new religious movements and mathematical modelling to come to reasoned assumptions regarding questions like:

- How did the movement grow in numbers and geographical spread?
- How much interaction was there between the various communities?
- How Jewish or Gentile were these communities?
- How significant was the presence of first-generation followers and their descendants?

Conversion and New Religious Movements

Conversion

The classical research paradigm to study conversion was psychological and individual, with a preference for the sudden and total conversion experience of Christians (James 1902). But the reality is that such conversions are a minority; far more people experience a more gradual process of conversion, even if they do experience a point in time at which the conversion is consciously acknowledged. Modern researchers, including psychologists of religion, stress the sociological aspects of the conversion process. Hood, Spilka, Hunsberger and Gorsuch (1996, ch. 8) contrast the two paradigms as follows:

Sudden conversion	Gradual conversion
• Middle to late adolescence	• Late adolescence to early adulthood
• Emotional, suggestive	• Intellectual, rational
• Stern theology	• Compassionate theology
• Passive role for convert	• Active role for convert
• Release from sin and guilt	• Search for meaning and purpose

Paloutzian (1996) acknowledges both paradigms of conversion and adds a third process: religious socialization of children who are raised in a certain religion. Focusing on conversion, Paloutzian (2005) tries to provide a multi-dimensional framework for religious conversion and spiritual transformation, by defining it as a change of a 'meaning-system'. This system includes attitudes and beliefs, values, goals, overall purpose, self-definition and ultimate concerns. Apart from the few total transformations that draw the attention of psychologists, there are many more conversions that consist of a partial change of the meaning system. But not every 'conversion' requires a meaning system change. The Amish have institutionalized a period of rebellion, before young adults are supposed to decide whether they wish to remain Amish. Evangelical and Pentecostal Christians, especially those practising adult baptism, teach that their teenagers and adolescents need to 'convert' and be born again, in order to become full members of the church they are raised in. Their 'conversion' is essentially a rite of passage in an existing meaning system. Finally there is the group that churches often claim as 'converted' but are better described as 'reaffiliated' from other churches, in case such people essentially maintained their meaning system. Thus an evangelical reformed man, who does not fit very well in his local church, does not really 'convert' when he joins a Baptist church (sometimes referred to as the 'recirculation of the saints').

Although a minority of people convert, something can be said about the type of people who are more likely to convert and the type of circumstances under which this is more likely to happen. In the case of established religions, apostasy (in the sense of becoming a-religious or non-observant) typically occurs in adolescence or early adulthood. But many return to their religious roots later in life, typically when they have families of their own. Only a minority of people raised and socialized in a certain religious framework leave it behind permanently. Converts to new religious movements are typically adolescents or young adults. People who convert once are far more likely to convert again than others, or to deconvert and return to the religion they were raised in, or remain seekers. Converts do not score differently on cognitive measures than non-converts, but they do on emotional measures (according to Paloutzian 1996, this is especially true for 'sudden converts'). They report more childhood and adolescent stress, prior drug use and psychiatric problems, as well as having less love and admiration for their fathers. This was true also for converts to established religions like Orthodox Judaism and Roman Catholicism, where the majority of members never changed their religion. There is, therefore, quite a difference in background between those who are raised in a certain religion and those who converted later from a different background.

The majority of converts are recruited through social networks. Lofland and Stark (1965) write about the following necessary and sufficient conditions for conversion to new religious movements: (1) enduring and acutely felt tensions, (2) a religious problem-solving perspective, (3) self-identification as a seeker, (4) encounter of the new religious movement at a turning point in life, (5) an affective bond with believers, (6) neutralization of attachments to persons outside the cult, and (7) intensive interaction with other converts. In an assessment of the model in the case of a Buddhist movement in America, Snow and Phillips (1980) conclude that affective bonds and intensive interaction are the two most important factors. Rambo (1993) proposes a seven-stage process for conversion in general, described by the keywords: context, crisis, quest, encounter, interaction, commitment and consequences.

Conversion to the Movement(s) of John and Jesus?

Some caution is needed before modern insights from Western countries are applied to first-century Palestine or the Roman Empire. I would like to see more results from cross-cultural research in pre-industrialized collectivistic societies. But the research discussed above can help us to ask some questions and clarify some matters. A key task for biblical scholars willing to use modern insights, such as Scot McKnight in *Turning to Jesus: The Sociology of Conversion in the Gospels* (2002), will be to classify the different 'conversion' situations in the historical analysis of Jesus and his earliest followers. Were the converts Jewish or Gentile? If Jews: were they observant or not? If Gentiles: were they god-fearers, pagans or 'unchurched'? Did they consider the movement they joined part of their religion or foreign to it? Did they decide themselves to join the movement, or was the decision made by their spouse, their parent(s) or their master?

In John's case, both the synoptic Gospels as well as Josephus indicate that a large proportion of Jews saw his activity as a legitimate part of their religion. John's movement seems to have been a reform movement that did not provide an alternative religion, but rather an opportunity to reaffirm and deepen one's existing beliefs. For many of his followers, it may also have been a stimulus to lead a life that is more in accordance with those beliefs. For some it may even have been a more profound change of behaviour, as they grew ashamed of their previous non-observant lifestyle. The same may have been true for the mission of Jesus before his crucifixion, although following Jesus on his journeys would be something different (Lk. 9.57-62).

After Jesus' death, his early followers developed a meaning system that – while still Jewish – included certain changes. This may well have been influenced by the resurrection experiences reported by Paul in 1 Cor. 15. The demographic analysis of that passage (see Chapter 4) suggests that most of Jesus' followers who participated in this process, the first-generation believers, are not to be characterized as converts at that point in time. They jointly developed as a group. The psychohistorian should employ different methods and analogies to understand their transformation. Those who joined later can be considered as 'converts'. They would include Jews, god-fearers and Gentiles; both devout and non-observant people; both primary and secondary converts. Finally, from the start there would have been children who never converted, but were 'socialized' in the new religious movement.

The important studies of A.D. Nock (*Conversion: The Old and the New in Religion from Alexander the Great to Augustine of Hippo*, 1933) and Ramsay MacMullen (*Christianizing the Roman Empire: A.D. 100–400*, 1984) focus on the conversion of Gentiles after the apostolic period. It should be noted that conversion in the third to the fifth century, to what then becomes the established and even favoured religion of Christianity, involves new motivations and processes that are beyond the scope of the present study.

New Religious Movements

Reinhold Niebuhr (1929, discussed in Hood et al. 1996, ch. 9) argues that people dissatisfied with the commonness and permissiveness of churches form or join sects with more demanding criteria for membership. Whereas the church is inclusive in its approach to members, the sect is exclusive. Contrary to the church, the sect denounces mainstream society. If a sect functions well and grows, it may have some members wishing to adapt more to society. If they do not leave the sect, but succeed in reducing the tension between sect and society, the sect has become a church. If some members are dissatisfied with that, they may split off as a new sect and the process may repeat itself. This approach explains well the splintering process of Protestant Christianity, but it is less able to explain other types of new religious movements. Glock (1964, discussed in Paloutzian 1996, ch. 6) suggests that people join a new religious movement in response to and in accordance with different needs. Sects (in the sense of religious groups that split off from mainstream churches) often attract people who are economically deprived. In response, the sect offers them spiritual rewards. A group that is *socially deprived* (lack of status or influence) in their current religion may split off and form a similar church of their own (but now with an increase in spiritual tension). People who are *organismically deprived* (physical ailments) may join a healing movement. In time such movements may die again or develop into a cult. People who feel *ethically deprived* because they deplore the morals of the larger church or society as a whole may join a reform movement, which is directed at changing the larger religion of which it sees itself as a faithful part. These movements often have a limited lifespan. Finally, people with *psychic needs* – sometimes attributed to their religious upbringing – may be prone to join a cult that completely replaces their previous religious framework.

The difference between a sect and a cult is that a sect arises from within a certain religion. It often tries to 'restore' that religion to its assumed original purity, although it can also wish to 'transform' it to respond better to society. Cults, on the other hand, are novel forms of religion. They often come from elsewhere, or from a particular charismatic leader who claims unique insights or revelations. Sects (and I am thinking of restorative sects in particular) tend to attract more men than women, people who are relatively more (extrinsically) religious and often enjoy less status, wealth and education. Cults on the other hand, tend to attract more women than men, often with more status, wealth and education.

According to Stark, in his discussion of Mormonism (2005), the prospects of a new religious movement to sustain a significant growth over a longer period of time are better if the following conditions apply:

- Cultural continuity with the conventional faith(s) of the societies in which converts are sought.
- Non-empirical doctrines (that cannot be proven wrong).
- A medium level of tension with their surrounding environment (strict, but not too strict), which must be maintained even as the movement grows.
- Legitimate leaders with adequate authority to be effective.
- A highly motivated, volunteer religious labour force, willing to proselytize.
- An adequate level of fertility at least to offset member mortality, combined with effective socialization of the children raised within the movement so as to minimize both defection and the appeal for reduced strictness.
- Competition with weak, local, conventional religious organizations, within a relatively unregulated religious economy.
- Strong internal attachments while remaining open social networks, able to maintain and form ties with outsiders.

The Movements of John, Jesus and the Early Jesus Followers

With the necessary caveats, I will now discuss the movements of John and Jesus in terms of new religious movements. Both Josephus and the canonical Gospels, in various places, claim that John's message was widely approved of by the Jewish populace. One could call it a reform movement that sought to reinvigorate Judaism with the vision of God's reign. According to Josephus (*Antiquities* 18.117), John's followers promised to live righteously, as governor Pliny's Christians in Pontus-Bithynia still did nearly a century later (10.96).

For many Jews, then, the Jesus movement in its first decades was still very Jewish, and its members continued to worship in synagogue and temple. It was special in the sense that it made a specific claim and required its members to live together in a certain way. Both these elements were not un-Jewish. But not everyone accepted the new movement. The persecution of which Paul speaks in Gal. 1.13 seems to have killed Stephen, later instances may have cost the lives of James the apostle and James the brother of Jesus (in 41 and 62 CE). It is not clear whether the persecution was solely a matter of the priestly authorities, or that more segments of Jewish leadership and society were involved. Josephus tells us that many considered James, the brother of Jesus, to be a righteous and pious Jew. The tension between Judaism and the followers of Jesus seems to have been influenced largely by local factors and incidents. In any case, to the young Paul, or Saul, it was clear that the movement was not compatible with his view of Judaism. When he joined the movement he was persecuting, it implied a partial but profound change of his meaning system. For others the change was far less dramatic.

The Jerusalem church, under the leadership of James, seems to have remained law-observant. As such, the Palestinian movement can (from a modern perspective) be described as a Jewish sect that may have been attractive especially to men with little wealth or status. On the other hand, the veneration of the crucified Jesus as the risen Lord fits better with the characteristics of a cult. In Jerusalem it seems to have attracted some priests and Pharisees, as well as Jews from the Diaspora visiting the city for the festivals or for a longer period. Over time and outside Palestine, the movement becomes more and more 'foreign' to Jews and can best be regarded as a cult. This is even clearer when we look at the position of the movement outside the context of Jews and god-fearers. For potential Gentile converts, it has all the characteristics of a new and foreign religious movement that has relatively high demands of its members and requires them to change their beliefs, behaviour and worship.

If the original core of followers consisted of poorly educated Galileans, then the influx of better-educated Jews and god-fearers from Jerusalem and the Diaspora injected a new type of authority. The authority based on personal knowledge of John the Baptist and Jesus gave way to knowledge of Jewish tradition and Scripture, such as possessed by Paul, Apollos or James (cf. 2 Cor. 5.16). As the movement spread into the Diaspora, the cult attracted some educated and wealthy Gentiles (quite likely more females than males). Their status in the city was considerably higher than that of the migrant Jewish followers of Jesus. As hosts they would have been co-leaders of the activities in their houses. As literate persons, they would have been able to read out letters and compose literary works themselves. As long as the movement operated out of the private homes of their more wealthy patrons, informal female leadership may have played an important role. As the original witnesses of Jesus died out, educated Gentiles would come to dominate the movement (see, for instance, Lucian's *Peregrinus*). Thus they became instrumental in the process through which some first-century traditions and writings of Jewish Christians were preserved while others were not. They also wrote much of the literature that interpreted these first-century writings and shaped the theology of emerging Christianity. It is quite understandable that they cherished the writings of Paul, which made it possible that Gentiles became full Christians and leaders of the church. Whereas the earliest followers of Jesus maintained continuity with Judaism, leaders such as Paul made it possible for god-fearers to become full members without becoming Jews, yet later leaders created cultural continuity with Gentile society (for instance by presenting Christianity as a monotheistic philosophy).

The Rise of Christianity

In 1996, sociologist Rodney Stark published a seminal study, *The Rise of Christianity*, in which he uses an exponential growth model, the sociology of new religious movements and basic statistical correlations to reconstruct the growth of early Christianity. He argues that Christianity as any new cult grew exponentially from a very low base. He believes that the mission to the Jews had been successful. As a cult, Christianity recruited people from higher social classes and women. As a result, the movement had a surplus of women, both leading to secondary converts (male spouses) and – in combination with strong family ethics – a significant birth surplus. Stark argues that the care given to non-Christians and the visible sacrifices made by martyrs contributed to its missionary success.

Reactions from Biblical Scholars

Stark's study has provoked many scholars to react or to integrate his findings. Some of the criticism is justified, whereas other points seem to follow from a lack of familiarity with statistics or the use of indicative numbers rather than best estimates.

In 1998, *The Journal for Early Christian Studies* ran a theme of Stark's book. Todd Klutz judges that the book was not without merit as a 'redescription' of Christian origins, but not as fundamentally new as Stark has 'tried to make us think'. Keith Hopkins uses Stark's framework to make calculations of his own. In his work, Hopkins used Stark's starting number, the principle of natural growth and the growth rate of 40 per cent. Hopkins also accepts Stark's point that 'Christianity should have appealed particularly to Jews rather than to pagans' and suspects that 'until about 150 CE, most Christians were ex-Jews or their descendants'. But Hopkins is less confident than Stark with regard to the claim that Christianity over-recruited from higher social classes. He points to pagan critics, such as Celsus, who accused Christians of recruiting 'tradesmen, illiterates, women and children'. His particular contribution is the calculation of the number of literate people in early Christian communities (using an estimate of 2 per cent of the adults who would be able to produce a literary work like a letter or a narrative). Elizabeth Castelli agrees with Stark that Christianity should be approached as any religious movement, and applauds his use of sociological models and quantitative methods. She takes issue, however, with Stark's assumptions regarding women in Early Christianity, which are often in conflict with the findings of feminist scholars. Castelli doubts the importance of natural growth and points to the ascetic movement among early Christian women.

Jack Sanders (1999) argues against the idea of a majority of Jews, or ex-Jews, among early Christians. He believes that most Jews in late antiquity remained firmly oriented to their religious culture and notes that surviving evidence shows a Jewish-Christian presence only in a few locations and also that most converts were non-Jews. He dismisses Stark's statistical argument, because, he argues, Jews were present everywhere around the Mediterranean. In an edited volume on *Religious Rivalries in the Early Roman Empire and the Rise of Christianity* (2006), there are four responses to Stark by Adele Reinhartz, Steven Muir, Roger Beck and Leif Vaage. Although critical remarks have been made, especially with regard to the mission to the Jews, the social class of converts and the position of women, it does seem that central elements of Stark's thesis have become accepted. In addition, Robert Wortham's 2006 article expands Stark's section on the Christian origins of Gnosticism. James Crossley's *Why Christianity Happened: A Sociohistorical Account of Christian Origins (26–50 CE)* (2006) expands the section on networks. Stark (2006) himself continues his study of the competition of mainstream Christianity with Judaism, mystery religions and variant forms of Christianity. Oskar Skarsaune (2007) concludes an edited volume on *Jewish Believers in Jesus* with an estimate of the number of Jewish believers by finding a middle road between Stark's analysis and the findings of various scholars studying specific cities and groups. Jan Bremmer (2010), however, in his valedictory lecture, believes Stark's numbers of Christians in the first three centuries are arbitrary and unconvincing. The heterogeneous spread of Christianity in different regions of the empire and in different times is not acknowledged enough by Stark. Furthermore, considering recent research, Stark's approximations of the percentage of Jewish Christians are not tenable and there is virtually no evidence that Jews still converted to Christianity from the late second century onwards. According to Bremmer, Stark's concepts are useful contributions to the field of research, but need to be developed further by specialists.

With these reactions in mind, I will discuss some of the most important contributions made by Stark.

Exponential Growth

Stark proposes to model the rise of Christianity as an exponential growth rate of about 40 per cent per decade. This is a mathematical abstraction of reality, as growth does not follow exact mathematical formulae. But it is important to note that the best possible description of such a growth process is a series of exponential growth (or decline) curves, depending on the internal and external dynamics of such a movement. As examples, Stark points to the growth of the Mormonism and the Moonies in America and worldwide, which he studied himself. These are interesting examples, as the Moonies represent a cult from outside the USA, and the Mormons one that is home grown on the foundations of Christianity. Mormonism accepts the Christian Bible, but adds the *Book of Mormon* to it, which is somewhat comparable to early Christianity, which accepted the Jewish Scriptures and added its own Jesus traditions. From its humble beginnings in 1830, Mormonism has grown at a rate of 30–50 per cent per decade to about 12 million in 2003, on the basis of a birth surplus and a conversion surplus, which in turn required an expanding geographical footprint. If this growth continues, numerically and geographically, Stark predicts that the movement will become a new world religion (2005).

From a macro-perspective, the growth of new religious communities (fictive kinships) does not follow marketing campaigns in the media or on the market places of antiquity, but follows personal relationships. That means that members may have relationships with outsiders, often relatives, friends and colleagues. Over time some of these outsiders will develop relationships with various cult members, adjust their own opinions and become insiders. This is in line with what we observe in modern-day conversion patterns, even if it is not in line with the self-presentation of converts. They often perceive their own conversion as a far more objective and individual decision.

In practical terms, a growth rate of 40 per cent per decade means that the assumed population doubles every 20 years, until the growth rate no longer applies, because the level of saturation slows it down (thus producing an S-curve), or because other more successful movements (or growing apostasy) start to cause a decline of the movement.

modelled growth

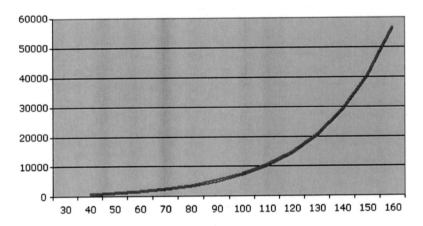

Again I should stress that the resulting growth curve is an abstraction of reality. If we plotted the actual numbers, which we do not have, on a graph, the curve would be far more irregular, as can be observed in areas where Christianity is currently growing fast (Jenkins 2006). Nevertheless, this irregular curve would wind around a middle line, the abstracted base growth rate, that would probably look very much like the line proposed by Stark, especially as the numbers increase and the movement is more spread out around the Mediterranean, so that individual and local variations are somewhat averaged out. Indeed, Stark's estimate of a 40-per-cent growth rate per decade is supported by census data from Egypt (239–315 CE) and Roman epigraphs (200–375 CE).

The Starting Number

Stark's starting number of one thousand Jesus followers in the year 40 CE is the 'round figure' of 1,000. It has no basis in reality, other than that the lowest numbers mentioned are the 120 in Acts 1.15 and 500 resurrection witnesses in 1 Cor. 15.6, and the highest numbers the 3,000 and 5,000 from Acts 2.41 and 4.4. The number of 1,000 is simply the result of projecting backwards the more secure numbers and growth rate from the third century with the equally rounded growth rate of 40 per cent per decade. But there is no need to assume that the growth rate was constant, as Stark very well knows on the basis of his statistics with regard to Mormonism. If growth had been slower in the first century, then a higher starting number would be possible and indeed required. It may even be possible that the movement first shrunk before it grew.

Furthermore, we have to distinguish between the stable 'members' and those with only a short-lived interest (cf. the parable of the Sower and the Seeds in Mk 4.1-20). The restoration movement of John and Jesus attracted the sympathy of large segments of the Jewish populace who had themselves baptized. It is even possible that some people initially responded positively to the community of Jesus followers without really joining it. The community may have continued the baptismal practice of Jesus and John, attracting some of the pilgrims who visited Jerusalem for the festivals, without yet developing the mechanisms to include and keep these people as members. It is also possible that many of these early 'converts' were merely sympathizers who returned home from Jerusalem when the festivals were over and Jesus had not yet returned as God's Messiah, or when the persecution that Paul writes about started. That would have thrown the movement back to the group of witnesses and their relatives (indeed a group of about a thousand people) as the steady base of the movement.

Birth Surplus

In order to maintain an average growth of about 40 per cent for several centuries, a new religious movement must have a birth surplus as well as a conversion surplus. Stark notes that Mormons have maintained a birth surplus above the American average throughout their history. I already noted that Jewish fertility must have been substantial through a positive attitude towards marriage and children (Tacitus, *Historiae* V.2). It is also possible that Jewish purity rules contributed to a more hygienic situation that moderated infant mortality somewhat. This contributed to an average growth of the Jewish population of perhaps some 10–13 per cent per decade for several centuries (derived from DellaPergola 1992). We also saw that in the early decades, there must have been many marriages with partners from outside the movement. This may have led to a substantially higher level of 'fertility' in the first decades (15–30 per cent).

On the other hand, as the movement became more and more a Gentile movement and marriages outside the group became less common, we should expect a more modest surplus. Furthermore, in her response to Stark, Elizabeth Castelli (1998) notes the tendency towards celibacy among women. This is already present in 1 Cor. 7, but more prevalent in the second century CE. It would be offset, however, by the high proportion of young adults among converts, appeals to ban extramarital sex for young males, perhaps the prevalence of freeborn people among Christians, and the possibility that at least some Christian masters encouraged their slaves to form stable (and more fertile) unions. To put this in perspective: if in the second century, the birth surplus contributed 10 per cent of the growth per decade, this means that in an average year, in a group of 100 persons (20 to 25 families), there was one birth more than there were funerals.

There may also have been birth deficits in times and places with high mortality, such as the Jewish wars, famines, persecutions and epidemics, although these effects may have been concentrated in certain regions and cities, such as Rome (64 CE), Palestine (66–73 CE and 132–5 CE) and Alexandria (115–17 CE).

Conversion Surplus

A conversion surplus is present if more people join than leave the movement. It is by nature less stable than a birth surplus. To reduce the number of people leaving, the movement needs to socialize its members well and maintain a strong cohesion. The attractiveness of the movement to outsiders depends on the outward orientation of the movement and external factors. Stark's suggestion that the care provided to outsiders in times of crisis contributed to the growth of the movement implies that such growth may have had its peaks and lows. Furthermore, it would provide a counterweight to the higher mortality under such circumstances. Internal crises may have reduced the cohesion of the movement and led to periods in which relatively more people left the movement. Such crises may have been the leadership crises after the deaths of James, Paul and Peter in the 60s CE, or ideological crises, such as when the Romans laid siege to Jerusalem and Jesus did not return as quickly as suggested in Mk 13.24-7 and predicted in Mt. 24.29-31 (as opposed to

Lk. 21.24). Overall, however, in the light of the movement's strong growth, we should assume that the first centuries were characterized by periods with relatively large conversion surpluses. To put this in perspective: if the conversion surplus contributed 10–35 per cent of the growth in a decade, this means that on average, in a given year, in a group of 100 persons, there are 1 to 3 more new converts than there were people who left the movement. From research into conversion processes, we would expect to see former converts to be most likely to deconvert, followed by a minority of adolescents raised within the movement. In Chapter 4, I argued that the original group of 500 seems to have known little apostasy.

Geographical Spread

Stark's argument on the basis of statistical analysis, that the mission to the Jews was successful drew much criticism, although Keith Hopkins (1998) suspects that 'until about 150 CE most Christians were ex-Jews or their descendants'. Stark returns to the issue in his 2006 study *Cities of God*. When Stark reviews the cities of the Roman Empire with an estimated population of 30,000 or more, he finds that (1) larger cities, (2) cities closer to Jerusalem, and (3) Hellenized cities were all more likely to have an early and significant Christian presence. But such cities were also more likely to have a Jewish community. Indeed, the key explanatory factor is the presence of a Jewish community. All major cities in the Roman Empire with a significant Jewish community had a church by 100 CE, as opposed to merely 18 per cent of cities without a (reported) Jewish community. This had grown to only 36 per cent by 180 CE. It is clear, therefore, that the network of Jewish Diaspora communities was the primary network through which early Christianity spread through the Roman Empire. I should emphasize that Stark uses accepted statistical methods to establish significant correlations, and to distinguish which variables are dependent (see the Statistical Appendix in *Cities of God*). In fact, Stark's method is rather robust for changes in the exact numbers and cannot be dismissed as Jack Sanders (1999) does. The correlation is there, and very unlikely to be accidental. But we can question the explanation that Stark gives for the correlation that he found. I believe that there are at least two reasons why this correlation does not necessarily prove that the majority of converts were Jewish:

- First, the first Jesus followers were Jews who migrated throughout the Roman Empire as other Jews did in those days. In this way, Christianity spread even without converts. In Chapter 4, I argue that many of the original group were young males, who needed to find a place to work, live and marry. Around the festivals, the community in Jerusalem met numerous Jewish pilgrims from the Diaspora eager to experience their religion in the Holy City. Some of them joined the movement in Jerusalem, others became contacts abroad. The persecution to which Paul refers in Galatians 1 may have driven the followers from the Diaspora back to their homes (as in Acts 11.19), over time joined by the young males. They provided the destinations and homes for the apostles, or 'missionaries' mentioned in 1 Cor. 9.5. A good example is Simon, a Diaspora Jew from Cyrene, who was in Jerusalem at the time of the crucifixion (Mk 15.21). Two of his sons were known to Mark's primary audience in the 60s or 70s CE: one with a Greek name, Alexander, the other with a Roman name, Rufus. It seems that the second name was given in Rome, where he lived with his widowed mother in the 50s CE (Rom. 16.3). She probably hosted Paul before in a different city, as Paul had not yet been in Rome. Andronicus and Junia(s), Paul's tribesmen, were among the primary witnesses; they, too, lived in Rome, after spending time in prison with Paul elsewhere (Rom. 16.7). Aquila was a Jew from Pontus, who moved to Rome and married Priscilla (both Roman names). They seem to have been followers of Jesus who moved to Corinth shortly before 50 CE (Acts 18.1). A little later they moved to Ephesus (1 Cor. 16.19), and then back to Rome (Rom. 16.3). Perhaps they returned to Ephesus (if 2 Tim. 4.19 reflects historical reality).

- Second, Stark argues that Jews were more likely to convert because of the existing ties with Jesus followers, and because they could preserve their religious capital when they joined the movement. But this is also true for the proselytes and god-fearers, Gentiles who associated to a larger or smaller extent with the Diaspora synagogues. As the Jesus followers migrated into the Diaspora in the 40s–70s CE, they would increasingly develop relationships with such god-fearers and we should expect that their relative importance among the converts grew as well. If the modern observation applies that converts are more likely to deconvert or reconvert, these groups would be more likely to join the groups of Jesus followers than those who had been born and raised as Jews. Furthermore, after the debates of the 40s and 50s CE (see Gal. 1–2) they could become full members and even leaders of the community without circumcision or observance of Jewish Law. Another likely group for conversion are the marginal migrants from the Hellenistic Eastern Mediterranean (including Jews) who moved west, and lived and worked side by side with the Jewish migrants who followed Jesus. Their lack of security and personal ties in a new city makes it likely that they would convert earlier than the established citizens of the city. An indication for this is the dominance of Greek among the believers in second-century Rome (Lampe 2003, 144).

A Spreadsheet Model of Early Christianity

For the purpose of this study the exact number of Christians in a given year is not relevant. The two questions that I have are the following:

- How long did the first-generation followers of Jesus and their descendants remain numerically significant in the movement?

- When did Gentile converts and their descendants become numerically significant in the movement?

In order to assess the consequences of the factors identified by Stark as well as those of scholars who criticized him, I have developed a spreadsheet model to simulate the growth of the movement which I presented at the SBL Annual Meeting of 2006 (with a very constructive response from Philip Jenkins). I have adapted the technique from economic modelling. Such modelling may follow these five steps:

1. Identify the factors involved: in our case these are the starting number of Christians, natural growth (fertility, percentage of marriages and mortality), conversion surplus, the relative attractiveness to Jewish and Gentile converts as well as to specific age groups, and the impact of specific events (such as the Neronian persecution and the first two Jewish Wars).

2. Create a spreadsheet model that separates input variables from calculations and output variables. This means that only the input variables are changed as part of the research. The outputs are defined as:

   - number of Christians in a given 5-year period between 35 and 200 CE
   - percentage of first-century believers and their descendants
   - percentage of Jews or Gentiles

Note: The two percentages are an abstraction on the assumptions that there was no intermarriage between first-century believers and new converts or between Jews and Gentile converts.

3. Investigate reasonable ranges for the input variables: this was done on the basis of ancient demographics (see Chapter 4), insights into conversion patterns and key assumptions of ancient historians. I suggest that the following represents a reasonable range of assumptions:

   - The starting number: 500–5,000, all Jews
   - Natural growth (on average 10–30 per cent per decade). Specifics include:

     Fertility: in correspondence with Egyptian average for married women (see Chapter 4).
     Percentage of marriages (depending on the propensity to marry and percentage of exogenous marriages): 40–60 per 100 adults.
     Mortality: in correspondence with the recommended model for Roman Egypt (see Chapter 4).

- Conversion surplus (on average 10–30 per cent per decade). Specifics include:

    Relative presence of young adults among all converts: 100–400 per cent. A relative presence of 400 per cent means that young adults between 15 and 30 years of age are four times more likely to convert than older people.
    Relative presence of Gentiles among all converts: 100–400 per cent. A relative presence of 400 per cent means that Gentiles (including god-fearers) are four times more likely to convert than Jews. The assumption is that the number of Gentiles and Jews known to the group largely follows its ethnic composition.
    Apostasy among first-generation believers and their descendants: 0–5 per cent per decade.

- The impact of specific events, which include:

    The Neronian persecution. Percentage of Jesus followers in Rome in 64 CE (2–10 per cent) and percentage killed (10–50 per cent).
    The Jewish War. Percentage of Jesus followers in Palestine in 66 CE (20–60 per cent) and percentage killed (20-40 per cent).

4. Design various internally consistent scenarios and analyse their outputs in terms of the available evidence: I designed three principle ways of looking at the growth of the first-century movement:

- A Jewish sect, starting with a relatively high number (2,400), high natural growth (25 per cent per decade), moderate conversion surplus (10 per cent per decade).
- A movement of Jewish migrants with a moderate start (1,200), with growth both from birth surplus and a conversion surplus (each 20 per cent per decade). In this scenario, Gentiles are more likely to convert than Jews, growing from twice as likely in 50 CE to four times as likely by the end of the first century.
- A missionary movement among Gentiles, starting from a small Jewish base (600) and with a moderate natural growth (15 per cent per decade) but with a high conversion surplus (30 per cent) with Gentiles four times as likely to convert than Jews.

5. Perform a sensitivity analysis of all input variables with respect to the selected scenario: for each input variable the effects are measured on the percentage of first-generation believers and their descendants, and the percentage of Jews, both for the year 70 CE.

Discussion of the Results

In this section I will discuss the outcomes of the scenario analysis and the sensitivity analysis.

Scenario Analysis

The preferred scenario is the one that best explains the literary evidence with regard to the presence of Gentiles among the believers. Although Christianity started with a core group of Jewish followers of Jesus and first attracted Jewish converts producing a Jewish offspring, it must soon have started to attract Gentile converts as well, indeed to such an extent that the movement eventually became predominantly Gentile. Suetonius, in a rather ambiguous passage, speaks about an incident among the Jews in Rome with regard to a certain 'Chrestus' during the reign of Claudius (possibly related to the departure of Roman Christians such as Aquila and Priscilla in Acts 18.2). Josephus, writing in the Diaspora towards the end of the first century, states that many Jews and many Greeks followed Jesus. Unless this is an interpolation, it may imply that in Josephus' day both groups were significantly represented among Jesus followers. Around 155 CE, Justin Martyr wrote that there were more Christians from among the Gentiles than there were from among the Jews or Samaritans (*First Apology* 53). Around 220 CE, when Stark suggests that the total number of Christians may be around half a million, Origen remarked that the number of Jewish Christians fell far short of the number of 144,000 Israelites saved in Rev. 7.4-8 (*Commentary on John* I.1.7).

	Literary 'evidence	Scenario 1	Scenario 2	Scenario 3
% Jews in Rome in 40s CE	High??	High	High	Moderate
% Jews at the end of 1st century	Moderate?	High	Moderate	Low
% Jews in middle of 2nd century	Low	Moderate	Low	Low
Number of Jews in early 3rd century	Far fewer than 144,000	c. 150,000	c. 50,000	c. 5,000

On the basis of the limited external evidence we have, the first scenario seems unlikely. The second scenario is the preferred model for theorizing about the growth of the movement, although the third scenario is not impossible. This confirms the critique on Stark that Jews were not as likely to convert as Stark assumed. With respect to the numerical development of Jews in the movement, the second scenario produces the following image (again the exact numbers are not relevant):

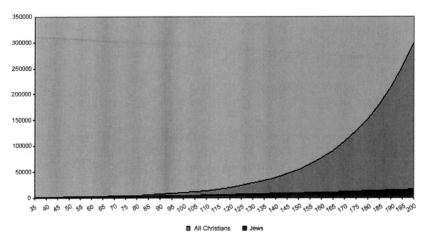

Graph: Proportion of Jews in the first two centuries (indicative only).

If we look in more detail at the first century of the same scenario, we can see that the same assumptions that produced a Gentile religious movement in the second century imply a mostly Jewish religion in the first century.

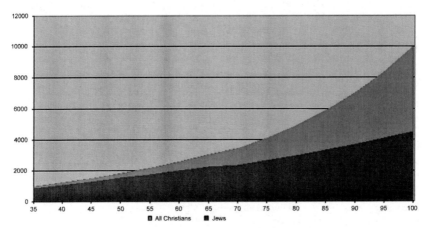

Graph: proportion of Jews in the first century (indicative only).

Finally, the percentage of first-generation believers and their descendants in the first century develops as indicated in the graph opposite.

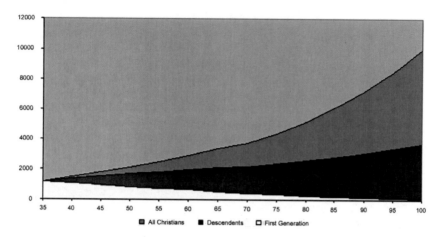

Again, the exact numbers are not really important. Furthermore, there is now a sharp dividing line because no intermarriage is assumed in the model. In reality, however, this is an increasingly large proportion of believers of mixed parentage (the same holds for the previous graph regarding the proportion of Jews). Finally I note that if we would use the third scenario, the situation until 70 CE would be quite comparable. In 70 CE the second scenario implies that 76 per cent of the believers were of Jewish descent while 58 per cent belonged to the group of first-generation believers and their descendants. In the third scenario this would be 63 per cent and 43 per cent.

Sensitivity Analysis

As a final step, the preferred scenario is tested on the robustness of its outcomes when the individual input variables are changed. The sensitivity of these indicative numbers to variations in the input variables is as follows:

Input factor to be tested	All values in 70 CE			1st gen. + descendants scenario value: 58%		% Jews scenario value: 76%	
	'low' input	scenario value	'high' input	low	high	low	high
starting number	900	1200	1800	50%	72%	72%	81%
fertility: marriage rate	45	50	55	52%	65%	73%	78%
victims in Rome 65 CE	10%	30%	50%	58%	58%	76%	76%
apostasy	5%	2%	0,5%	53%	61%	74%	77%
young new converts	100%	200%	400%	56%	61%	74%	77%
Gentile new converts	100%	200%	400%	58%	58%	71%	80%

The sensitivity analysis shows that the scenario is rather robust for reasonable changes of individual input factors. This is true for the third scenario as well. The percentage of first-generation believers and their descendants is mostly dependent on the assumed starting number, whereas the percentage of Jews until about 70 CE is even more stable and only somewhat dependent on the over-representation of Gentiles among new converts.

Conclusions

Without attaching too much value to the numbers themselves, we can now draw the following conclusions:

- In numerical terms, it is likely that first-generation believers and their descendants dominated the movement until the Jewish War.
- In numerical terms, it is likely that Gentiles dominated the movement only from the end of the first century onwards.

The Composition of the Diaspora Communities

The proportion of Jewish followers would have been different between Palestine and various Diaspora cities. We may assume that the movement in Palestine was overwhelmingly Jewish. In the Diaspora, however, we should expect mixed communities of both Jews and Gentiles – but note that there would have been significant variation from city to city.

If we assume that the major cities were first reached by Jewish migrants who followed Jesus and who attracted god-fearers and other migrants to their community, we may assume that prior to the Jewish War, the percentage of Gentiles among Diaspora believers steadily increased to about half the total number. As a result of the Jewish War, and in line with the fate of many other Palestinian Jews, many Palestinian believers would have fled to Diaspora cities or have been shipped off as slaves. This migration is remembered in a document of the Syrian Church, preserved in China in the following words: 'The Jews were defeated, many killed or scattered across the world, helping to make more disciples for the Messiah' (Palmer 2001, 67). This may have restored the Jewish majority among believers in the main Diaspora centres. Towards the end of the first century, however, the Gentile believers were in the majority in almost all the Diaspora communities.

The Literary Evidence in Paul's Letters

The question is, however, how this relates to the literary evidence. Many scholars regard Paul's letters to the Thessalonians, Philippians and Galatians as letters written to Gentile communities. This is disputed by Malina (2006), who believes Paul saw himself as the apostle to the *Jews* living among the nations, although I believe he is taking the argument too far. I have set out a middle position in my essay 'The Jewish Recipients of Paul's Letter to the Galatians' (in Porter 2009), in which I argue that the problems of Gentile-Jewish table-fellowship in Antioch are also behind the problems in the ethnically mixed Galatian communities. If we strip away Paul's rhetoric and reconstruct the position of his opponents, it is likely that their focus was not on Gentiles, but on Jews: Peter and the other Jews were asked to observe purity rules which conflicted with table fellowship as it was practised in Antioch. I assume that Paul's problem with this position was that it undermined the communion in the mixed Diaspora groups. If Jews were to remain law-observant (the demand of James), and if the Diaspora groups were to function as a single community (Paul's requirement), then this would *de facto* mean that the Gentiles would have to live in accordance with the Law. That would reduce the attractiveness of the movement for the Gentiles. James's position is perfectly sensible given his work among the Jews in Palestine; Paul's position is understandable given his focus on the nations. Even Peter's awkward position is in line with his responsibilities as a leader in the movement as a whole. If I am correct, then Antioch, the Galatian communities, Corinth and Rome all seem to suffer from this conflict because all of them were such mixed communities, as predicted by the model for the year 55 CE (on *average* 60 per cent Jewish and 40 per cent Gentile).

For the city of Rome, Lampe (1989/ET 2003) and Hvalvik (2007) have used prosographic information to analyse the 26 names of the people greeted in Rom. 16. Lampe concludes that at least 12 of them were personal acquaintances of Paul who migrated to Rome from the east; he also believes the majority of the ones greeted came from the east. Hvalvik deduces that eight of them were probably Jewish: five he regards as certain because they are known Jews or called Paul's tribesmen, furthermore Rufus and his mother (cf. Mk 15.21) and Mary. To Hvalvik this suggests that there would have been around 30 per cent of Jews among the Roman followers of Jesus. Apart from the question whether the list of greetings is representative, the names are a poor marker of ethnicity. Many Jews used Graeco-Roman names in the Diaspora, like Simon who gave his sons Greek and Roman names: Alexander and Rufus; others 'internationalized' their names (Miriam to Maria, possibly Jehunni to Junias). Indeed, the five 'certain' Jews are called Priscilla, Aquila, Andronicus, Junia(s) and Herodion: all Graeco-Roman names. The interpretative key to the list in Rom. 16 is the word 'tribesmen': if it means 'Jews', then why does Paul use the word for only two of the five known Jews? The very fact that they were apostles before him already indicates that they were part of the first, and Jewish, community of followers in Jerusalem. Furthermore, if Jews were as common among the Diaspora communities as the model suggests, why would he make specific mention of their Jewish background at all? It would make sense, however, if he referred to them as fellow members of the tribe of Benjamin (Phil. 3.5). If there were already three Benjaminites among the 26 names, there would have been many more Jews among them.

Geographical Spread and Group Size

Whereas the community of Jerusalem started with a large group, and probably remained the far largest community until the first Jewish revolt, the Diaspora communities had to start from zero. As the expansion of the movement first followed the Jewish Diaspora, we should expect to find more than 90 per cent of Jesus followers in the largest cities with a sizeable Jewish presence, nearest to Jerusalem (population sizes and distances in miles taken from Stark 1996). In the table below, I give an indicative estimate of the expected size of Christian communities, if their growth reflects the correlated factors demonstrated by Stark.

City:	Population (indicative)	Jewish Population (absolute)	Distance to Jerusalem	Expected size in 60 CE (indicative)	Expected size in 80 CE (indicative)
Rome*	650,000	++	1,480	100	400
Alexandria**	400,000	+++	350	100	200
Ephesus	200,000	+	640	100	200
Antioch	150,000	++	250	200	400
Corinth	100,000	+	830	100	200
Smyrna***	75,000	+	820	50	100
Damascus	45,000	+	130	50	100
Other cities****	Small to medium	Small or non-existent	Varies	10–30 cities with 20–50 members	20–50 cities with 20–100 members
Total Diaspora (indicative)				1,500	4,000

* Higher growth rate as the city was known to attract new cults, the reputation of the movement gained in the Neronian persecution, and the influx of Jewish slaves (including Christians) following the first Jewish revolt.

** Lower growth rate assumed because of strained relations between Jews and Gentiles culminating in the 38 CE pogrom. Early church only attested in Codex Beza. Jewish population (including Christians) decimated in the second Jewish revolt of 115–17 CE

*** Attested in Revelation.

**** Harnack counts another 25 places in the Diaspora that are attested to in first-century literature. There would have been more places, but some perhaps only temporarily.

The numbers in the table of course should not be considered as accurate in any detail, but they do add up to a plausible overall portrait, showing that only some communities had several hundred members, whereas most were smaller than 100 (see Verhoef 2005, for a description of a small community like Philippi). It seems, then, that a significant proportion of the community is greeted in Rom. 16 (28 individual adults and five groups). To put such a number in perspective: a community of 100 members in 60 CE would typically consist of:

- 40 children, 30 young adults aged 15–30, and 30 adults over 30.
- The community could come together in a few house-groups.
- There could be some 10 young males unmarried, and some 5 older females widowed; about 20 married couples, and some 5 married women whose husbands did not believe.
- Between 50 and 60 members were Jewish migrants, 40 to 50 were Gentiles (local god-fearers and some fellow migrants from other countries).
- Of the 40 to 50 Jewish migrants, about 5 had been part of the original group of resurrection witnesses, another 10 had one or two parents among them and some 15 of them had one or more grandparents among this group.

To illustrate the demographic development in an imaginary group of 100 members over the period of one year, the following indicative scenario may be considered:

- Marriage: two girls came of age and married: one with an adult male in this group, one to an outsider (who agreed to join the group). A young adult male married a believing girl from another group in another city.
- Birth surplus (+1): the 25 married female members would give birth to about six children. About two or three children would die as well as one or two adults.
- Conversion surplus (+2): about one young adult would leave the movement in which he or she was raised; perhaps two recent converts too. There would be some four new converts, for example: one young Jewish male who married a girl from the group, a widowed mother with a child from among the non-Jewish migrants, and the god-fearing husband of one of the female members of the group.
- Migration deficit (–1): one family of three migrated to another city. One young male married a girl in another community. Another went looking for a bride in Rome. A couple without children and two young males arrived from other communities, one as a slave.

Many Christianities?

The emphasis of research in the larger part of the twentieth century was on the creative forces in the early history of what is now called Christianity, as well as on the distinct circumstances under which each of the Gospels was composed. As a result, scholars have come to speak of many different 'Christianities', such as Pauline Christianity, Matthaean Christianity, Jewish Christianity and Johannine Christianity. The parallel referred to is Judaism: 'just like there are many Judaisms, there were also many Christianities.' As a counterweight to such claims, a provocative set of essays, edited by Richard Bauckham, appeared in 1998: *The Gospels for All Christians: Rethinking the Gospel Audiences*. Indeed, there is not much sense in writing a book for your local community if only ten other people can read it. It is more sensible for an author to write for people where the author is not present or whom the author will leave. The question then is whether the movement that was spread across the Mediterranean is to be regarded as one movement in which writings could circulate freely or as several movements with distinct readerships.

While I readily recognize the diversity of early Jesus followers, the question is whether it makes sense to assume a set of different Christianities (in the sociological sense) if we take the numbers into account. In the first century CE there were some 1,000–10,000 followers of Jesus, and half of them below 25 years of age. The 'many Judaisms', however, could recruit from a population of several millions of Jews. Furthermore, the model indicates that there was a high level of interaction between the groups of Jesus followers, situated as they were within the established patterns of travel and communication, and within the geographical footprint of the Jewish Diaspora. I have also demonstrated that the influence of the first generation of Jewish followers of Jesus and their children and grandchildren is likely to have remained significant in most of these Diaspora groups throughout most of the first century. They contributed to the social cohesion of the movement. A good example is the speed with which the Gospel of John seems to have reached Egypt.

It is hard to overestimate the difference between the larger part of the first century, when primary witnesses were still around, and when Diaspora communities were dominated by Jewish migrants who could trace their roots back to earliest Jesus followers, and the early second century when the communities in the Roman Empire came to be dominated by educated Gentiles (Origen, *Contra Celsum* III.10–12) and distanced themselves from law-observant Jewish followers of Jesus. The first-century movement of Jesus followers is therefore best described as one of the diverse Jewish movements, comparable to other groups like the Pharisees, or the Essenes. The conflicts early followers had (such as the one described in Galatians) are intra-movement conflicts, not inter-movement conflicts. Only towards the end of the first century, when the movement had grown significantly and the larger part of it had become dominated by Gentiles, does it make sense to speak about different Christian movements, or 'Christianities'.

Conclusions

Modelling the movement of Jesus followers as a new religious movement allows us to make reasoned assumptions about its growth and composition. Although exact figures are not available, a plausible scenario emerges in which the first-century movement that produced the letters of Paul and the surviving first-century Gospels can be characterized as follows:

- The movement started out as a missionary movement of Jewish migrants, growing through both a birth surplus and a conversion surplus.
- Gentiles, probably god-fearers and fellow migrants, were more likely to convert than Jews.

- First-generation believers and their descendants had a significant presence in the major Diaspora centres.
- Gentiles came to dominate the movement towards the end of the first century CE.

Chapter 6

THE MEMORY OF JESUS IN PAUL'S LETTERS AND THE GOSPELS

In Chapters 4 and 5, I have argued on the basis of demographics and insights in successful new religious movements that, first, it is likely that a significant number of first-generation witnesses and their descendants were present in both Palestine and the Diaspora throughout the first century. Second, because of the additional migration of Jews from Palestine in relation to the Jewish War, the proportion of Gentiles in the major Diaspora communities in the 50s and 70s CE may have been of comparable significance. This changed, however, around the end of the first century when believers of Gentile descent are likely to have become the majority.

In this chapter, I will assess how these findings can help us design a strategy to extract the most reliable information about Jesus from the letters of Paul and the first-century Gospels. It is important to note that these are written documents from an age in which most people were illiterate. I will therefore first discuss this aspect before turning to the few Jesus traditions that we can find in the oldest written documents, the letters of Paul. After that, I will look at the way in which Jesus' followers may have conserved, created and shaped the memories of Jesus that found their way into first-century Gospels.

Orality and Literacy

According to Hopkins (1998), some 20 per cent of the adult males could read and only 2 per cent were sufficiently literate to compose a letter or treatise. In a community with about 100 members divided over two or three house-groups, this would give us about six potential readers and perhaps one person who could write more than a basic note. Although I believe that the scriptural basis of Judaism and early Christianity may have enticed more members to learn how to read, it is easy to see that the smaller communities had to rely to a very large extent on oral communication to transmit Jesus traditions (as envisaged in 2 Tim. 2.2 and partly in 2 Thess. 2.15, see Gerhardsson's 1998 republication; Dunn 2005) or news from other Jesus followers. Even when a letter was sent, it required trusted persons to authenticate and complement it (as envisaged in Acts 15.25 and Col. 4.9). The physical letter, often quite short, gave the envoy the authority of the sender. The author of Acts 15 envisages that the important letter about the requirements for Gentile believers had just over a hundred words in which the oral communication of the envoys was emphasized. The lengthy letters of Paul were clearly exceptional pieces of communication (Richards 2004).

In the first century, therefore, oral traditions memorized by many were authoritative. A man like Papias, who lived when most primary witnesses had died, remembered what he had learned from the last survivors, and how he eagerly related what his visitors had learned from such primary witnesses: 'For I did not suppose that information from books would help me as much as the word of a living and surviving voice' (quoted in Eusebius, *Church History* 3,39.4 and 3,39.7).

How Many People Could Write?

Around 50 CE, when Paul's letters were written (by himself and some co-authors or scribes) and when some of the written sources of the Gospel narratives were put into writing, there were probably somewhat more than a thousand Jesus followers in the Aramaic-speaking regions and somewhat less than a thousand in Greek-speaking areas (see Chapter 4). If we assume that an author would be a male over 30 years of age, and take Hopkins's 2 per cent, then about three people could compose such a work in Aramaic and another three in Greek. Around 80 CE, when 'many' had attempted to write Gospel narratives (Lk. 1.1), some three people could do so in Aramaic and about twelve in Greek. In total, over the years, we would reach about 30 potential authors for the Greek writings composed in the last three decades of the first century. Of course, not everyone who could write such works would actually do so, but it is interesting to note that the number of authors assumed by New Testament scholars for the writings that may have been composed in this period (and the sources incorporated in them) stands at about half that number. We can conclude, therefore, that the preserved writings cover a significant part of the authors in the Hellenistic Diaspora. Unfortunately, all that we have from the Aramaic-speaking regions amounts to some fragments of the Hebrew Gospel preserved by later authors (Edwards 2009), and the possibility that parts of Aramaic or Hebrew works were translated into Greek and used in the Greek Gospels (Black 1946; Martin 1974, 1987 and 1989; Casey 1998 and 2002; Edwards 2009). Using the same assumptions, the total number of potential male authors over 30 years of age, capable of composing a work in Aramaic between 40 and 70 CE, is about six.

Again these numbers are only indicative. The number for writers in Greek could be lower, if we believe migrants had insufficient command of the language or if we exclude those with deteriorating eyesight (glasses were not yet invented). The numbers could be higher if we allow for female authors, or for the combination of younger writers who teamed up with older authorities (the traditional Mark/Peter model), who would know better than modern people how to compose oral works. It is possible that the Jewish world was not a typical Mediterranean society and did provide their children with more training in reading and writing (in Hebrew or Aramaic). But after all such sophisticated work on the numbers, we are still left with a first-century movement dominated by oral authority and very few people who could write or copy texts in a professional way. As they stood at the beginning of the transmission chain, it is easy to understand Origen's complaints of errors and changes that resulted in much textual variation in, for instance, the Gospel according to Matthew (*Letter to Africanus*, in Grafton and Williams 2006, 125).

Scholars need to take into account not only the ancient practices of reading, writing and copying (Gamble 1995; Millard 2000), but also the number of potential authors in a certain community, before speculating about first-century Pauline or Johannine schools engaged in literary production. We also need to be sensitive to the very reasons for writing a 'speech' in the form of a letter or a narrative like a Gospel (see, for example, *The Written Gospel*, ed. Bockmuehl and Hagner, 2005, and Thatcher's *Why John WROTE a Gospel*, 2006).

Written Sources

When someone, or a group of people, has reason to compose an overall narrative out of a set of traditions, another process takes place, which Quintilian's *Institutio Oratoria* discusses under the headings 'finding', 'arrangement' and 'wording'. The Gospel narrative, Richard Burridge (1992/2004) argues, would have been perceived by people in the first century as ancient biography. In a biography of a famous person (general, emperor, philosopher), the author and his audience expect something about the achievements of that person, plus some stories about his ancestry and birth and about the way he died, that underline his greatness – they care far more about the classification of the person's character than about its development. Depending on his reasons for writing, the 'biographer' had to find and select material, decide between what seemed to be two different versions of the same saying or event, and think about what was missing (a standard school exercise was the writing of an appropriate but fictive context for a preserved saying). Next, the author had to arrange the material and his own thoughts in a way that conveyed his interpretation of his subject's achievements and his message to his audience. The author was not supposed to write about the days in which nothing of significance happened. Tedious repetitions were to be avoided. Whereas the positions of birth and death were pretty standard, there were various ways to arrange the achievements. Some were mainly chronological, others topical (Philo's *Moses*). The interpretations and messages could be woven into the narrative (Philo) or follow it (Plutarch's *syncrises*). Thirdly, the narrative had to be worded eloquently. The ancients appreciated a unity of style and correct language. Interpretations could be added as commentary or could be put into the thoughts or words of the narrative's characters. The text could be plain or loaded with symbolism. The text should be easy to read out loud to a larger audience in an acceptable time-span (it was still an oral culture), and – if performed without the benefit of reading from paper – organized in a way that was easy to remember. A few good speeches would add to the liveliness of the performance, and it was understood that such speeches were not verbatim reports. Hence, it is not very surprising that many within the early movement could live with deviating narratives (although the late second-century Roman elder Gaius rejected the Gospel of John because it deviated too much from the Synoptic Gospels). Once the work was ready, the author was no longer in control of it. In antiquity it was up to the reader to copy the works he desired. Only if there were readers who continued to copy the work would the writing survive the material on which it was written. Although there were copy-shops where professional scribes performed such tasks at a significant cost, a less wealthy Christian community could also ask one of its more literate members to undertake this work. But an amateur copyist could easily make mistakes and a community or a copyist with an interest in the subject could also be tempted to make changes to the text.

In evaluating our sources we should take into account the genre of the work, the author's strategy in composing it, and the public's willingness to reproduce it. There are huge differences in this respect between the Gospels of Matthew, Mark, Luke, John and Thomas, as well as with the book of Acts, but this is beyond the scope of the present study. We should also take into account whether they invited some kind of review by the first generation; to this end they should have circulated early and widely, and claimed some level of historicity. The latter can be done through the conventions of a genre, like biography, or by claiming eyewitness support (see Bauckham 2006, critically discussed by various scholars in JSHJ 2008/6 and JSNT 2008/31).

Non-Christian Sources

Any source is by definition selective and biased. It is unfortunate, therefore, that we have only a few non-Christian sources. They are, strictly speaking, not about the historical Jesus, but about the way that others remembered him. Josephus, writing from Rome in the late first century, knew both the community led by James in the 60s CE and the Roman community after the Jewish revolt. According to Josephus, the followers of Jesus saw him as the brother of James, as a teacher and a miracle worker (unless this is an interpolation), and as the Messiah who was crucified under Pilate but rose after three days. The positive feelings that many Jews had towards the historical Jesus and the law-observant community led by his brother James are probably reflected in a Syrian letter from 72 CE by Mara bar Sarapion (Merz, Rensberger and Tieleman 2010). The author refers to Jesus as a wise man and as a 'king', whom the Jews had executed, but who lived on because of the new laws that he made (that his followers proclaimed). The destruction of the Jewish nation and the scattering of the Jews among the nations are seen as divine retribution for the murder of Jesus. This reminds us of Josephus' report that some Jews saw the hand of God in the downfall of Herod Antipas because of his murder of John the Baptist (*Jewish Antiquities* 18.116). The references to Jesus in the works of second-century Roman authors such as Tacitus, Suetonius, Pliny and Celsus are all about Jesus' followers and hence further removed from Jesus than the writings of those followers themselves.

Jesus Traditions in the Letters of Paul

The oldest New Testament sources are the letters of Paul, a man who had not known Christ personally and who wrote around the 50s CE, some 20 years after the crucifixion. There is no doubt that these letters represent the views of a man with strong convictions that were sometimes at odds with those of other early followers of Jesus. Many, like James Dunn (2009), have called Paul the second founder of Christianity. We need to be careful, therefore, in our reading of his letters and use of the information they contain. How much of it is specifically Pauline and originated with him? Furthermore, some people published letters under his name and authority. Scholars generally believe that the following letters are indeed authored by Paul: Romans, 1 and 2 Corinthians, Galatians, Philippians, 1 Thessalonians and Filemon; it is to these letters that I will confine myself in this study. Before looking at the information in his letters, I will first discuss the nature of the relationship between Paul and his audiences.

The Context of Paul's Letters

In a regression analysis of the influence of Pauline visits and the presence of a synagogue, Stark (2006) concludes that Paul had no (zero!) statistical effect on the spread of early Christianity to the major cities of the Roman Empire. In other words, not a visit by Paul but the presence of a Jewish community determined whether Christianity would reach such a city in the first century. In Chapter 5, I concluded that the spread of Christianity across the Diaspora followed existing patterns of Jewish migration. It is likely that migrants from Palestine brought their beliefs about Jesus with them to major Diaspora centres like Rome, Alexandria and Antioch.

A closer look at Paul's mission confirms this: all major cities had a Christian community before he visited them (Rome, Ephesus, Antioch, Corinth and Damascus), whereas other major cities were not visited by Paul (Alexandria and Smyrna). Major cities without a Jewish community (such as Apamea, Pergamum and Sardis) were never part of Paul's missionary outreach. According to Acts, his first missionary journey, when he visited minor cities in Cyprus and in southern Galatia, was made under the leadership of the Cypriot Jew Barnabas. In the major cities where Paul was active (Antioch, Corinth and Ephesus), he was never the unchallenged leader, as is clear from his own letters. Some believers in 1 Corinthians traced their convictions back to Paul, Cephas/Peter or Apollos, others to Christ. Such individuals may have meant this quite literally: they or (one of) their parents may genuinely have known Peter or even the historical Jesus. Paul had to boost his claims as a resurrection witness to be able merely to enter into an argument with leaders such as Peter and the Apostles (1 Cor. 9.1-2). He seems to have ranked among minor leaders such as Apollos (1 Cor. 3.4). Only the communities in some medium-sized cities in Macedonia (Philippi and Thessalonica and perhaps Beroea, too) seem to be rooted in a mission led by Paul. But also these cities, situated as they are on the Via Egnatia between Italy and Asia Minor with Jewish communities, would someday be visited by Paul's opponents (Phil. 3.2).

The conflict between Paul, James and Peter did not concern Paul's Christology but the applicability of Mosaic regulations to Gentile and Jewish followers of Jesus. From his letters to the Corinthians, it seems that Paul's teachings on the ethics of the community, the rites of baptism and Eucharist and the death and resurrection of Jesus were more or less compatible with those of Peter and the other apostles, and those of James and the brothers of Jesus; these views at least did not cause the controversy. The real controversy concerned the question whether Jewish believers could have table fellowship with Gentile believers who did not live in accordance with the Jewish Law (Gal. 2.11-14; see Van Os 2008).

Paul's initially strong language in his letter to the Galatians is already toned down in his letters to the Corinthians and Romans, written shortly thereafter. It is striking to see how much the author of Acts is downplaying Paul's original position, possibly to save Paul from disapproval by the Jewish leaders of the movement at the time when Acts was written. Against Paul's own words in Gal. 2.1-13, he secures the approval of Peter and James for the mission to the Gentiles (Acts 15.6 makes Peter the apostle to the Gentiles, and 15.13 leaves the decision to James). Where Paul emphasizes that Titus did not have to be circumcised, Acts 16.3 relates how Paul has Timothy circumcised. Paul makes a big deal about his conflict with Peter and the men of James in Antioch, but Acts 18.22 reduces this to 'spending some time there'. Finally, Acts 21.21 makes out Paul to be subservient to James as one who would not make Jews abandon purity laws or circumcision, things which Paul clearly propagates in his letter to the Galatians, and about which he is neutral in his letters to the Romans and the Corinthians. In the days when Acts was written, probably after the influx of refugees from the first Jewish revolt, clearly the compromise was that Gentiles did not have to become Jews, but that Jewish believers were still encouraged to be law-observant. Paul's influence, therefore, was limited in the first century. When 2 Tim. 1.15 was written, it was remembered that the community in and around Ephesus ('all of Asia') had denounced Paul. But the letters he wrote proved decisive when the growing influence of Gentiles made a different compromise necessary. That compromise was already foreseen by Paul 40 years before: Gentiles and Jews would be freed from the Mosaic Law and form a new race as Christians. If I may add this point to Dunn's 2009 study of the early church: Paul was not 'the second founder of' *first-century* 'Christianity' but of *second-century* Christianity, at which point in time his teachings provoked bitter opposition to law-observant groups. It seems, for instance, that the position of Acts 15 (Jews saved as Jews, Gentiles saved as Gentiles) is still upheld by the anti-Pauline Pseudo-Clementine *Recognitions* 1.27–71, which F. Stanley Jones (1995) believes to be a Jewish Christian source from Jerusalem around 200 CE.

Paul wrote letters to exercise his influence in communities where he was not present. He did not rely on oral communication only, but believed he could improve his case by asking his envoys or the addressees to read out his own thoughts (cf. 2 Cor. 10.10). This is understandable in view of the innovative and controversial character of his views on the position of Gentiles and Jews in the *ekklesiai* and his particular command of Scripture that could not easily be replicated by envoys.

The reason why Paul's letters were preserved is therefore twofold: (1) There were very few writers and Paul's lengthy writings were exceptionally rich in theology when compared to the standard short notes that people would give to their messenger; (2) Paul's theology satisfied the social needs of the dominant members in the second-century Diaspora churches.

Information in Paul's Letters

The information about the earthly Jesus in the undisputed letters of Paul is relatively scarce. Some have argued from silence that this is all that Paul knows about Jesus because he was not interested in the earthly Jesus (2 Cor. 5.16). But that conclusion is not tenable. Paul had spoken with Peter, John and James. He had worked with people who were followers of Jesus before him, such as Barnabas, Priscilla and Aquila, and knew others such as Andronicus and Junia(s) (Rom. 16.7). Indeed, by the same logic, Paul would know very little about himself, as he discloses little personal information in his letters. Furthermore, as argued above, Paul's letters were exceptional; they cannot have been the vehicle for passing on information about Jesus. Paul himself occasionally refers to oral traditions (1 Cor. 11.23 and 15.1, 11), a word of the Lord (1 Thess. 4.15), or instructions of the Lord (1 Thess. 4.2).

What Paul does mention to his audiences is that Jesus is the Son of David according to his flesh and the Son of God according to his spirit (Rom. 1.3-4). God sent his Son, born from a woman, and born under the Jewish Law (Gal. 4.4), in a body of flesh (Rom. 8.3). Jesus has brothers (1 Cor. 9.5), one of whom is James (Gal. 1.19). Jesus called the Twelve, even if only Cephas/Peter and John are mentioned (Gal. 2.9). His ministry was to the Jews (Rom. 15.8). As a son, Jesus seems to have prayed to God as Father/Abba (Gal. 4.6). He condemned divorce (1 Cor. 7.10). He instructed that people should live their lives in holiness and honour and probably also with love for one another (1 Thess. 4.2-9). Jesus spoke about a coming on the clouds to resurrect the dead (1 Thess. 4.15-16). Jesus' Spirit is God's Spirit (Rom. 8.9). Jesus was persecuted (1 Thess. 1.6) and crucified (Phil. 2.8), because of the Jews (1 Thess. 2.15). He celebrated a last supper with his friends on the night that he was betrayed, and asked that henceforth the bread be broken in his memory, and the cup be drunk as the sign of the new covenant in his blood (1 Cor. 15.23-5). He died as a righteous one on behalf of sinners (2 Cor. 5.15, 21), freely and obediently (Rom. 5.6-19), as a paschal lamb (1 Cor. 5.7), and an act of love (2 Cor. 5.14). He died, was buried and rose from the dead; he was seen by Peter, James, the Twelve, the apostles and several hundreds of his followers (1 Cor. 15.1-7).

Searching for the Origins of Paul's Information

When assessing information in Paul's letters we can apply rhetorical analysis to sieve out the most reliable information. If the information is not argued by Paul but presupposed, the information is older than the letter. If the information is used in support of the argument, when writing to a non-Pauline community, or a community in which Paul's authority was contested, it can be considered common knowledge within a larger part of the movement. If that community had access to first-generation believers, or followers of Cephas/ Peter or James, the information was likely to have been shared by followers both in the Diaspora and in Palestine.

Of course, information that passes these filters (and most of the information set out above actually does) does not have to be historically accurate. The analysis shows only that such information was likely assumed to be true by Jesus' family and friends in the early years after the crucifixion. The next step would be to look at the content of the information in relation to the functioning of social memory, which I will discuss as part of the next section. There is an important difference between general information (such as Jesus had a brother called James, or that the family thought it was possible that they were of Davidic descent) that could actually be verified in the 40s and 50s CE, and information about specific words and actions that were seen or heard only once by a limited number of witnesses (like the exact words spoken by Jesus during the last supper).

Jesus Traditions and Social Memory

The first-century Gospels include stories about Jesus, sayings of Jesus, and sayings set within stories. The Jesus Traditions in the Synoptic Gospels are set in a narrative structure that follows the Gospel of Mark. Matthew saw no reason to change this structure but does reorganize the stories and sayings within that structure. Luke made some changes and added a lengthy account of Jesus' journey to Jerusalem. Both Matthew and Luke add a birth narrative and several accounts of the resurrection appearances. The Gospel of John contains only a few episodes, each with lengthy and unique discourses. Only a few of these episodes are found in the Synoptic Gospels. Contrary to the Synoptics, most of these episodes are set in Jerusalem. The Gospel of Thomas does not follow a narrative structure.

As I argue above, they could not have been written solely for their local community, but they were influenced by the specific beliefs and circumstances of their authors and the community in which the work was first conceived. This is not the place to argue the provenance of the Gospels in detail, but it is necessary to be explicit about my assumptions. I date (a version of) the Gospel of Mark prior to the Jewish War (some scholars believe that most of the narrative was written as early as the 40s CE, e.g. Robinson 1976, Wenham 1992, Casey 1998, Crossley 2004). Mark is followed by the Gospels of Matthew in the 70s CE and Luke in the 80s CE. Around the end of the first century the Gospel of John and, perhaps, the Gospel of Thomas were written. It is possible that under the name Q scholars have reconstructed much of a collection of sayings that we find both in Matthew and in Luke, which may therefore be of similar antiquity as the Gospel of Mark. From other Gospels that potentially were written in the first century, we have only small fragments. Some second-century documents also contain older traditions.

If we accept the priority of Mark and Q, it can be argued that Matthew and Luke had limited freedom in adapting their sources (but possibly more freedom in extending them). The limitations are seen in their conservative use of the sayings of Jesus, such that we can indeed reconstruct something like Q. At the same time, however, Matthew can rework the prediction of the destruction of Jerusalem in Mk 13 such that it seems that the Son of Man will come immediately after the city is destroyed (Mt. 24.29), whereas Luke, whom I date years later, writes that the Gentiles will first rule the city until their times are fulfilled (Lk. 21.24).

The author of Acts shows the standard freedom of speech-writing in late antiquity, but the (same) author of the Gospel according to Luke is fairly conservative with the words of Jesus, merely working them up from the version in which they were memorized (and probably translated and written down before him). The *author* behind the speeches in the Gospel according to John uses the freedom of speech-writing even for speeches of Jesus, and acknowledges the role of the living Spirit in that process (Jn 16.13-15), but the compiler of that Gospel seems to have been far more conservative with respect to the author's work (Bas van Os 2009, building on Anderson 2006). Perhaps the discourses in the Gospel of John should be read like Plato's Socratic dialogues: in both cases the authors use the freedom of speechwriting to make their own points.

Conserving and Creative Forces

Before the Jesus traditions were used by the evangelists, they were created, shaped and passed on by the earliest followers of Jesus. In this process there were both conserving and creative forces at play. As anthropologists have demonstrated, in oral cultures there exist mnemonic systems and secured transmission chains to preserve certain specific traditions – shaped to be remembered. In 1998, two earlier works by Birger Gerhardsson (1961 and 1964) were republished as evidence of a renewed interest in the relevance of conserving forces in antiquity in general and in rabbinic Judaism in particular. Students were supposed to repeat before they could create. The rabbis knew specific techniques to control the passing on of the sayings and narratives that were part of the 'oral Thora'. Likewise, Jesus could have taught his disciples to memorize his instructions, and his disciples could have used the same techniques to pass on traditions about Jesus. I would think that something similar may be behind the image painted in 1 and 2 Timothy, where the author pens the following words in Paul's name: 'and the things you heard from me among many witnesses, commit these to faithful men who will be competent to teach others' (2.2).

Gerhardsson's model, however, does not explain the differences in wording between, for instance, the Synoptic Gospels. James Dunn (2003), therefore, uses a less formal understanding of oral transmission. Samuel Byrskog (2000) and Rafael Rodriguez (2010) propose seeing history and story in interaction, especially in oral history and communal performance, with each controlling and shaping the other. Richard Bauckham (2006) zoomed in on the role of eyewitnesses in this process. This is particularly relevant given the findings in Chapters 4 and 5 above with regard to the presence of first-generation believers. According to Bauckham, several features in the Gospels and Acts indicate that these eyewitnesses were both informers and guarantors of Jesus traditions. Interesting for this study is the fact that Bauckham included a chapter in which he engages with the work of psychologists with respect to the reliability of eyewitness memory. Equally interesting is that Judith Redman (2010) has an article in the *Journal of Biblical Literature* that evaluates Bauckham's work on the basis of psychological research. She concludes as follows (196):

> ... psychological research makes it clear that Bauckham's work in *Jesus and the Eyewitnesses* does not provide strong evidence for the historical accuracy of the Gospels. Although it is clear that transmission of stories in oral cultures is remarkably accurate once a community decides that something should be preserved and skilled oral tradents are entrusted with the task of preserving it, many of the inaccuracies in eyewitness memory come into being within hours, days, or weeks of the event being witnessed. Furthermore, these eyewitness accounts come from within a faith community formed around the subject of the stories, which adds a particular source of bias not present in other histories of the time.

Neurobiologists, psychologists and sociologists teach us that memory is not just about the conservation of historical facts, but a creative process in itself: much of what we remember is shaped by what we and our peers believe could or should have happened and the way in which we 'store and retrieve' our memories. Although it is somewhat difficult to suggest things that are contrary to what people remember, it is easy to suggest things that fit with what they remember and that they would like to be true. Cognitive science teaches that new ideas are likely to be quickly disseminated and remembered in social networks if they are minimally counter-intuitive – remarkable, but not too much (Czachesz 2003, 2007). The enormous growth of miracle stories in the apocryphal Gospels and acts is easily understood as part of this process, especially in the second century when the primary witnesses had died and the movement became dominated by Gentiles. Even quite bizarre stories became only minimally counter-intuitive as more and more divine powers were ascribed to Jesus and the apostles. It is quite conceivable that some of these stories originated as fictional literature (for instance, as Christian alternatives for the late antique novels), but were later included in works claiming to be historical.

Anthony LeDonne (2009, 70–4) applies the theory of social memory to Jesus traditions. He notes that memories are frequently 'refracted' under the influence of existing 'typologies' as well as later perceptions and events. At the same time, people need a level of 'mnemonic continuity' to maintain integrity between past and present. In order to assess the relationship between the memory of the group and the historical reality that is remembered, the historian should know the history, beliefs and perceptions of the group in order to follow and take into account the cycles of refraction. He concludes (268):

> The historical Jesus is the memorable Jesus: he is the one who set refraction trajectories in motion and who set the initial parameters for how his memories were to be interpreted by his contemporaries. If this is so, then the historian does not 'find' Jesus in spite of the refractions of the evangelists. Rather the historian discerns his historical presence and impact on the basis of these refractions. It is because these refractions exist that we can confidently postulate the mnemonic sphere in which the memories of Jesus were located.

Conclusion

Unfortunately, we do not yet have the precise theory about the development and 'psycho-history' of the early Jesus followers that allows us to reassess the relation between the history of Jesus and the stories of the evangelist. But I do hope that the present study can contribute to such a framework. For Part Three, however, I will take a rather traditional historical-critical approach towards the historicity of Jesus traditions. First, I will concentrate on traditions in the oldest layers. I will give priority to Jesus traditions in Paul's letters, Mark and Q, and then to additional traditions in Matthew and Luke. Although I recognize the potential for historical information in John, Thomas and other early sources, this will have to be argued in every single case.

The oldest information in Paul's letters concerns data that are supposed to be common knowledge in the wider movement that included the Twelve and the brothers of Jesus. In each instance we will have to ask ourselves whether such information is best explained as going back to Jesus, or to post-Easter innovation by Jesus' family and friends. In Part Three, I am particularly interested in the potential impact that Jesus may have had on:

- The veneration of God as an intimate father of the fictive 'brothers and sisters' who followed Jesus (Chapter 7).
- The social cohesion between his followers and the inclusion of both Jesus' family and the Twelve within the group (Chapter 8).
- The interpretation of their spiritual experiences as the works of the Holy Spirit or the Spirit of Jesus (Chapter 9).
- The idea that Jesus was crucified and raised in accordance with God's will, and the remembrance of his death as beneficial to his followers (Chapter 10).
- The identification of Jesus as both the suffering Messiah and the Lord who will descend from heaven on the Last Day (Chapter 11).

To explore the relationship of these elements with the historical Jesus, I will use the Synoptical-century Gospels, giving priority to earlier layers over later; and to general information over specific words and deeds. For the time being, a historical-critical approach should be employed to extract the most reliable information, using the criteria of multiple attestation, dissimilarity and contextual credibility. The latter criterion should include psychological credibility. In all cases the specific bias of the evangelist needs to be taken into account.

PART THREE

PSYCHOLOGICAL ANALYSES
OF JESUS AND HIS IMPACT

Introduction to Part Three

Based on the findings in Part Two, I conclude that it is likely that the historical Jesus did indeed have an impact on the beliefs and traditions of his followers, but that we need to proceed with caution because over time their memory of him would have been significantly affected by their beliefs and circumstances. In order to demonstrate the usefulness of psychological methods, I employ a three-step approach:

- First, I identify in the undisputed letters of Paul certain beliefs that are likely to be pre-Pauline and shared by many first-generation believers – beliefs that cannot be explained easily on the basis of contemporary Jewish or Hellenistic thinking, but could conceivably go back to the historical Jesus. This may remind some of the Second Quest's criterion of double dissimilarity.
- Second, I have selected various empirically tested theories that are central in the contemporary psychology of religion and likely to be helpful in theorizing about the relationship between these beliefs and the historical Jesus, given the rather secure facts that he was a religious man, who joined the movement of John the Baptist, earned a reputation as a healer and an exorcist, had to cope with the death of John and who nevertheless went to Jerusalem for what was to be his final Passover.
- Third, I have applied each theory in combination with the established criteria of historical-criticism to relevant traditions about Jesus (foremost in Q and Mark) to come to a psychologically plausible theory of how the historical Jesus could have contributed to these beliefs.

Contemporary Methods Available in the Psychology of Religion

The psychology of religion has two sides, which are already reflected in the systematic work of Edwin Diller Starbuck (*The Psychology of Religion: An Empirical Study of the Growth of Religious Consciousness*, 1899) and the more intuitive work of his teacher William James (*The Varieties of Religious Experience*, 1902). Whereas James set out to understand individuals, Starbuck set out to describe generalized patterns that apply to larger groups. Although it would seem that a study of the historical Jesus would focus on an individual, the opposite is true, as there is too little data to psychoanalyse Jesus. As Runyan suggested, other methods may be more appropriate for historical research, especially in the absence of ego-documents and childhood data. In the case of a religious movement like early Christianity and a religious person like Jesus of Nazareth, such methods should be sensitive to the religious dimension.

The psychology of religion re-emerged as a discipline in the 1980s (Paloutzian (1996; Wulff 1997). It involves the scientific research of subjects like the religious development in different life phases, religious experience, attitudes and behaviour, conversion, and the relationship between religion and mental health. Hood, Spilka, Hunsberger and Gorsuch (1996) emphasize empirical research in their approach. The *Handbook of Religious Experience* (edited by Hood, 1995) gives an overview of such experiences in different faith traditions, discussed in the light of different established psychological theories. A recent update of the field is the *Handbook of the Psychology of Religion and Spirituality*, edited by Paloutzian and Park (2005).

Although the field of psychobiography is dominated by the psychoanalytical methods of Freud, Jung and Erikson (Runyan 1988, 237), it has been noted that their intuitive psychoanalytical theories have not been successful in providing a framework for the psychology of religion. Pehr Granqvist (2002, 72–5) suggests that in the case of monotheistic religions like Christianity, the combination of attachment theory, coping theory and role theory may provide a better framework for an empirically based psychology of religion. I believe this might be true on an individual level, but a religious person is also part of a religious group and of society as a whole, which are the subject matter of sociologists and anthropologists. To take these into account, I have added Rational Choice Theory and Anthropological Psychology to the theoretical framework that I will use in Part Three (see illustration below).

A theoretical framework to study the psychology of a religious person

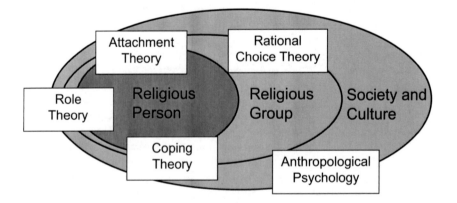

Five Essays

Starting with Attachment Theory and progressing clockwise, each of the five chapters of Part Three will explore how a specific theory can help to theorize about the impact that Jesus had on his earliest followers:

- Using Lee Kirkpatrick's research on Attachment Theory and Religion, I will ask in Chapter 6 whether it is possible that Jesus' experience with his human parents is related to his portrayal of God as a Father, and how this may clarify the impact this may have had on the veneration of God as a Father by his earliest followers.
- In Chapter 7, I will use Rational Choice Theory, developed by sociologists such as Rodney Stark, to look at the relationships between Jesus' family and his followers as well as with the movement of John the Baptist, and what this may tell us about the eschatological ideas that they and Jesus himself may have shared.
- In order to explore Jesus' reputation as an exorcist and a healer and the impact this may have had on the spiritual experiences of his followers, I will use Anthropological Psychology in Chapter 8. This is not a particular theory, but rather a sub-discipline, described by Erika Bourguignon, that combines psychological and anthropological insights from various researchers.
- In Chapter 9, a key period in Jesus' mission will be brought into focus in which he had to cope with rejection, the execution of John the Baptist and the associated threats to his own life. Kenneth Pargament has researched how religion and coping can interact in situations of grief and crisis. A key element is the significance that religious persons attribute to a certain situation. I will use his work to investigate whether this may explain that the death of Jesus was interpreted as being in accordance with God's will and to the benefit of his people.
- Finally, I will use Hjalmar Sundén's Role Theory to explore how Jesus' followers came to attribute to him a specific combination of roles: the suffering servant, the royal Messiah and the coming Lord. Sundén noted that, especially in times of stress, people within a certain religious tradition can come to relate their own situation to the narratives and roles in that tradition. How much, then, of the roles ascribed to Jesus by his earliest followers can have had a basis in the last part of the life of Jesus himself?

The concluding section returns to the question of Christology, raised in Chapter 1: How much of early Christian beliefs originated with the historical Jesus, and how much originated after Easter, among his earliest followers?

Chapter 7

ATTACHMENT TO THE FATHER

In Chapter 2, three psychobiographical studies of the historical Jesus are discussed. All three psychological portraits emphasize the family background of Jesus as an important element for analysis, and especially his relationship to his human father or to the concept of fatherhood. All three use assumptions about Jesus' relationship with his father to explain his adult personality and actions. But the link between Jesus' relationship with his father and his adult personality and actions is too weak, and information about his childhood too selective and biased to lead to scholarly consensus. Miller's analysis concludes the relationship was good, Capps says it was bad and Van Aarde sees it as non-existent.

The situation is perhaps better if we try the combination of two different links that are better supported: the link between the historic Jesus and the veneration of God as a Father by his earliest followers, and the link between Jesus' attachment to God as a Father and his relationship with his human father. Both Paul and the Jesus traditions speak frequently about God as a Father. The childhood evidence is still lacking, but psychologists of religion have studied the link between divine and human attachment figures, and their results can say something about what is more or less likely with respect to the relationship between Jesus and his human father.

The Veneration of God as a Father by Early Jesus Followers

The emphasis on God as a Father is recognizable throughout early Christian literature. This is already true for Paul's undisputed letters. At the start of each letter, grace is offered from 'God our Father and Christ the Lord' or a close variant thereof (1 Thess. 1.1, Gal. 1.3, 1 Cor. 1.3, 2 Cor. 1.2, Rom. 1.7, Phil. 1.2 and Phlm. 1.3). In these letters, God is referred to as the Father of the believers, or the believers as children of God, two or three times as often as he is the Father of the Israelites in the entire Hebrew Bible. Whereas in most instances in the Hebrew Bible, the collective Israel is the child of God, the emphasis in early Christianity is on each of the followers as a child of God (as in Hos. 1.10). For Paul, this relationship with God is new and transformative. He considers his pre-conversion period as a time in which he was a slave of the Law, in fear of transgression and condemnation by the King of Israel. This may tell us more about Paul than about the average follower of Jesus, but it is clear that for followers like Paul, the familiar idea that God was the Father of Israel turned into an extraordinary and transformative idea that God was his personal and merciful Father. In 2 Cor. 6.18 he boldly extends the promise God made to David concerning his House (2 Sam. 7.14) to all believers, they will be 'sons and daughters' of God and heirs to his Kingdom.

The grace-formula indicates that 'Father' may have had a function in the blessings that believers used in their regular practice. There are two passages in letters written in the 50s CE that demonstrate that Paul's audiences, too, addressed God as Father:

> But when the fullness of time had come, God sent his Son, born of a woman, born under the law, in order to redeem those who were under the law, so that we might receive adoption as children. And because you are children, God has sent the Spirit of his Son into our hearts, crying, '*Abba!* Father!' So you are no longer a slave but a child, and if a child then also an heir, through God. (Gal. 4.4-7)

> For you did not receive a spirit of slavery to fall back into fear, but you have received a spirit of adoption. When we cry, '*Abba!* Father!' it is that very Spirit bearing witness with our spirit that we are children of God, and if children, then heirs, heirs of God and joint heirs with Christ – if, in fact, we suffer with him so that we may also be glorified with him. (Rom. 8.15-16)

In Rom. 8, Paul clearly assumes that his audience uses 'Abba, Father' as a standard opening address in their prayers. The veneration of God as the Father of the believers most likely precedes Paul, as 'Abba' is the Aramaic equivalent of 'father'. The use of the Aramaic in Paul's Greek letters most likely indicates that the word belongs to the tradition passed on by the first followers of Jesus who spoke Aramaic. Furthermore, the word was used both in Galatia where Paul had preached, as well as in Rome where Paul had not yet been.

In these two passages, Paul traces the veneration of God as a Father back to Jesus. For Paul, they are 'predestined to be conformed to the image of his Son, in order that he might be the firstborn among many *adelphois*' (Rom. 8.28). The idea that Jesus is the firstborn suggests that for Paul a new family was revealed with Jesus' resurrection (Rom. 1.4). For Paul, it is baptism in Christ (dying and rising with him) that ended former ethnic, social or gender-related boundaries and makes all believers children of God (Gal. 3.26-9). It is Jesus – for Paul the Son of God *par excellence* – who achieved the adoption of his followers as children; it is in his Spirit that his followers address God as 'Abba, Father'.

The movement of early Jesus followers perceived itself as a family. This language is also found in other cults and associations in the Graeco-Roman world, although perhaps not taken as far as Paul does in these letters. It is this form of fictive kinship that must have been attractive to migrants and slaves, and widows and orphans, cut off from their original families. On the basis of Paul's letters, I conclude that the veneration of God as a Father was of great importance to the early followers of Jesus, that it preceded Paul, and is to be traced to the original Aramaic-speaking followers, possibly to Jesus himself.

Geza Vermes (1993, ch. 6, 'Abba, Father': The God of Jesus) analyses the roughly 60 times in the Synoptic Gospels that Jesus calls God 'Father' from a Jewish perspective. Vermes notes that the Father imagery in the Hebrew Bible, the intertestamental literature and the Qumran writings is certainly present but relatively sparse. It is far better attested to in rabbinic literature, including the expression '(my) Father who is in heaven'. As such, both Christian and rabbinic origins of the veneration of God as 'the loving and affectionate Protector of the individual member of the family' are likely to be situated in the religious feelings that Jesus and some first-century *hasidim* shared. With respect to Jesus and his followers, Vermes summarizes his findings as follows:

> The concept of God as Father of Jesus, of his followers, and of the whole created world, is deeply implanted in the Gospels. It figures in various literary forms – parables, sayings, prayers – and in all the layers of the Synoptic tradition – in Mark and the triple transmission, in Q, and in the separate Matthean and Lucan versions. As customary, the purpose is not mystical or theological, but existential and practical: by envisaging the Deity as a caring parent, Jesus intends to impress on his disciples their appropriate attitude towards God, and since the notions of Father and son are correlative, propose a model for the behaviour of 'brothers and sisters'.

Note that the idea of brothers and sisters changed over time. Jews were used to call each other 'brothers and sisters', mostly in an ethnic sense derived from a (perceived) common ancestry. An equivalent term for this use is 'children of Abraham' (Q 3.8, Jn 8.33). Jesus and Paul use it to refer to 'children of God', even though here, too, there are differences. For Jesus it involved all Jews who wanted to do the will of God (see the discussion of Mk 3.35 below). It is quite possible that many Jesus followers in the 50s CE still saw other pious Jews as their brothers and sisters. In the accounts of the death of Jesus' brother James in 62 CE by Josephus and Hegesippus, it seems that many Jews accepted the movement as led by James in Jerusalem as part of Judaism.

As Jesus' relationship with his heavenly Father was common among his followers, but not common among first-century Jews, Vermes may well be correct in saying that Jesus transferred this type of attachment to God to his followers. The next question is how Jesus may have developed such a relationship with God and how this may be related to his relationship with a human parent. In the remainder of this chapter, I will first assess what Jesus' earliest followers remembered about the composition of his family. Next I will discuss and apply John Bowlby's Attachment Theory, which started as the study of attachment patterns in young children, but expanded to include other attachment figures in later age, such as close friends, romantic partners and God.

Jesus' Family

The most direct data about the family of Jesus consists of the remarks in the letters of Paul about James and the brothers of Jesus in his day, as well as the remark from Josephus about the death of James around 62 CE, when Josephus himself lived in Jerusalem (before his departure to Rome). The demographical analysis in Chapter 4 showed that it is quite unlikely that these were older brothers of Jesus. It is far more likely that they were his younger brothers. His mother is not mentioned in these sources and it is quite likely that she had already died by the time that Paul wrote about the resurrection witnesses in 1 Cor. 15.

The authors of the synoptic Gospels and the compiler of the Gospel of John are considered to be indirect witnesses, writing 20 to 60 years after the events they relate. While this is true for specific events or sayings for which these writers were not present, it is possible that they had firsthand information about the brothers of Jesus. Given the small size of the movement, the fact that the brothers visited various groups of Jesus followers in the 50s CE and survived into at least the 60s CE, it is quite likely that one or several Gospel writers had met one or more brothers of Jesus. It is extremely likely that one or several Gospel writers had met other Jesus followers who had known some of these brothers very well, and that their Gospels were read and copied by people who had.

With that in mind, it is fruitful to assess what the writers of the first-century narrative Gospels, who seem to have had a biographical interest in Jesus, assumed about his family situation. I will take into account only statements made in the context of his ministry; following the death of his mother there was no surviving witness of Jesus' birth.

- In the narrative of the author of Mark, Jesus came from Nazareth (but this could also be read as his name) to be baptized by John (Mk 1.9). Some unspecified time later, when John is arrested (1.16) Jesus lives in Capernaum (2.1), either in his own house or that of a disciple such as Peter (1.29). When he comes 'home' in 3.19 the crowds keep him from eating and his mother and siblings come to fetch him (3.31), presumably from another house in the neighbourhood. In 6.1-3, Jesus returns to the small village of Nazareth, the place where he grew up. Some people recognize him and say: 'Is not this the carpenter, the son of Mary and brother of James and Joses and Judas and Simon, and are not his sisters here with us?' The statement clearly implies that only the sisters lived in Nazareth with their husbands. At the end of the Gospel, Mary the mother of little James and Joses stands at the cross (15.40), Mary the mother of Joses saw where his body was laid in the grave (15.47), and Mary the mother of James finds the empty tomb (16.1). Whether this is Mary the mother of Jesus is not clear in the narrative, but James and Joses seem to be persons known to the audience and the only ones mentioned are Jesus' brothers from 6.3. Perhaps the author does not call her the mother of Jesus, because the Markan Jesus gave up his mother and brothers in 3.35 and 10.29.

- In Mt. 4.12-13 Jesus moves from Nazareth to Capernaum after John's arrest, as one of the four prophesied places of origin (Bethlehem, Egypt, Nazareth and the land of Zebulon and Naphtali). In Mt. 13.55, when Jesus visits his hometown, he is called 'the son of the carpenter'. Mark's information about his brothers and his sisters ('all' his sisters this time) is repeated, but Joses' name is changed into 'Joseph'. Joses seems to have been a diminutive of that name, and it is quite plausible that the boy would have been called Joseph after he came of age. Likewise, the woman at the cross is called Mary the mother of James and Joseph in 27.56; again she is not identified as the mother of Jesus.
- Contrary to Matthew, Lk. 4.16-30 places Jesus' visit to Nazareth in the time immediately following his baptism, implying that he had already moved to Capernaum at the time of his baptism. In Lk. 4.22 Jesus is called 'the son of Joseph'. The author of Acts 1.14 adds that Mary the mother of Jesus as well as his brothers had joined the Twelve and other disciples after the crucifixion.
- In Jn 1.45 Jesus is called the 'son of Joseph from Nazareth'. But like Luke, the author seems to assume that Jesus' mother and her sons lived in Capernaum (2.12), where the people also knew his father Joseph (6.42, but this might also be explained as a transposition of the Nazareth episode). Jn 7.1-10 again implies that his brothers lived together and went together to Jerusalem for the Festival of Booths. At that point in time, they did not follow Jesus. John clearly identifies a Mary at the crucifixion as Jesus' mother (19.25-7) and has the moving scene in which Jesus gives her his disciple John as a son in his place (for an analysis of this relationship between them, see Chapter 8).

To sum up: all authors assume that Jesus was raised in Nazareth but lived in Capernaum with his mother and younger brothers at some point in his life. Three out of four authors assume this to be the case prior to Jesus' baptism, whereas the dissenting author of Matthew clearly uses the places of Jesus' origins in a symbolic way. The author of John places the relocation even before the death of Joseph.

The reason for the family to move to Capernaum may have been economical. If Joseph and Jesus were carpenters, or construction workers, Nazareth with perhaps a hundred families was most likely too small to sustain them (especially as the family kept growing). But they may have worked in a wider region. In the 20s CE the economic activity shifted from Sepphoris (near Nazareth) to the shores of the Sea of Galilee: an area stretching from Herod Antipas' new capital Tiberias to Bethsaida Julias, the enlarged capital of the territory governed by his brother Philip. Whether Jesus worked on government projects in the cities is a point of debate (there was no daily commuter traffic in antiquity). All I am saying is that the economic activity shifted towards the Sea of Galilee and that some people looking for work in construction may have felt the need to relocate.

There is not much reason to distrust the information in Mark regarding the names of Jesus' mother and brothers, nor the idea that Jesus had sisters who had married in Nazareth (for an impression of what this may have meant in the light of Graeco-Roman demographics and mortality, I refer to Chapter 4). The name Joseph for Jesus' father is given only in the three later Gospels, but it is found in very different stories and corresponds with the names of one of Jesus' brothers in Mark. These general data concern not only the historic Jesus but also his brothers who were still around in the 50s and 60s CE. They are therefore likely to be correct, even if only the names of James and Jude are independently attested to in other early sources.

Attachment Theory

John Bowlby, who had studied under Freud's pupil Melanie Klein, put forward his basic theory about childhood attachment in his groundbreaking work *Attachment* in 1969. In later works, he discusses psychological states that may be related to attachment, such as anxiety and fear (*Separation*, 1973), and sadness and depression resulting from the loss of an attachment figure (*Loss*, 1980). Bowlby also wrote a well-researched biography of Charles Darwin (1990) in which particular attention is given to the tragic loss of Darwin's mother when he was eight years old and Darwin's failure to recall much about her or her death. Bowlby attributes much of Darwin's later mental and medical problems to this unresolved loss.

The theory can be summarized as follows: virtually every infant will attach itself to one or more specific primary caregivers and seek to maintain a level of proximity. In a stress situation an infant will normally seek out the attachment figure, whose response will result in a tension reduction effect and allow the infant to continue its exploration of its environment. If caregivers are sensitive to the signals of the infant, and respond appropriately, the infant will develop a 'secure attachment'. This is the case for most infants tested, although in certain situations (such as among the Ganda in Uganda and in communal kibbutzim where children do not sleep in their parents' home), significant minorities were not securely attached. Secure attachments contribute to children's competences to regulate their negative emotions, relate to peers and teachers and to develop cognitive abilities. If a child is not securely attached, it can develop two types of behaviour that may cause problems in childhood or later life: anxiety and avoidance. Anxiety can be regarded as a hyper-activation of the signals that a child gives to (potential) caregivers. Avoidance manifests itself as deactivation of such signals. The loss of an attachment figure causes stress but can be resolved over time if alternative attachment figures respond appropriately to the child.

Attachment theory combines the theoretical strength of psychoanalytical approaches with an enormous amount of research as the theory lends itself well to empirical testing, pioneered by Mary Ainsworth and her colleagues (Kirkpatrick 1995). According to the overviews provided in the *Handbook of Attachment: Theory, Research and Clinical Application* (ed. Cassidy and Shaver 1999), its basic premises have been confirmed in empirical studies in diverse cultures, including pre-modern cultures (Van IJzendoorn and Sagi), and even among primates (Suomi).

Jesus

Whether or not Jesus was securely attached to his mother and father cannot be decided from childhood information. The single first-century tradition, about the 12-year old Jesus in the temple, does not pass the criteria of historical criticism. But empirical research suggests there is a relationship between attachment in childhood and in later life. Jesus' earliest followers did leave us traditions that say something about the adult relationship Jesus had with his family and friends and with God.

When assessing Jesus' views and behaviour as an adult, I will start with the traditions in the oldest layers, Mark and the double tradition (Q), and assume that the sayings (Q) and major events (such as the last supper and the resurrection experiences in 1 Corinthians) have benefited more from the conservative forces in oral transmission than from the minor events. For comparison, I will mention the ratings given by the Jesus Seminar for the sayings that I quote, in four categories: 'undoubtedly Jesus', 'probably Jesus', 'like Jesus' and 'not Jesus' (Funk and Hoover 1993).

Adult Relationships

The relationship between attachment and adult relationships has been researched extensively. It was found that childhood memories tend to correlate with a person's mental 'working models' of self and others in later years (Feeney 1999):

- Memories. Secure individuals tend to remember their parents as warm and affectionate, avoidant individuals to remember their mothers as cold and rejecting, and ambivalent ('anxious') individuals to remember their fathers as unfair.
- Beliefs and attitudes. Secure adults generally score high on self-worth and have a positive opinion of most others. They are normally interpersonally oriented and liked by others. Most avoidant adults lack confidence in social situations and perceive others as not dependable or trustworthy. Ambivalent adults tend to see others as difficult to understand and feel that people have little control over their lives.
- Goals and needs for a romantic partnership. Secure adults generally seek intimacy, while trying to balance autonomy and closeness. Most

avoidant adults maintain distance and prefer autonomy and achievement. Ambivalent adults tend to sacrifice autonomy and desire extreme intimacy, while fearing rejection.
- Strategies. Secure adults will generally acknowledge distress and more often than not manage to employ their negative feelings in a constructive way. Avoidant adults will tend to cut off anger and withhold intimate disclosure. Most ambivalent adults will alternate between compliance and anger.

It should be noted that these elements are statistically correlated, but are in no way absolute links. Later experiences (such as the loss of a parent, or the experiences in key friendships and romantic relationships) can influence the 'working models' of adults. Important for our subject is the finding that secure persons are also more likely to be caring and sensitive towards others who need care (such as younger siblings or children).

Jesus

With respect to the four aspects discussed above, the information about Jesus' adult attachments, other than with his family, is as follows:

- Memories. The Jesus traditions do not include sayings about his childhood. I suggest this says something about the nature of oral sayings that were preserved, not about Jesus' memory. There are a number of general sayings regarding intra-family conflicts resulting from following God, but these do not concern memories of his childhood. Below, I will comment on the conflict Jesus had with his mother and brothers during his mission. In Lk. 11.12-13 (a Q-saying scored as 'like Jesus' by the Jesus Seminar), Jesus does observe that fathers respond to and provide for their children.
- Beliefs and attitudes. Jesus seems to have been interpersonally oriented and affiliated himself with a significant number of people (see Chapter 8). With a group called 'The Twelve' he shared his life for the duration of his ministry. He seems to have been closer to some of them. He seems to have noted people's afflictions and they came to him for teaching and healing (see Chapter 9). After his crucifixion, many people mourned him. But he also had to cope with rejection (see Chapter 10) and this is reflected in a number of sayings.
- Goals and needs for a romantic partnership. Whether Jesus was married or not is not of direct importance to our discussion here: marriage in late antiquity was not an expression of an intimate relationship and reflects more the economic than the emotional ability to bond. Although married couples could become intimate partners over time, it was not a condition to enter the marriage. More important in antiquity was one's ability to forge adult relationships with friends, such as Jesus did with the Twelve, and – so it seems – in particular with Peter, James and John.

- Strategies. In Mark, Jesus is generally composed even in the face of criticism, but sometimes reported as angry or emotional (Mk 3.5 and 14.34).

I conclude that the information about Jesus' adult attachments is too fragmentary to classify him as either securely attached or as avoidant or ambivalent.

Attachment to God

Since the 1990s, attachment theory has been applied in studies of religious attachment, mostly in (post-)Christian Europe and America. These are discussed in Granqvist (2002) and Kirkpatrick (2005). Kirkpatrick (52) notes that Christian faith is often viewed as a relationship with God, Jesus or Mary. In order for the divine person in such a relationship to be classified as an attachment figure such as a mother or a father, the following conditions must be met. The attachment figure should provide feelings of comfort and security. He or she must be a secure base from where the world can be explored and a haven of safety in times of distress. Separation from an attachment figure should cause distress. An instrument to measure attachment to God was developed by Brennan, Clark and Shaver (1998): the *Attachment to God Inventory* (AGI). It contains 14 items on the Anxiety subscale and 14 items on the Avoidance subscale. Avoidance of God is expressed in statements such as: 'I prefer not to depend too much on God', or 'I just don't feel a deep need to be close to God'. Examples of statements indicating anxiety about God are: 'I often worry about whether God is pleased with me', and 'I fear God does not accept me when I do wrong'.

Although we cannot ask Jesus to fill out the questionnaire for us, there is quite a bit of information about Jesus' relationship with God. I have reviewed Q and Mark, with the following questions in mind:

- Did Jesus perceive God as a responsive attachment figure?
- Did Jesus turn to God in times of distress?
- Did Jesus perceive himself as worthy of God's love?

Did Jesus Perceive God as a Responsive Attachment Figure?

We can be reasonably confident that this was indeed the case. Jesus frequently compared God to a loving or caring father. In Q (in the edition of Robinson, Hoffman and Kloppenborg 2002), this is seen in the following sayings:

> Love your enemies [and] pray for those [persecuting] you, so that you may become sons of your Father, for he raises his sun on bad and [good and rains on the just and unjust]. (Q 6.27-8, 35c-d)

> Be full of pity, just as your Father … is full of pity. (Q 6.36)

Are not [five] sparrows sold for [two] cents? And yet not one of them will fall to earth without [your Father's] <consent>. But even the hairs of your head all are numbered. Do not be afraid, you are worth more than many sparrows. (Q 12.6-7)

[So] do not be anxious, saying: What are we to eat? [Or:] What are we to drink? [Or:] What are we to wear? For all these things the Gentiles seek; [for] your Father knows that you need them [all]. But seek his kingdom, and [all] these shall be granted to you. (Q 12.29-31)

What person of you, whose child asks for bread, will give him a stone? Or again when he asks for a fish, will give him a snake? So if you, though evil, know how to give good gifts to your children, by how much more will the Father from heaven give good things to those who ask him! (Q 11.12-13)

In the memory of his followers, Jesus frequently used the word 'Father' for God, and always in a positive sense: the Father provides for his children even if they do wrong. This is not in contradiction to human fathers, but rather exceeds the innate goodness of a human father towards his children. The Jesus Seminar rated all these sayings 'like Jesus', with the exception of 12.6-7, which received the rating 'probably Jesus'.

I also note that when Jesus speaks of the punishment by God, he invokes the image of a king.

Did Jesus Turn to God in Times of Distress?

In several instances we read that Jesus went into solitary places to pray:

- Mk 1.35. Jesus' mentor John was arrested, and Jesus had taken the risky step to continue John's preaching together with other disciples of John. When people in his audience experience healing at his hands, and a crowd comes to him, he flees the house and withdraws for prayer in the wilderness.
- Mk 6.30. After John's execution and the return of his disciples, he wants to go to a deserted place and rest. His plan seems to fail because crowds see them leave and follow them along the shore. But after having spent time with them, he sends away the crowd and the disciples, and goes up the mountain to pray in solitude (Matthew makes this point explicit).
- Mk 9.2. In the face of the increasing risk that he too will suffer and die, he takes Peter, James and John with him on a high mountain, where they have a religious experience that comes to be referred to as the transfiguration.
- Mk 14.32-6. Expecting his arrest, he goes to the garden of Gethsemane on the Mount of Olives to pray in an emotional way (see also Heb. 5.7). First in the presence of Peter, James and John, and then alone. Mark describes Jesus as praying to his divine 'Abba':

They went to a place called Gethsemane; and he said to his disciples, 'Sit here while I pray.' He took with him Peter and James and John, and began to be distressed and agitated. And he said to them, 'I am deeply grieved, even to death; remain here, and keep awake.' And going a little farther, he threw himself on the ground and prayed that, if it were possible, the hour might pass from him. He said, 'Abba, Father, for you all things are possible; remove this cup from me; yet, not what I want, but what you want.'

The historicity of the above episodes and their details is disputed, but it seems likely that at least the overall picture is 'like Jesus'.

Did Jesus Perceive Himself as Worthy of God's Love?

When we turn to Jesus' prayer life in Q and Mark, we see that the Fatherhood of God was not only a theoretical construct for Jesus. He addressed God as his Father with whom he could be intimate and who would answer his prayers. This can be seen in the following two passages (of which the beginnings were rated 'like Jesus' by the Jesus Seminar):

At <that time> he said: I praise you, Father, Lord of heaven and earth, for you hid these things from sages and the learned, and disclosed them to children. Yes, Father, for that is what it has pleased you to do. Everything has been entrusted to me by my Father, and no one knows the Son except the Father, nor [does anyone know] the Father except the Son, and to whomever the Son chooses to reveal him. (Q 10.21-2)

[When] you pray, [say:]
   Father
   – may your name be kept holy! –
   let your reign come:
   Our day's bread give us today;
   And cancel our debts for us,
   as we too have cancelled for those in debt to us;
   and do not put us to the test!
   (Q11. 2b-4)

It seems that Jesus perceived not only his own relationship with God as that of a son and a father, but also that he could bring his followers into that relationship (remember Vermes' analysis that this was not very common among first-century Jews). Evidence from the letters of Paul reviewed at the start of this chapter confirms that his way of addressing God was indeed passed on in early Christian communities.

To conclude: It seems to be reasonably certain that Jesus perceived God as an attachment figure such as a father, and that he was securely attached to him. In attachment terms, Jesus shows little avoidance and anxiety towards God: he experiences God as an available attachment figure to whom he can turn in times of distress. Jesus sees himself as being loved and supported by God. Jesus does not describe God as a transcendent impersonal force, but as a person. He does not compare God to a romantic partner, friend, sibling or mother, but to a father and a king. The designation 'king' stresses his power towards the world at large and to the benefit of his loved ones. But Jesus and his followers never address God as 'king' in their prayers. For them, he is primarily addressed as 'Father'. As such, he is like human fathers. But while they are good to their children despite their sinfulness, God is abundantly good to his children because he is perfect.

I note that certain traditions in special Luke (like the parable of the prodigal son) could well be from Jesus or like Jesus. This would reinforce the conclusions we can draw on the basis of Mark and Q.

Attachment to God and Parents: Compensation or Correspondence?

Having God as an attachment figure does not necessarily indicate that a person was securely attached to primary caregivers as a child. Research shows that people with a strong religious attachment typically have developed such an attachment via two very different mechanisms: Compensation and Correspondence. Attachment to God is sometimes found to compensate for insecure attachment to other humans, often derived from avoidance and/ or anxiety in the relationship with parents (Granqvist and Hagekull 1999). This is often combined with another effect: people with insecure parental attachment are more likely than others to experience sudden conversion or deconversion, especially in adolescence, in the opposite direction of parental beliefs and convictions. Such sudden conversions of the 'sick soul' are to de distinguished from the more gradual conversions of the 'healthy minded' (Granqvist 2003).

In contrast, securely attached people often maintain a measure of correspondence between their parents' religion and their own. Their own religious beliefs gradually develop out of those of their parents. If they are religious, then young adults often display a correspondence between their Internal Working Model of their parents and that of God. Note, however, that this correlation is weaker at a later age. Securely attached people are able to attach to other humans. If they are religious, they often display low avoidance and anxiety towards God.

To summarize: the majority of adolescents and young adults is securely attached and shows a level of correspondence with their parents' beliefs. A minority, with insecure childhood attachment, is more likely to turn away from parental beliefs, sometimes converting to another religion.

Analysis of Jesus' behaviour and sayings in Mark and Q reveals that Jesus experienced not only a strong attachment to God, but also a secure one. This would suggest that Jesus developed this attachment on the basis of the correspondence mechanism. It would also suggest that Jesus was able to attach to other humans. In order to test this finding, I will investigate three questions:

- Did Jesus come from a religious family?
- Did Jesus experience a sudden conversion when he was baptized by John?
- Did Jesus break with his family when he joined John's movement?

Did Jesus Come from a Religious Family?

Van Aarde is correct when he criticizes reconstructions of Jesus' relationship with his father on the basis of the conflicting birth narratives of Matthew and Luke. In these narratives, Joseph and Mary are portrayed as religious people, who live righteously and expect the coming of the Messiah. But the fact that these narratives do not pass the tests of historical criticism does not mean that Jesus was not raised in a religious family. It only means that we have to look elsewhere for evidence. Also the story about the visit to Jerusalem for a religious festival in Lk. 2.41-52 is historically suspect, as it seems to be a typical portrayal of Jesus as a precocious 12-year-old, very similar to Josephus' self-portrayal in his *Vita*, Chapter 2 (7–9). One could argue that both Matthew and Luke could not force their audiences, many of whom had known the brothers of Jesus, to accept the general idea that the family was religious. The counter-argument is that it may have been socially desirable for the brothers to display their parents as devout Jews, and therefore this argument cannot be decisive. But many families were indeed religious, and supporting evidence, I suggest, can be found in the fact that both Jesus and James seem to be quite familiar with parts of the Mosaic Law and the way that scribes argued about the application of such rules in daily life. Both did not see the mission of Jesus as abolishing the Law, but as fulfilling it. Furthermore, the early church in Jerusalem seems to have valued James for his knowledge and observance of the Law, making him a 'pillar' of the church with Peter and John (Gal. 2.9). It also seems that James sent envoys to convince Jewish believers in the Diaspora to uphold the Law (Gal. 2.12). Again it is hard to imagine that James could have developed all his expertise only after the death of Jesus, when James joined the movement. Furthermore, the archaeology of first-century Nazareth suggests that the tiny peasant village held to Jewish burial, dietary and purification practices (Reed 2000, 51; Crossan and Reed 2001, 35–6). Given the complete lack of evidence to the contrary, it is therefore best to assume that Jesus' family was to a significant degree a religious family, like so many other Jewish families in first-century Galilee.

Did Jesus Experience a Sudden Conversion?

On the basis of criteria of historical criticism (Meier 1994, 100–105; Webb 2009), most scholars agree that Jesus was probably baptized by John (which is not the same as saying that the baptism stories and the temptation stories that followed Jesus' baptism are accepted as historical). It is tempting to see Jesus' baptism by John as a moment of conversion accompanied by intense psychological distress (the temptation in the desert by Satan). John the Baptist, however, did not call the Jewish people to a new religion, but to a purified life. Both the Gospels and Josephus describe the popular appreciation of John as a member of the Jewish religion. Rather than a conversion in religious outlook, for most people, his baptism intensified existing religion, and awakened an existing expectation of the coming of God's reign. Large numbers of Jews (Q 3.7-9 and Mk 1.4-5) did indeed come forward for baptism and appreciated John as one of the Jewish prophets. Jesus did so, too, as we can read in Q 7.24-35 and 16.16 (rated as 'probably Jesus' and 'like Jesus' by the Jesus Seminar). If Jesus came from a religious family, then his baptism by John was not a conversion to a religion other than that of his parents. This is also the understanding of the author of the Gospel of the Hebrews, in which also Mary and Jesus' brothers wished to be baptized by John. Mk 1.9-13 and Q 4.1-13 do not describe Jesus' baptism as a response to psychological distress. Jesus simply came to be baptized like so many other Jews. Baptism did not make Jesus a member of a selective new religion: Jesus addresses his Jewish audience as children of God, without asking whether they had been baptized. It is therefore incorrect to see Jesus' baptism as a moment of *conversion*. But there may have been a *sudden* spiritual experience associated with the idea of God's fatherhood, and I will come back to this point later in this chapter.

Did Jesus Break with His Family?

In the following instances in Q (rated 'like Jesus' and 'probably Jesus', by the Jesus Seminar), Jesus claims that his message will split families and set children against their parents, and also that to follow Jesus means that one's parents should be abandoned or hated:

> For I have come to divide son against father, [and] daughter against her mother, [and] daughter-in-law against her mother-in-law. (cf. Mk 13.12: 'Brother will betray brother to death, and a father his child, and children will rise against parents and have them put to death.') (Q 12.53)

> [<The one who>] does not hate father and mother <can>not <be> my <disciple>; and [<the one who>] <does not hate> son and daughter cannot be my disciple. (Q 14.26) (cf. Mk 10.29b-30a: 'there is no one who has left house or brothers or sister or mother or father or children or fields, for my sake and for the sake of the good news, who will not receive a hundredfold.')

Do these texts suggest that the following of Jesus is equivalent to breaking with one's family, or are they only an Oriental way of saying that religion is more important than family? The fact that Jesus calls God 'Father', and those who follow him his 'brothers and sisters' suggests that these words, as a generic concept, had a positive connotation for Jesus. From the letters of Paul we know that early Christians continued to call each other brothers and sisters. The relationship between biological and spiritual brothers and sisters plays a role in Mk 6.20-35:

> ... and the crowd came together again, so that they could not even eat. When his family heard it, they went out to restrain him, for people were saying, 'He has gone out of his mind.'

[story about the scribes attributing Jesus' healings to the power of Beëlzebub]
Then his mother and his brothers came; and standing outside, they sent to him and called him. A crowd was sitting around him; and they said to him, 'Your mother and your brothers [and sisters] are outside, asking for you.' And he replied, 'Who are my mother and my brothers?' And looking at those who sat around him, he said, 'Here are my mother and my brothers! Whoever does the will of God is my brother and sister and mother.'

Basically, the story says that Jesus spent the whole day at the beach, preaching the Gospel, and was again late for dinner (presumably with his mother and brothers in their Capernaum house). His family was angry with him and came to fetch him from what may have been Peter's house in Capernaum (mentioned in Mk 1.29). Their public display of disapproval of his mission could not occur at a more damaging time, at least in Mark's narrative. While the scribes accuse Jesus of being a demoniac, his family comes to say that he is out of his mind. The Markan Jesus reacts with the statement that his true family consists of those who do the will of God (a statement rated 'like Jesus' by the Jesus Seminar). The rebuke is similar to calling Peter 'Satan' in Mk 8.33. Note that this did not happen after Jesus' baptism by John, but after John's arrest, when Jesus and his friends felt compelled to continue John's mission (Mk 1.14-15, Mt. 3.2). The conflict is therefore not related to Jesus' membership of John's movement *per se*.

This passage is often taken as a prime example of Mark's technique to make a 'sandwich' out of two stories. In this case a story about scribes who called Jesus a demoniac is inserted into a story about Jesus and his family. The story about Jesus' family is often taken as historical because of the negative portrayal of his family. Matthew and Luke play down the harshness of this pericope. Even the translators of the NRSV cannot cope with the implication that Mary also called her son 'out of his mind' and add the word 'people' in their translation. But the third person plural ('they') in the original Greek refers back to his family who went out to restrain him. The story would also be transmitted despite the evidence it gives against the virginal conception of Jesus: how is it possible that even Jesus' mother and brothers turned against him, if they had known about his miraculous birth? The problem with that argument is that there is no evidence that Mark assumed a virgin birth, so how can we argue that he was embarrassed by this story? Joel Marcus (1999) argues that the story fits well with Mark's theme of incomprehension on the side of Jesus' brothers and the Twelve. Joel Marcus even suggests that the story is to be situated in the dispute with the men of James about the applicability of the Law in the Diaspora communities, but notes the lack of evidence for this thesis (279–80). The story may also have been composed with a view to the conflicts later followers of Jesus experienced with their own families (as in the sayings quoted at the start of this section).

Nevertheless, there is additional evidence that Jesus' family did not support Jesus in his mission. In Jn 7.5 a comment is given that his brothers did not believe in him. There is a tradition, preserved in Q, in which Jesus is called 'a glutton and a drunkard, a friend of tax collectors and sinners' (Mt. 11.19,

Lk. 7.34, rated as 'like Jesus' by the Jesus Seminar). Taken out of its first-century Palestinian context, as is done by Matthew and Luke, these words are simply polemics. In context, however, the designation 'a glutton and a drunkard' is a technical term for a rebellious son:

> If someone has a stubborn and rebellious son who will not obey his father and mother, who does not heed them when they discipline him, then his father and his mother shall take hold of him and bring him out to the elders of his town at the gate of that place. They shall say to the elders of his town, 'This son of ours is stubborn and rebellious. He will not obey us. He is a glutton and a drunkard.' Then all the men of the town shall stone him to death. So you shall purge the evil from your midst; and all Israel will hear, and be afraid. (Deut. 21.18-21)

It is quite possible that both Lk. 7.34 and Jesus' response in Mk 3.35 are related to public disapproval of Jesus as a stubborn and rebellious son who did not obey his mother, but rather ate and drank with tax collectors and sinners. The (later) Mishna (*Sanhedrin* 8) on this passage specifies that the commandment applies to a rebellious adolescent (not yet fully bearded), who seeks the companies of sinners and is denounced by both his parents, father *and* mother. One parent alone was insufficient for a condemnation. Jesus, of course, was an adult male. But Jesus' defence in Mk 3.35 seems to build on the same idea: his mother condemns him, but he is doing the will of his 'Father in heaven' (as Mt. 12.50 words it).

If there was a conflict between Jesus and his family; it did not constitute a full break. As we saw in Paul's letters, his family joined the Twelve as followers of Jesus shortly after the crucifixion, with James included in the list of primary witnesses. It is even possible that his mother was present at his crucifixion. In attachment terms, it seems that Jesus was neither anxious nor avoidant, but rather sought to balance autonomy and affection in his relationship with his family. For the time that his family stood between him and his mission, he decided to go his own way, without thinking negatively about the terms father, mother, brother or sister. He remained open to restore the relationship and apparently did so prior to his crucifixion.

The likely scenario that emerges from these analyses is that the Jesus who was so attached to God was securely attached to his primary caregivers as a child, came from a religious family, and submitted to baptism as something that was still compatible with his home religion.

The Role of the Father

McDonald, Beck, Allison and Norsworthy (2005) tested the influence of religious parents on avoidance and anxiety towards God in a group of over a hundred students at a Christian university. Many came from religious homes, in this case Christian homes. The study investigated the influence of three factors on avoidance of and anxiety towards God: family spirituality, family intimacy and family support of autonomy.

- Family Spirituality. The participants were tested with regard to their perception of the emphasis on religious practice at home, as well as the spirituality and hypocrisy of each parent. Low avoidance scores correlated strongly with (1) the emphasis on religious practice at home, (2) a high score on father spirituality, and (3) a low score on father hypocrisy. There was also a moderate correlation with mother spirituality, but the influence of mother hypocrisy did not pass the statistical hurdle to be counted as significant. Anxiety was not strongly correlated with the student's perception of his family's religiousness.
- Family Intimacy. Both maternal and paternal care, as well as their warmth and affection, correlated with low avoidance of God as an attachment figure. Again anxiety was not strongly related to these factors.
- Family Support of Autonomy. An authoritarian father correlated strongly with the avoidance of God as an attachment figure; the influence of an authoritarian mother was not significant enough. There was also a moderate correlation between rigid family structures and avoidance of God, whereas families who facilitated independence in their children also stimulated them to seek God's presence. With regard to the anxiety score, the role of the mother appears to be more important. An over-protective mother is more likely to instil anxiety in a child about God than an authoritarian father, perhaps because the influence of the mother on the working models of the child is often more fundamental in early childhood than the influence of the father. Lower anxiety scores were also moderately correlated with the support given by families and their facilitation of independence.

Jesus

The study suggests that securely attached young adults with a sincerely religious and supportive father are more likely to have a secure attachment to God as a father figure. But we should be careful to apply these results to Jesus. They are based on a single study among North-American students that should be confirmed by other studies with other groups, before they can serve as a basis for historical reconstruction. Furthermore, the silence in the sources about Jesus' childhood and Joseph is deafening. All we can say is that the burden of evidence is on those who do not approach Joseph as a religious Jew and a normal father.

The Loss of Siblings and Father

Bowlby argues that the way an individual responds to loss is related to his attachment system, to the effect that those who are not securely attached are more likely to suffer psychological and physical distress following the loss of an attachment figure. He also believes that the relative absence of distress may be caused by a defensive reaction that may eventually break down and cause intense grief, and that the suppression of grief can adversely affect a person's health. Subsequently, many counsellors have tried to persuade people to express their emotions and somehow come to closure in cases of loss. In reaction to this, a number of authors in *Continuing Bonds* (ed. Klass, Silverman and Nickman 1996) stress the continued presence of the attachment figure among many of the bereaved, like spouses and children, or parents and siblings in case of the loss of a child. This experience seems to correlate with the belief of the bereaved in an afterlife (Normand, Silverman and Nickman 1996; Conant 1996). In a study of adult daughters who lost their father, a minority experienced an intrusive presence, correlated to relation problems with their father, or feelings of guilt originating in the period of the illness of which their fathers had died (Tyson-Rawson 1996). Israeli families in which one or more older children were lost evaluated their deceased children more favourably and as more available than their living children (Rubin 1996).

In sum, people need to find new ways to deal with the unavailability of early attachment figures. Some will continue to speak to or pray to their lost father or mother. In some cases, people have difficulty in finding this balance (Fraley and Shaver 1999). Unfortunately, these studies all concern modern societies in which mortality (and especially mortality among children) is very low.

Research also suggests that people with an attachment to God are likely to turn to God in times of bereavement or unusual stress. 'The loss of a principal attachment figure, such as a parent or a spouse, may activate a search for a *substitute* or *surrogate* caregiver, or at least increased reliance on a previously secondary figure', such as God (Kirkpatrick 2005, 64–5). In such circumstances, a person experiences God as 'an antidote to fear and anxiety'. In the case of bereaved siblings, a majority in various studies reported feelings of guilt, ultracentrism (as opposed to egocentrism), increased faith and sense of spirituality, as well as an increased ability to give and receive help among family and peers (Hogan and DeSantis 1996). Some of these outcomes are probably related to a majority of securely attached and religious persons who went through an effective process of mourning among those studied.

Jesus

As the demographic analysis in Chapter 4 has shown, it is likely that Jesus experienced the death of several siblings as well as the loss of his father as an adolescent and/or young adult. As part of a religious family and as one who was later to address God as 'father', it is likely that the experience of loss contributed to Jesus' attachment to God. There is, however, no evidence in the Jesus traditions to confirm (or dispute) this, except the indication that Jesus shared the faith of many Jews in an afterlife (Mk 12.27, rated 'like Jesus' by the Jesus Seminar).

With regard to family and the Twelve, it is likely that Jesus was an attachment figure to them. The fact that they jointly mourned him and experienced his continuing presence may have contributed to the social cohesion between the two groups.

Back to Jesus' Baptism and Psychobiography

In the analysis presented earlier in this chapter, I argue that Jesus' baptism was not a conversion experience. It is, however, likely that it was a profound religious experience. But no early follower was present (as implied by Jn 1.29-34) at the event and no saying of Jesus recalls it. The description of Jesus' baptism in the first-century Gospels rather looks like what later followers believed could or should have happened. From a historical-critical point of view there is little to work with. On the other hand, however, it is likely that the experience of baptism by John was shared by most, if not all, of the earliest Jesus followers. Although few, if any, would have witnessed the baptism of Jesus, it is inherently likely that some of them spoke about it with Jesus. The presence of such witnesses within the movement makes it likely that memories about Jesus' baptism were preserved within the movement. Furthermore, it was a celebrated event that was translated into the later practice of the movement to use baptism in the name of Jesus as an initiatory rite. Stories about Jesus' baptism would therefore be of great importance in the movement. They would have to fit on the one hand with the people remembered and on the other hand with the meaning that the rite had acquired.

Dunn argues that the most important elements of this event for Jesus were the related experiences of God's Spirit and Jesus' son-ship (1975, 62–7; 2003, ch. 11). Dunn stops here, as he sees too little basis for 'speculation as to whether this experience of Jesus was the climax or decisive "clincher" of a growing experience of God, or whether it was something abruptly new and totally unexpected'. Not content with this situation, Miller (1997, ch. 3) explores the psychological matrix of the event and calls it the 'turning point' in Jesus' life and his 'second birth'. He sees it as a sudden conversion, in which John emerges as a 'surrogate parent to Jesus'. Jesus would have experienced 'an inner conflict', leading up to his desire to be baptized. The problem with Miller's reconstruction is that it misreads the type of movement John started, and what conversion could have meant for his followers. There is no evidence of an inner conflict leading up to Jesus' baptism (rather the contrary: he struggled with it afterwards). Neither is there any indication that Jesus came to see John as a surrogate parent – the whole story and subsequent evidence is about God as Jesus' parent. Van Aarde (2001, ch. 3) stays closer to the story when he sees Jesus' baptism as the experience during which the fatherless Jesus was cleansed of his illegitimate birth and accepted by God as his child. But the problem with all these interpretations is that there is nothing in John's baptism that connects the ritual with the experience of God as a father. The preserved traditions about John suggest that John's emphasis was on God's kingly role (his imminent reign), not on his fatherly role. I will suggest two trajectories that may help to us to think about Jesus' baptism:

- First, baptism in the letters of Paul re-enacts not only Jesus' crucifixion and resurrection, but also the reception of Jesus' Spirit of son-ship (Rom. 6–8, 1 Cor. 12.13, Gal. 3.26-4:7). This of course influenced the way in which his followers spoke about Jesus' baptism. But there is no other contemporary source to which we can attribute this development, other than to the baptism of Jesus. The most economic and plausible explanation is that Jesus did indeed look back on his baptism as a spiritual experience of son-ship.
- The second trajectory takes place within Jesus' own mission: John baptized for the remission of sins. The core of the controversy stories in Mk 2.1-17 is about Jesus' work as one who comes to forgive sins and to heal sinners (even if only verse 17 is rated 'probably Jesus' and 'like Jesus' by the Jesus Seminar). Here we see that it is Jesus who associated the forgiveness of sins with a healing experience.

If we are to concoct a theory as to why early Jesus followers associated baptism with the forgiveness of sins and the reception of a Spirit of son-ship, while recognizing that the veneration of God as a father was not common in the first century CE, we should evaluate whether a plausible connection between these concepts can be found in the historical Jesus. Here Attachment Theory can be of help. I suggest that the general words of forgiveness spoken by John to Jesus upon his baptism may have unleashed deeper emotions, if Jesus suffered from guilt. Such feelings are often suppressed and can lead to strong psychological reactions when released. Furthermore, if these feelings of guilt were associated with the loss of his father, we may have a link between the concepts of forgiveness and son-ship. If Mary (and Jesus) were focusing on the needs of the younger children in their family when Joseph died, it is possible that Jesus did not experience the mourning process needed to come to terms with his father's death. If Jesus needed a word of forgiveness from his father, and if God spoke that word through John, then God assumed the father-role for Jesus. God may have been a secondary attachment figure for Jesus prior to his baptism, but if Jesus discovered God as his father, then the strong and secure attachment he may have felt towards Joseph may have been transferred to God. As this was a healing experience for Jesus, he may have characterized it as the work of God's Spirit (Mk 3.29). When later in his life he took it upon himself to continue John's work, it would be his contribution to transfer the idea of God as a loving father to his followers, who were therefore his younger brothers and sisters (Rom. 8.29). As the demographic analysis in Chapter 4 shows, a very significant proportion of young adults were indeed fatherless. The impact this had on Jesus' followers is clearly visible in the letters of Paul, where God is still invoked as 'Abba, Father'. Thus a psychologically plausible theory can suggest a historical kernel behind the experience Jesus had following his baptism (hearing the voice, experiencing the spirit, and the temptation in the desert).

The type of guilt I am thinking of here is the guilt people feel towards the deceased or towards their responsibilities as survivors. A mourner frequently asks why that other person died and not him or herself. For example, when an accident occurs in which both could have been killed (like in Luke 13.4 – which may have been a building accident). In such situations, people may think things like: 'If I had only done this or that differently, then he would not have died.' An eldest child can feel obliged but incompetent to take over the responsibility for younger siblings. Indeed, in pre-industrial societies with high infancy mortality, we often see infants die when a parent falls away, simply because of the reduction in income, food and care.

Robert Webb (2009) concludes that it is probable that Jesus had an inaugural experience and that it is somewhat probable that it included divine son-ship and Spirit anointing. But he sees it as merely possible that this did indeed happen at baptism. Contrary to Meier, he believes that the historian can investigate the historicity of Jesus' experience, but 'psychological speculation on *why* he had the experience (e.g., the death of his father at a young age created the need for a "father figure") would be psychologizing, and this should be avoided'.

Again we see the aversion of psychology. But part of the task of a historian is the generation of plausible theories that explain what we can observe, and the psychological experience of the divine father is one of the most remarkable beliefs among early Jesus followers that should be explained. I do agree with Webb that there is no evidence to confirm the suggestion that the loss of his father contributed to a spiritual experience of son-ship when Jesus was baptized, let alone to suggest that feelings of guilt may have played a role. But I offer this theory as an example of the contribution that this particular psychological method can make in the generation of hypotheses. Apart from revelation *ex nihilo* (which escapes the work of historians) other potential explanations, or combinations of explanations, need to be evaluated as well. Perhaps the family of Jesus did descend from David (Bauckham 1990) and cherished the promise of God to be a father of David's offspring (2 Sam. 7.14, Rom. 1.3). This would, however, require an additional theory as to why Jesus came to universalize this concept to include all those who do the will of God. Perhaps Jesus' family belonged to the Hassidic movement that started to see God as a father. This would explain Jesus' universal concept of God's fatherhood, but not the connection with baptism in the writings of his followers, or the way that they remembered Jesus as the one who revealed his Father to his followers (Jn 1.18; see also the designation 'Father of the Lord' in 2 Cor. 1.3, 11.31).

Conclusion

The analysis of Jesus' attachment to family and God suggests that the correspondence hypothesis can fruitfully be explored: Jesus was a religious Jew who came from a religious Jewish family. His particular life experiences may have deepened his faith, but he did not break away from the faith of his ancestors. Perhaps through the loss of his father he became strongly and securely attached to his heavenly Father. He was able to share this experience with his followers, who came to perceive the idea of God as a loving and caring parent as a key aspect of their faith. He represented the Father, as the eldest son among his brothers and sisters. As a securely attached person, he was probably able to be sensitive to their attachment signals. But if Jesus remained a caregiver in these relationships, while he was going through a turbulent period of mission, he may have sought his own caregiver more and more in his heavenly Father.

Attachment Theory also sheds some light on the appeal of this concept to his followers. About half of the young adults between 15 and 25 years of age were indeed fatherless. In times of social turbulence and social pressure in combination with an oversupply of unmarried young males and middle-aged widows, the idea of God as an attachment figure and his people as brothers and sisters may have caught on quickly with a significant number of people, through the mechanisms of both correspondence and compensation. Later on, when the movement spread as a cult in the Diaspora, the correspondence mechanism may have been dominant for those reared within the movement. The compensation mechanism may have been more significant among those who converted from the outside.

Chapter 8

THE RATIONAL CHOICE OF JESUS' FRIENDS AND FAMILY

The starting point for this chapter is the fact that both the Twelve and the brothers of Jesus were part of the same missionary movement (1 Cor. 9.5), that Jesus' brother James was included in the tradition of the witnesses of the risen Jesus (1 Cor. 15.7) and that all proclaimed the innovative idea that Jesus was their Messiah who had died for the sins of his people (1 Cor. 15.3 and 11). Furthermore, James was actually involved in the leadership with Cephas/Peter and John (Gal. 1.19 and 2.9), and sent envoys to Diaspora communities (Gal. 2.12). Apart from the Pauline corpus, the New Testament only contains letters in the names of Peter, John and Jesus' brothers James and Jude.

This is remarkable, as the brothers were clearly not included among the Twelve chosen by Jesus, and even seem to have been critical of his mission during his lifetime (Mk 3.21, Jn 7.5). How is it possible that they formed one group after the crucifixion, shared in the same experiences and interpreted these experiences and the life of Jesus in very similar and innovative ways? Not all of this can be explained from a post-crucifixion (or even post-resurrection) perspective. In this chapter, I wish to use Rational Choice Theory to explain the social cohesion and the shared religious ideas between the two groups.

Jesus

In the previous chapter, I used Attachment Theory as the most appropriate tool to tease out of the sayings of the adult Jesus what we can reasonably assume about Jesus' childhood attachments. As I found only evidence of a 'normal' attachment pattern, it seems reasonable to approach Jesus at the start of his ministry as a normal person, rather than a 'sick mind' looking for compensation in a surrogate father figure. How then does a 'normal' person develop religious beliefs and even a sense of revelation? Rational Choice Theory is a promising tool to address this issue. It assumes that most people are 'sane' (as in 'normal'), and observes that most people in this world are to some extent 'religious'. It assumes that many people perceive that religion brings them certain benefits, observing that on balance research shows a positive correlation between mental health and religiousness (Stark 2005, 88). It makes sense, therefore, to investigate the religious choices people make from a rational perspective. In this sense, the theory studies the behaviour of rational people as opposed to the psychopathological approach to religious behaviour often taken by social scientists who do not share the religious convictions of the people they study. It was this attitude that was criticized by Albert Schweitzer in his review of the psychiatric study of Jesus (see Chapter 1): an opinion that is deluded in modern society may have been normal in another time and place.

Rational Choice Theory

Rational Choice Theory is a sociological, theoretical framework developed out of economy and psychology (exchange theory). It assumes that people strive for what they perceive to be benefits in a way that they believe will deliver those benefits. It is sometimes described as the American challenger of the European Secularization thesis (Davie 2007). The latter has clearly lost its predictive and universal value (although Davie argues that it may remain relevant for the European situation). The current discussion is about the question to what extent Rational Choice Theory can claim universal applicability. This argument may over time be outdated, as Rational Choice Theory is well suited to generate and reject hypotheses on the basis of empirical research. In other words: the theory will develop to take into account more factors in a more sophisticated way. For now, it is probably prudent to say that the theory can already account for general tendencies in the North American situation, and is expanding to cover more specific situations as well as other cultural contexts.

One specific area, in which the strength of the theory was demonstrated, was the *Rise of Christianity* (Stark 1996) in the Graeco-Roman Diaspora (see Chapter 5). The 'unregulated religious economy' of the Roman Empire, in which many different 'religious firms' competed to provide benefits to adherents, lends itself well to the type of analyses that Rational Choice Theory offers.

Stark and Finke (2000) propose that religious organizations mainly originate through sect formation, and that most religious groups will begin in a relatively high state of tension. Second, they argue that people joining new religious movements are seeking a higher tension (between the group and the world), which is both more demanding as well as more rewarding than the mainstream variants of their religion. But, thirdly, people do not join such movements quickly as most people want to preserve their social and religious capital. It is therefore more likely that one will join a movement if there are already strong personal ties with members of that movement, and if the movement allows them to preserve their religious culture. Typically this happens if a movement is able to present itself as a purified version of the existing religion.

The Religious Economy of First-Century Judea and Galilee

In an appendix to *Acts of Faith* (2000), Stark and Finke present a theoretical framework consisting of 99 propositions and 36 definitions. A number of these are relevant with respect to the rise of new religious groups within an existing religion.

> Proposition 71. To the degree that a religious economy is unregulated, it will tend to be very pluralistic.
> - *Definition 34.* Pluralistic refers to the number of firms active in the economy; the more firms there are with significant market shares, the greater the degree of pluralism.

> Proposition 79. The capacity of new religious firms to enter relatively unregulated markets successfully is inverse to the efficiency and variety of existing religious firms.

In early antiquity, religion was often polytheistic and integrated with the institutions of the family, the tribe and the nation. This changed through the Hellenization of the Near East and the integration of the entire Mediterranean basin in the Graeco-Roman world. Although we can debate the questions whether paganism constituted a single religion, whether the identification of local deities with Graeco-Roman gods constituted a form of syncretism, and whether the cities and states in late antiquity favoured certain gods, it is undeniable that in late antiquity a number of new cults arose. Through migration and conversion, initiates of Isis, Mithras, Cybele, Dionysus/ Orpheus and Jahweh could be found throughout the empire (Tripolitis 2002; Burkert 1987; Turcan 1989/ET 1996). In terms of Rational Choice Theory, it is reasonable to assume that their rise was related to the growing pluralism of the Graeco-Roman cities and the lack of strength of local deities for producing religious benefits in this new context. For Palestine, however, the situation was different. The Hasmonaean state was born in the fight against the religious aspects of Hellenization. The victors held the offices of high priest and king and strongly promoted a Jewish way of life in the territories they conquered. Even though the Jewish areas of Palestine were heavily influenced by Hellenism, archaeological remains reveal a uniform pattern of burial, dietary and purification practices throughout Judea and Galilee (Reed 2000, 27–30). In other words: many aspects of society are related to religion, or 'sacralized'. It seems therefore that the following propositions apply:

> Proposition 72. The capacity of a single religious firm to monopolize a religious economy depends on the degree to which the state uses coercive force to regulate the religious economy.

> Proposition 73. To the degree that a religious firm achieves a monopoly, it will seek to exert its influence over other institutions, and the society will thus become sacralized.

- *Definition 35.* Sacralized means that there is little differentiation between religious and secular institutions and that the primary aspects of life, from family to politics, are suffused with religious symbols, rhetoric and ritual.

Note that older Jewish communities outside Palestine have their own history of interaction with their Gentile context. There were varying degrees of acceptance of and adherence to Mosaic Law. Malina and Pilch (2006, 14–17) even argue that circumcision was not generally practised in the Diaspora before Palestinian Jews promoted it there. Neusner (1969, 183) makes the interesting comment that in the Eastern Diaspora, Christianity spread first to those Jewish communities that were not under the influence of the early rabbis, the *Tannaim*: 'One must infer therefore that wherever Tannaite influence gained ground among the local Jewish community, as in Nisibis and Nehardea, there Christianity made slight progress, if any, for a very long period of time.'

Generally, Rational Choice Theory predicts that religious commitment will be higher in unregulated religious economies than in a monopolized market. But a high commitment can also result when a religious firm embodies a group in social conflict with other groups, as for instance in the 'pillarized' situation of the Netherlands in the middle of the twentieth century, when there was an oligopoly of Catholic, Reformed and re-Reformed churches which organized their followers in semi-independent 'sacralized' societies, including Christian institutes for education, Christian health care, Christian cultural activities, Christian labour unions, and Christian sports associations (Stark and Finke 2000, 241–3).

Proposition 75. To the degree that religious economies are unregulated and competitive, overall levels of religious commitment will be high.

Proposition 76. Even where competition is limited, religious firms can generate high levels of commitment to the extent that the firms serve as the primary organizational levels for social conflict.

In the case of first-century Palestine, the situation may have been similar because of the social conflicts between Hellenism and Judaism, and between Samaritans and Jews. In the Roman province of Syria, Judea and Galilee were two Jewish regions among other regions and Gentile cities, with recurring conflicts between various segments of the population. It is this exceptional status of Palestinian Judaism that we need to keep in mind when we look at the following propositions:

Proposition 42. Among religious organizations, there is a reciprocal relationship between the degree of lay commitment and the degree of exclusivity.

Proposition 43. All religious groups can be located along an axis of tension between the group and its sociocultural environment.
- *Definition 25.* Tension refers to the degree of distinctiveness, separation, and antagonism in the relationship between a religious group and the 'outside' world.

- *Definition 26*. Churches are religious bodies in a relatively lower tension with their surroundings.
- *Definition 27*. Sects are religious bodes in relatively higher tension with their surroundings.

Proposition 80. Religious organizations mainly originate through sect formation.

Proposition 81. Sect movements that endure and grow will tend to reduce their tension with the sociocultural environment, thereby moving away from the market niche(s) in which they originally were based (a process referred to as sect-to-church transformation).

Proposition 83. As religious groups move into range of the largest niches and abandon their original market niche(s), they tend to suffer schisms as sect movements break away to serve members with higher tension preferences.

Proposition 92. Most sects do not reduce their initial level of tension and do not grow, and the high-tension end of the church-sect spectrum will therefore abound in small, unsuccessful religious organizations.

When we apply these propositions to first-century Palestine, we can see that there were several types of tension at play. The cultural tension between Jewish and Hellenistic thinking, the cultic tension between purity and impurity and the political tension between God's reign (which could take place via his legitimate king or high-priest) and the reign of Rome or its vassals. In the movement(s) of John the Baptist and Jesus, we also see an ethical tension, as they asked their followers to do more than the Law required.

When the Maccabees took control of the state and the temple, it seems to have been inevitable that their movement would include most of the populace and lose some of its initial tension. This is an important point as their dynasty did not descend from Aaron and therefore had no hereditary claim to the high priesthood. Their religious fervour legitimized their role in the eyes of pious Jews. It seems that the Sadducees were prevalent among the Jerusalem aristocracy, emphasizing the cultic provisions in the Law of Moses, but denouncing the existence of angels, the *eschaton*, or life after death. In other words, they maintained their religious firm through a cultic tension with non-Jewish society. The temple was needed to provide purification. On the other hand, the political tension and the cultural tension with the Graeco-Roman world were reduced. At this point in time, we see the rise of the Pharisees and the Essenes. The Essenes denounced the legitimacy of the temple authorities and formed a group that maintained a higher tension in every aspect: cultural, cultic and political. Their movement remained small and disappeared after the first Jewish revolt and the destruction of the temple. The Pharisees promoted purity in daily life and stressed Jewish beliefs alongside temple worship. Josephus reports that the population credited the Pharisaic interpretation of the Law over that of the Sadducees, although the actual number of Pharisees remained small. They started out in a higher cultural and cultic tension, but not politically. Over time, when the Pharisaic movement reorganized Judaism after the destruction of the temple, it seems that the cultural and cultic tension was reduced somewhat. In later centuries, Rabbinic Judaism was to become the dominant force of Jewish continuity in the Diaspora. The legitimacy of the temple-church hierarchy was further diminished when the Roman vassals and governors started to appoint the acting high priest. Inasmuch as Zealots are to be seen as groups of people motivated by a zeal to force God's reign upon Jewish society, they too should be seen as groups that maintain a higher tension with society, in this case a religio-political tension. Finally, some prophets like Theudas and 'the Egyptian' seem to have formed short-lived, non-violent groups who believed that God would intervene in history. Such groups seem to have sought a higher tension both in terms of culture and politics.

The Movement of John the Baptist

In his 'socio-historical study' of John the Baptist (1991), Robert Webb concludes that John's movement was 'dispersed and passivist', as opposed to the 'corporate and activist' approaches of some other prophets. John did not form an alternative community. People could continue to worship in synagogue and temple. At the same time, however, his baptism constituted an alternative purification rite that competed with the purification rites of the Pharisees and the temple-church. It was also a singular event of initiation, as it let people re-enter the Promised Land, out of the wilderness and through the River Jordan in anticipation of God's imminent reign. It was not an initiation into another religion or religious community, but into a future remnant of Israel that would escape the wrath of God when he established his reign. As such, John did not create a new religion, but rather 'reformed' a significant number of Jews who chose to be a subgroup within their religion, called to a higher level of tension. This elevated tension was foremost ethical, as expressed in the words 'repentance' and 'conversion'. At the same time it created a conflict between John and the Tetrarch Herod Antipas, whom he criticized for his behaviour in matters of divorce and marriage. Whether all people who were baptized by John actually succeeded in living out John's ethics cannot be deduced from the evidence, but without a more permanent religious incorporation it is likely that over time many preserved little more than a memory of John's call and their good intentions in answering it.

John, Jesus and Social Capital

A basic statistical fact that can be observed throughout human history is stated in proposition 30:

Proposition 30. Under normal circumstances, most people will neither convert nor reaffiliate.
- *Definition 21*. Conversion refers to shifts across religious traditions.
- *Definition 22*. Reaffiliation refers to shifts within religious traditions.

As discussed in previous chapters, the movement(s) of John and Jesus remained within Judaism. Joining the movement is best characterized as 'affiliation', not conversion. Whether it is also '*re*-affiliation' depends on the question of whether one was religiously affiliated before and whether such affiliation effectively ended with the new affiliation. I noted above that joining John or Jesus did not imply that people stopped going to the synagogue or temple. But I also note that for the most involved disciples (as opposed to the sympathizers) affiliation with Jesus did not come free. The itinerant mission meant that they were away for weeks or longer from their work, home and family (Mk 10.28-30).

The phrase 'under normal circumstances' implies that people need sufficient motivation to follow a religious group or leader. Mark's highly suggestive account of the calling of the first disciples can easily be misread as the first encounter between Jesus and his first followers (1.16-20). This is not what Mark says, but only the readers of Lk. 4.38 and Jn 1–4 are told that there were previous relationships between the men, both as followers of John as well as inhabitants of Capernaum. Whether the details are true is of less importance, but the idea of previous relationships is exactly what Rational Choice Theory predicts:

Proposition 29. In making religious choices, people will attempt to conserve their social capital.
- *Definition 23*. Social capital consists of interpersonal attachments.

Proposition 31. To the extent that people have or develop stronger attachments to those committed to a different version of their religion, they will reaffiliate.

These propositions apply three times: (1) the decision of the brothers of Jesus to join the Twelve, (2) the decision of the Twelve to join Jesus, and (3) the decision of Jesus to join John the Baptist. If there was a pre-existing social network comprising the brothers, Jesus and the Twelve, these three (re-)affiliations would make sense. Jesus would then have joined John as a disciple, partly because he knew many of his followers, either as his relatives, or as his fellow townsmen. That implies that the brothers of Jesus also would have known the Twelve quite well before they decided to join them and form one group of Jesus followers. Furthermore, the knowledge of such a social network was to persist well into the 60s and 70s CE, when many members were still alive. Statements in Paul's letters or (the sources of) the Gospels would also be 'falsifiable' as they do not regard a single saying or event. In other words: whether John and Mary stood at the cross cannot be proven, but whether Mary lived with John for some time following Jesus' death must have been known to quite a number of early Jesus followers.

In *The Rise of Mormonism* (2005, ch. 2), Stark compares Joseph Smith with the (assumed) founders of Judaism, Christianity and Islam. He points out that the first followers of Joseph Smith were his own family members, eleven in total. The others were two individual friends and ten members of the Whitmer family. Stark believes that this is comparable to the family-based beginning of Moses, Jesus and Mohammed. I would add the example of Mani, of whom a Middle-Persian fragment says that he first converted his father and family leaders (M 49 II). When Stark and Lofland studied the emergence of the Unification Church ('The Moonies') in the United States, they found that 'all current members were united by close ties of friendship *predating* their contact with Dr. Kim'. Dr. Kim was a Korean member who had come to the United States. 'By the time we arrived to study them, the group had never succeeded in attracting a stranger' (Stark 2005, 61). Stark (1999, 17) explains the dynamics of reaffiliation as an application of the theory of deviant behaviour:

> People conform when they believe they have more to lose by being detected in deviance than they stand to gain from the deviant act. ... A major stake in conformity lies in our attachment to other people. Most of us conform in order to retain the good opinion of our friends and family.

Rather than applying historical-critical methods to test each individual Jesus tradition, I will therefore propose a social network that makes sense of as much first-century data as possible. Again I do not claim that all details are accurate, but rather that the general picture is plausible in the light of Rational Choice Theory. The potential relationships that I can find are the following:

1. Jesus and his family may have come to Capernaum not only because of economic reasons, but also because of existing relations. If so, a possible candidate is the family of Zebedee. It is not impossible that the sister of Mary at the cross in Jn. 19.25 is the same as the wife of Zebedee, the mother of John and James standing at the cross in Mt. 27.56. Zebedee was a fisherman from Capernaum who operated his ship with his sons and his hired workers (Mk 1.20). When Jn 19.27 says that John, probably still in his teens, took Mary in his house after the crucifixion, Mary came to stay at the house of her sister.
2. According to the synoptic Gospels, John and James worked side-by-side with Simon (Peter) and Andrew (Mk 1.16-20). Simon had married a girl from Capernaum and the brothers lived with Simon's mother-in-law (Mk 2.29). It is not implausible that they continued her deceased husband's fishing operations.
3. Simon and Andrew originally came from Bethsaida, from where they seem to have known Philip (Jn 1.44).
4. John, James, Simon, Andrew and Philip knew Nathanael from the village of Qana not too far away from Nazareth. The six are said to have been followers of John the Baptist in Jn 1.35-51. The Gospel of John suggests

that Jesus' family knew him as well: apart from Jesus and Mary, also the brothers of Jesus and Jesus' fellow disciples were invited to a wedding in Qana (2.2,12). Nathanael is also mentioned in the story about seven disciples (including Thomas) who go fishing in Jn 22.

5. Levi the son of Alphaeus (Mk 2.14) was a customs official for Herod Antipas. The first Gospel identifies him as Matthew. Another 'son of Alphaeus' was James. The two may have been brothers. An interesting suggestion follows from the Aramaic form of the name: Halphai, which may be equivalent to Chalpho (both attested in Capernaum inscriptions, Reed 2000, 156). Thus the 'Greek' names Alphaeus and Clopas may refer to the same Aramaic name. This suggests the possibility that Levi and James were sons of Joseph's brother Clopas. It's therefore not impossible that Simon the son of Clopas, who is said to have succeeded James as the leader of the Jesus followers in Jerusalem in the 60s CE, was their (younger) brother. In that case Joseph and Chalphai would each have named one of their sons James, and another Simon.

6. Another pair of brothers among the Twelve may be discovered in the name Thomas, or 'Twin'. This would give an interesting explanation for the difference between the apostle-lists in Mark and Matthew who have Thomas and Thaddaeus on the one hand, and Luke on the other who has Thomas and Judas. If Thaddeus and Judas were twin brothers, this would explain the two variants quite naturally: during Jesus' mission Judas was called the 'Twin' in order to distinguish him from Judas Iskarioth who seems to have been more important (as the keeper of the purse). After Judas Iskarioth fell out, Judas may have come to be known by his real name (Judas). His brother Thaddaeus may then have been referred to as the twin brother of Judas. This rather imaginative suggestion gains a little support from Syriac tradition, which speaks of co-operation between Judas Thomas and Addai/Thaddaeus.

None of the above suggestions can be proved or disproved on the basis of historical-critical criteria, but they illustrate the possibility that the most important members of the Twelve were brothers, cousins and friends who were well known to both Jesus and his brothers. From the perspective of Rational Choice Theory such a situation is probable and helps us to understand why Jesus joined them as a disciple of John the Baptist, why Jesus could readily call upon them to continue John's work after John's arrest, and why the group could merge so well with the brothers of Jesus after the crucifixion. Furthermore, Acts 1.22-3 suggests that all of the Twelve and also other followers were baptized by John and saw that as the proper start of their own movement.

Acts 6.9 suggests another social network for the earliest Greek-speaking followers of Jesus in Jerusalem. Stephen has an argument with members of the 'Synagogue of the Freedmen' comprising Jews from Cyrene, Alexandria, Cilicia and Asia, which ultimately leads to his death (so the author of Acts tells us). It is not implausible (but unprovable) that this synagogue was the home of people such as Simon of Cyrene (Mk 15.21) and Paul of Tarsus in Cilicia, or Stephen himself. Paul's role as persecutor may have resulted from the argument within his own synagogue that enabled him to identify the 'suspects'.

John, Jesus and Religious Capital

Social capital is not the only factor that Rational Choice Theory takes into account. Another form of capital is the time previously invested in one's religious framework.

- *Definition* 24. Religious capital consists of the degree of mastery of and attachment to a particular religious culture.

Proposition 34. The greater their religious capital, the less likely people are either to reaffiliate or to convert.

Proposition 33. In making religious choices, people will attempt to conserve their religious capital.

To build up a comparable 'status' in a new religion requires 'investments'. This implies that converts with little religious capital have to give up less than converts with a great deal of religious capital. As a result, persons with a great deal of religious capital are less likely to convert to a new religious movement, unless they can preserve their investments and reuse their capital in the new movement with which they affiliate themselves. Again these are general statistical relations that hold true for larger groups of people. An individual conversion is dependent on a larger number of factors.

As a result of the two factors discussed here, most converts of new religious movements in modern studies are the 'unchurched', those who had little religious or social capital invested in their previous religious affiliation. Another group consists of those who can preserve their religious and social capital by reaffiliating, for instance if there is a steady flow of 'conversions' from one church to another within the same religious tradition. If significant numbers of people are dissatisfied with their current church or their own status in that church, but have no alternative that would preserve their social and religious capital, they – as a group – can form an alternative church or sect. In case of the movement(s) of John and Jesus, we would therefore expect that the majority of recruits would either be Jews with little religious capital (such as 'sinners toll-collectors') or people who saw John as a spokesman for what they already believed.

There is another interesting phenomenon to be observed. In a fast-growing movement with many people with little religious capital, new converts with a great deal of reusable religious capital may quickly attain a high status. This applies to Paul (Phil. 3.5). It may also apply to James the brother of Jesus who is referred to as an authority by Paul who promoted the correct application of Jewish Law (Gal. 2.9, 12), and remembered in Acts 15.13-21 as one who rules in a question on the basis of his scriptural knowledge (see also logion 12 in the *Gospel of Thomas*). This is consistent with the assessment in Chapter 7 that Jesus probably came from a religious home. If the religious capital of James contributed to his leadership position in the movement after the crucifixion, it is likely that Jesus' religious upbringing gave him a certain level of authority among followers of John with less religious capital.

Jerome (*Dialogue against the Pelagians* 3.2) quotes a passage from a Hebrew Gospel in which Jesus' mother and brothers propose to be baptized by John. Jesus then asks for what sins he should be baptized, 'unless spoken in ignorance'. This text is mostly dated to the first half of the second century, but Edwards (2009, 94–6) argues that it belongs to an old Hebrew Gospel that influenced the Gospel of Luke. Webb (1991, 83; 2009, 103–104) believes this text is evidence of a movement to distance Jesus from John to the point that he had not been baptized at all. But the text does not say that Jesus was not baptized and Jerome quotes this text in the context of his argument that nobody can avoid sinning. The enigmatic words of Jesus should probably be understood in the light of what follows: 'Even the prophets, after they were anointed with the Holy Spirit, were guilty of sinful words.' Read in this way, the text might perhaps go back to a time when Jesus' baptism was explained as fulfilling all righteousness, even covering wrong words spoken by Jesus in ignorance. Whether the text is from the mid-first century or the first half of the second century, I note that Aramaic-speaking followers of Jesus, the part of the movement in which family members of Jesus had been leading figures into the early second century (Bauckham 1990), told a story in which Jesus' mother and brothers were positive about John's baptism. I do not claim that James or Jesus received any formal religious training like Paul may have had (Gal. 1.14, Phil. 3.5), but rather that it is plausible that they were thoroughly socialized into their religion by their parents and felt confident within their tradition, and that their tradition was close to that of John. This again helps to understand why the Twelve and the brothers of Jesus could form one group after Jesus' crucifixion.

Both Jesus' religious upbringing and his affiliation with John and his followers suggest that Jesus shared or came to share John's religious beliefs. Furthermore, the continuing importance of John's baptism among Jesus' followers suggests that some of this influence was present until the very end of Jesus' mission (Meier 1994, 176). Apart from the general religious outlook of religious first-century Jews, there are certain specific ideas of John that are worth noting as likely beliefs that Jesus and his followers shared with John. These ideas include the following (Webb 1991, chs 6 and 8):

- John expected God's intervention and reign.
- John urged people to convert to live in accordance with God's will, and to be purified in anticipation of that kingdom.
- John believed God forgave such people their sins.

- John believed that God, or his agent, would come to purify with spirit and fire. Those who had turned to God would be restored with God's spirit. Those who remained polluted would be judged with his fire.

Revelation and Prophecy

In his 2005 *The Rise of Mormonism*, Stark compares the revelations of Joseph Smith with those of Moses, Jesus and Mohammed. Again, the key assumption is that 'normal' people can have mystical experiences, or revelations. Indeed, in order to be followed by others for a longer period of time, in a way that lays the base for future growth, it is essential that his followers experience the leader or prophet as sane. No one likes to believe he or she is following a lunatic. On the basis of the similarities in the traditional accounts of these four founders, and in the light of Rational Choice Theory, Stark formulates another twelve propositions. The question is whether these similarities can be proven on historical-critical grounds, but we can at least discuss how the propositions work out in the case of Jesus.

1. Revelations will tend to occur when (a) there exists a supportive cultural tradition of communications with the divine and (b) the recipient of the revelation(s) has direct contact with a role model, with someone who has had such revelations.
5. Novel (heretical) revelations will most likely come to persons of deep religious concerns who perceive shortcomings in the conventional faith(s).
6. The probability that individuals will perceive shortcomings in the conventional faith(s) increases during periods of social crisis.
7. During periods of social crisis, the number of persons who receive novel revelations and the number willing to accept such revelations are maximized.

These propositions clearly apply. In a sacralized society, any social crisis is immediately a religious crisis as well, as the leaders of the church-state are unable to provide adequate answers. First-century Palestine went through a number of social crises and many first-century Jews cherished their prophetic tradition. The prophets in the Jewish Scriptures often spoke out explicitly against the priestly and royal authorities. As a result there arose a number of first-century 'prophets' who believed they understood God's will and predicted how God would intervene (Webb 1991, ch. 9). Many times, they attracted a modest following, until their predictions were proven false. This reality is reflected in the words that the author of Acts puts into the mouth of Gamaliel (5.34-37). In Jesus' case, the prophetic culture was embodied by John the Baptist. As a deeply religious person, John may have turned to the prophetic tradition to understand God's will for his day, leading to his conviction that he should prepare the nation for the coming of God's agent. If Jesus believed John's prophetic message came from God, he may have been stimulated to believe that some of his own experiences were also a kind of communication with God.

2. Many common, ordinary, even mundane mental phenomena can be experienced as contact with the divine.
3. Most episodes involving contact with the divine will merely confirm the conventional religious culture, even when the contact includes a specific communication, or revelation.
4. Certain individuals will have the capacity to perceive revelations, whether this be an openness or sensitivity to real communications or consists of unusual creativity enabling them to create profound revelations and then to externalize the source of this new culture.

To put things in perspective: Compared to Mohammed and Joseph Smith, John and Jesus seem to have claimed very few 'direct' revelations from God. Rather, they speak their own mind and most of what they say seems to have been within the range of Jewish beliefs of the time. But their conviction that God's reign 'was near', and that they had a specific role to play in God's plan (even if they still had doubts about the specifics), implies that they both experienced some kind of communication with God. It led John to become a baptizer, and Jesus to be a healer (see Chapter 9) and to risk his death when he went to Jerusalem for his last Passover (see Chapter 11).

With regard to John the Baptist, Jeffrey Trumbower (1994) and James Dunn (1994) argue that John was profoundly influenced by respectively Isaiah (Dunn) and Malachi (Trumbower). Dunn notes in particular Isa. 40.3 ('Prepare in the wilderness the way of the Lord') and the oracle about the Coming One in Isa. 30.27-8. 'His tongue is like a devouring fire, his breath is like an overflowing stream that reaches to the neck', and he will come 'to sift the nations with the sieve of destruction'. Dunn notes that also the Qumran community applied such texts to their own time and situation. Trumbower observes that 'the Maccabees, Theudas, Jesus ben Ananias, Jewish revolutionaries and the sectarians ... all used Scripture to understand their own times'. In John's case, he concludes as follows:

> I think the evidence indicates an appropriation by John of the text of Malachi, perhaps from his own reading of the text or from his having heard it read and interpreted. He saw himself as Elijah, dressing like him and beginning his career at the place where the old prophet had been taken up to heaven. Baptism (perhaps his own novel idea based on the Jewish tradition of periodic cleansings) was a preparation for the imminent judgment, in the hope that at least those who repented and were baptized could avoid the unquenchable fire of God's wrath, ideas which echo Mal. 3.19 and 24. In line with Mal. 3.1-3, John predicted a 'Coming One', either an agent of Yahweh or Yahweh himself. This 'Coming One' (not identical with Elijah) would suddenly come into the Temple, execute judgment and act as a refining fire.

If Trumbower is correct in his main thesis, John's conflict with Herod Antipas over his divorce takes special significance, as Mal. 2.13-16 contains the harshest condemnation of divorce in the Hebrew Bible. I suggest that also John's saying about the cleansing of the threshing floor (Q 3.17) becomes more specific: the day that the evildoers are burned up like stubble or chaff (4.1) is the same day that the Lord will come to cleanse his temple

(3.1-2). It is not impossible that with the expression 'threshing floor' John consciously evokes the story that the temple was built on the threshing floor of the Jebusite Araunah (2 Sam. 24). There the Angel of wrath had stopped in the days of David, just before the plague reached Jerusalem. He stopped because of the altar that David built to the Lord. Now that the temple worship was polluted (Mal. 1.7) and the 'covenant with Levi' corrupted (2.4), the Angel of the covenant threatens to come to finish the job (3.2). But 'return to me, and I will return to you, says the Lord of Hosts' (3.7). If John's call for repentance and conversion ('return') is read in the light of Malachi, conversion simply means the resolve to live life in full accordance with God's will, without cutting corners.

Another point to be observed is the fact that the prophetic revelation was not only communicated through words, but also through symbolic action (a practice also observed in other prophets). John baptized people in the wilderness, as they re-entered the Promised Land through the river Jordan (Webb 1991, 364). In the light of Malachi, this symbolic act may be seen as part of a programme: first the commitment to the Law of Moses is reconfirmed, and then the Lord or his agent will cleanse and re-establish his temple.

With regard to Jesus, I observe that both first-century prophets such as John and the early followers of Jesus appropriated prophetic Scriptures. The most economic and plausible hypothesis about Jesus would then be that he did so too. Not all references in the Gospels to the Jewish Scriptures are creations of Jesus' followers; it is likely that some do go back to Jesus. It is possible that some of his actions (such as the cleansing of the temple) stood in the tradition of symbolic prophetic acts, which are found in the Hebrew Bible, among the first-century prophets and among the followers of Jesus (as illustrated by Acts 21.11). This is a reason to question Capps's interpretation of the cleansing of the temple as an impulsive act (see Chapter 2). I will come back to this point in Chapter 11.

The remaining propositions with respect to revelations regard the social network in which revelations are received:

8. An individual's confidence in the validity of his or her revelations is reinforced to the extent that others accept these revelations.
9. A recipient's ability to convince others is proportionate to the extent to which he or she is a respected member of an intense primary group.
10. The greater the reinforcement received, the more likely a person is to have further revelations.
11. The greater the amount of reinforcement received and the more revelations produced by a person, the more novel (heretical) subsequent revelations will become.
12. As they become successful, religious movements founded on revelations will attempt to curtail revelations or at least prevent novel (heretical) revelations.

These propositions are related to the idea that revelation is often the interpretation of mental processes that can be made in various ways. One of the factors is social acceptance. If Jesus was part of a network that accepted John's prophetic interpretation, and if Jesus had a respected position resulting from his religious capital, and if his initial revelations were well in line with the beliefs of the group, it is likely that the group around him approved of his inspired insights. This group consisted of his cousins and friends who followed John. At the start of his mission, it did not include his younger brothers; even though they shared Jesus' religious beliefs, they did not share his emerging perception of his own role.

As Jesus learnt to trust the mental processes through which he experienced God's guidance, he will most likely have relied more on them, especially in times of distress and danger. As I will argue in Chapters 10 and 11, these mental processes did not reveal God's specific plan with Jesus' role in one great moment of insight. The process is more interactive and adaptive. As the group shared certain experiences with Jesus, they also participated in this interactive process. After his death, they continued to turn to the Scriptures and the 'spirit' to understand Jesus' role. It was only towards the end of the first century that conservative forces tried to curtail such prophetic activity (on this dynamic with respect to the Gospel of John, see Tom Thatcher 2006).

New Religious Ideas and Practices

In this last section, I return to the propositions listed in Stark and Finke (2000). Why did followers continue to preserve and develop Jesus' religious ideas and practices?

> Proposition 21. All religious explanations, and especially those concerning otherworldly rewards, entail risk.

> Proposition 22. An individual's confidence in religious explanations is strengthened to the extent that others express their confidence in them.

Religious movements, as in the case(s) of John and Jesus, make promises about the future that cannot be verified by followers today. Those who believe risk the 'investment' that they are making today. Those who do not believe risk the promised returns on that investment. Being risk averse, people will try to find different ways to gain confidence in a religious explanation. If respected others underwrite the religious explanation, and are willing to make the investment, a person gains confidence in its underlying value (this is similar to the pricing mechanisms for public shares in dot.com enterprises today).

Another way to gain confidence is the participation in rituals and prayers. These convey the paradigms and opportunities through which certain mental processes can be interpreted as mystical experiences and certain events as divine intervention:

Proposition 23. Confidence in religious explanations increases to the extent that people participate in religious rituals.
- *Definition* 17. Religious rituals are collective ceremonies having a common focus and mood in which the focus is on a god or gods, while the common mood may vary.

Proposition 24. Prayer builds bonds of affection and confidence between humans and a god or gods.
- *Definition* 18. Prayer is a communication addressed to a god or gods.

Proposition 25. Confidence in religious explanations will increase to the degree that miracles are credited to the religion.
- *Definition* 19. Miracles are desirable effects believed to be caused by the intervention of a god or gods in worldly matters.

Proposition 26. Confidence in religious explanations will increase to the degree that people have mystical experiences.
- *Definition* 20. Mystical experiences are some sense of contact, however fleeting, with a god or gods.

The early followers of Jesus shared both Jewish rituals and prayers. In addition, as we can see already in Paul's letters, they shared specific rituals and prayers inspired by John and Jesus: initiatory baptism, common meals, and praying to God as 'Abba'. The recurrent meals probably provided for a more enduring bond than the one-off experience of John's baptism could have done. The groups thus came together regularly and they actively sought 'spiritual gifts' and shared an increasing number of traditions, both about Jesus and about his followers, which reported the miracles that God had performed in their lives. The stories about Jesus' healings and miracles (see Chapter 9) were widely believed, even by Jesus' opponents.

Proposition 27. Confidence in the explanations offered by a religion will be greater to the extent that its ecclesiastics display levels of commitment greater than expected of followers.

Proposition 28. Vigorous efforts by religious organizations are required to motivate and sustain high levels of individual religious commitment.

People know and knew that religious leaders often benefit from the sacrifices of their followers. As a result, their beliefs are no longer evidence of the truth of their preaching. The test is whether the leader is prepared to invest more than his immediate returns. Perhaps the biggest 'investment' that a leader can make is his own life. Both John and Jesus, as well as some of the most prominent early followers such as James, Peter and Paul, sacrificed their lives. If such sacrifices are made willingly, they are a powerful testimony to the sincerity of the religious explanations given by these leaders. If such sacrifices are themselves part of the religious explanation offered by the leader before his or her death, they are a testimony to the validity of that explanation as a whole.

In the end, the movement of Jesus' followers was far more successful than the movement of those who followed John but not Jesus. Rational Choice Theory points to a number of factors to explain the difference. Contrary to John's 'dispersed and passivist' movement, Jesus' followers were quickly organized as a fictive family of children of the Father, with clear leadership roles for the Twelve and Jesus' brothers. They regularly convened for common meals and prayer, and thus helped their members to share mystical experiences and to 'recognize' divine intervention in their lives.

Conclusion

Rational Choice Theory does not explain what happens in the life of an individual who starts a new religious movement or who decides to join such a movement. But it does observe some factors that are at play in such processes in a way that lends itself to empirical verification. On this basis, the theory can propose or support plausible hypotheses with regard to Jesus and his earliest followers. These include the following:

- Jesus, his brothers and his friends belonged to a social network that to a large extent preceded their religious affiliation.
- Jesus and his family shared many of the beliefs of John the Baptist.
- John's prophetic interpretation of Jewish Scripture influenced Jesus' prophetic awareness.
- The social crisis in Palestine and the legitimacy problems of the existing temple-church and the Herodian dynasty contributed to the prophetic roles of John and Jesus, as well as to their reception and reinforcement.
- The religious experiences that John and Jesus transferred to their followers as well as the ultimate sacrifices they made contributed to the enduring confidence that their followers had in their teachings and later developments thereof.

Chapter 9

THE SPIRIT OF JESUS' HEALINGS

Psychohistory or psychobiography of people in non-Western or pre-modern societies has suffered from the fact that its main tool, psychology, has developed within the modernity that it helped shape. The tension is especially felt when we study societies or individuals with very different attitudes towards the individual, the group and the spiritual world.

In the last decades, however, cross-cultural psychology has broadened the field in which psychological theories are tested. A good example is the comparison of the results of Bowlby's 'Strange Situation' test in different cultures (see Chapter 6). Psychological anthropology goes a step further, as it takes the specific culture as its point of departure and tries to describe and understand its specific psychological dynamics as part of that culture (Erika Bourguignon 1979, 13). In this chapter, I will investigate the usefulness of anthropological and psychological concepts to understand the development of the role of the Spirit in the ministry of Jesus and his earliest followers.

How Did the Holy Spirit Become the Spirit of Christ?

When James Dunn (1975) discusses Jesus' experience of God, this is organized in two chapters: one on 'sonship' and the other on 'spirit'. Both elements come together in the baptismal practices of his earliest followers, who also described Jesus' own baptism by John in these terms. In Chapter 7 above, I discuss how Attachment Theory sheds some light on the experience of God as a Father, and I offer some suggestions about the possible relationship that this may have had with baptism. But how is it possible that the baptismal experience was associated with the reception of the Holy Spirit? And what about this remarkable passage in Paul's letter to the Romans about the close relationship between son-ship and Spirit (8.9):

And you are not in the flesh but in the Spirit,
since the Spirit of God dwells in you.
But if anyone does not have the Spirit of Christ,
he does not belong to him.

This, almost casual, use of the expressions 'Spirit of God' and 'Spirit of Christ' as synonyms does not belong to Paul's argument and can therefore be assumed to belong to a vocabulary that he shared with his audience. Writing to an audience in a city that he had not yet visited, Paul can assume that they will agree that the experience of the Spirit is the sign of one's life in Christ. The attribution of certain religious experiences to the indwelling of the Spirit of God and the equation of that spirit to the Spirit of Christ was quite likely not a Pauline invention. Furthermore, there are some passages in Paul that seem to equate the life-giving and glorifying Spirit to the risen Christ (1 Cor. 15.45) or the Lord (2 Cor. 3.17).

This raises a number of questions with regard to the early movement and the ministry of Jesus:

- What kind of religious experiences did these early followers of Jesus have that they associated with the indwelling of his or the Holy Spirit?
- How did these experiences of the outpouring of God's or Jesus' Spirit originate and spread?
- How can Jesus have been associated with the Holy Spirit?

Before discussing each of these questions in more detail, I will discuss some current applications of anthropological concepts on the study of the historical Jesus and Paul.

Spirits, Altered States of Consciousness and Shamanism

Altered (or alternative) States of Consciousness (ASC) can be induced by individual practices (like fasting and meditation), group dynamics and/ or the use of stimulants such as drugs. In about half the surveyed human societies, including most 'circum-Mediterranean societies', such states are wholly or partly attributed to spirit possession. Statistical analysis shows that such societies are typically large, sedentary and complex, with slavery and polygynous marriage (Erika Bourguignon 1973, 20). It is hypothesized that the rigidity of such societies is an important factor in the occurrence of possession trance. Bourguignon (1973, 12) stresses that

> ... although the *capacity* to experience altered states of consciousness is a psychobiological capacity of the species, and thus universal, its utilization, institutionalization, and patterning are, indeed, features of culture, and thus variable.

In other words: general psychobiological insights can help us understand the intrinsic dynamics of these experiences, while specific cultural-anthropological knowledge is needed to understand their manifestation and significance.

ASC is not only an anthropological concept; it can also be studied from a neurobiological perspective. Eugene d'Aquili and Andrew Newberg (1999; see also the updated summary in Newberg and Newberg 2005) explain

ASC, the experience of the divine, and the transformation of the self from a neuropsychological perspective. They argue that 'God appears to be "hard-wired" into the brain' (206). Mystical experiences are therefore relatively normal and not necessarily psychopathological. They can be induced by myth, meditation and group rituals.

John Pilch (2000 and 2004) suggests that the healings and visions in the Gospels and the book of Acts can be understood as ASC experiences. Stevan Davies (1995) argues that Jesus' speech induced ASCs that led to healings and exorcisms. In Chilton and Evans's *Authenticating the Activities of Jesus* (2002), Bruce Malina uses 'cross-cultural social psychology' to argue for the historicity of Jesus' walking on the sea of Galilee as an ASC, as Pieter Craffert (2008) does with respect to the transfiguration story.

Shamanism

In the last decade, the concept of shamanism has gained some currency in the study of the historical Paul and Jesus. John Ashton (2000) proposes to analyse Paul's religious experience as if he were a shaman (although realizing that he was 'not really' one, 29). He also argues that Jesus is a much stronger candidate for identification as shaman (62). The starting point for this is perhaps the realization that Jesus' claim to fame in Palestinian society was his work as a 'magician' (Morton Smith 1978), 'exorcist' (Graham Twelftree 1993), or 'miracle worker' (Twelftree 1999). This is best demonstrated in Pieter Craffert's *The Life of a Galilean Shaman* (2008). Craffert (420–2) claims that historical Jesus research is 'trapped in the historiographical framework from which it emerged more than a hundred and fifty years ago'. It assumes 'that a historical figure could not have been like the Gospel portrayals and consequently that the Gospels have developed in a linear and layered fashion from the authentic kernels to the elaborate literary constructions as they are known today'. He believes that the

> shamanic complex as an ASC-based religious pattern ... describes religious entrepreneurs who, based on regular ASC-experiences, perform ... healings, exorcisms, and the control of spirits, but also act as prophets, teachers, and poets, in their communities. This is a social type model that without much difficulty can account for the wide spectrum of Gospel evidence ascribed to Jesus of Nazareth.

I very much appreciate the work of Craffert as a way of making scholars aware of the modern and post-modern mindset that we bring to historical Jesus research. It is indeed possible that more sensitivity to cultural differences would lead us to different conclusions. The strength of this approach is that it highlights the perceived mechanisms of spirit possession in Paul's letters and the Gospel narratives that might otherwise be neglected. Having said that, I am not yet convinced of the wholesale application of the concept of shamanism to the historical Jesus. The word shaman has been taken from its Arctic origins to refer to a social type that can be found in a larger group of societies (Lewis

1971/2003). But the question is, of course, whether this specific social type existed in first-century Palestine. According to Fiona Bowie (2000/2006, ch. 7), the shaman 'functions as a healer and a psychopomp' through 'the ability to control the spirits'. In a 'trance séance', the shaman 'makes contact with the spirits, sending out his or her soul to heal, exorcise, mediate, divine, or perform acts of vengeance'. The séance may be accompanied by 'drumming, singing, dancing, and the wearing of an elaborate costume all adding to the dramatic effect'. Such mechanisms look less applicable to the situation in, for example, Corinth, where the Holy Spirit dwells in all believers, or in the life of Jesus, who did not organize trance séances as part of his healings. Lewis (1986/1996, ch. 7) makes a distinction between exorcism and adorcism in traditional Christian (Ethiopic), Islamic and Buddhist societies. The exorcist expels evil spirits (like Jesus is said to have done), which Lewis contrasts to the shamanic leader who bases his or her treatment on 'adorcism' or spirit accommodation. Furthermore, the concept of shamanism suggests that the established and traditional role of an individual can explain the spiritual experiences in Paul's letters. But it is rather the innovative character of the communal experience of the Holy Spirit in Corinth and other early communities of Jesus followers that should be explained. This may also be true for Jesus, if the reports are correct that his preaching and exorcism were seen as unusual. Finally, shamans are usually trained by older shamans. But while Craffert does point to John the Baptist as Jesus' teacher, there are no reports that John ever healed or exorcised his followers. One of the key questions for this chapter is therefore how Jesus came to act as a healer and an exorcist.

To summarize: anthropological concepts, such as spirit possession and ASCs, remind us that literal and literary truths are not the only ways that Paul's letters and the Gospels may have been 'true' for a first-century audience. I am not convinced, however, of the usefulness of the shaman as a social type in first-century Palestine. I believe we first need a careful historically and anthropologically informed understanding of what is going on in Paul's letters and the Gospels.

What Kind of Religious Experiences Did These Early Followers of Jesus Have That They Associated With the Indwelling of His or the Holy Spirit?

In his 2002 study, Gordon Fee characterizes the concept of the '(Holy) Spirit' in the Pauline corpus as *God's Empowering Presence*. Fee concludes (896–9) that the Spirit plays 'a crucial role' in Paul's religious experience of Christ and hence in his understanding of the Gospel of Jesus. Furthermore, both the experience and the understanding are 'thoroughly eschatological': the experience both confirmed and modified Paul's pre-existing ideas about the *eschaton*; it proved that the eschatological scenario had been set in motion and guaranteed the outcome by its power. The experience was powerful in both the life of the individual and the community as it was the prophesied 'return of God's own personal presence to dwell in and among his people'. Fee argues that Paul holds certain 'Trinitarian presuppositions' in the sense that while God is one and personal, the spirit can be understood as the Spirit of God, as the Spirit of Jesus or as a distinct person. Believers 'are "Spirit People" first and foremost', '… in the likeness of Christ to the Glory of God'. Endowing these believers with *charismata*, the spirit's presence 'helps to build up the believing community'.

The Diaspora Meaning of 'Holy Spirit'

Spirits were everywhere in the cultural tapestry of the Mediterranean in late antiquity. Varying from the ghosts of the deceased to the good or evil spirits that functioned between gods and humans. Apart from their appearance in histories, folktales and novels there is an enormous amount of literature dealing with the ways and means of influencing the spirits. There was a wide variety of opinions about such beings, based upon Greek philosophy, as well as perceived wisdom from the Egyptians, Chaldaeans or Jews (for a selection of sources, see Georg Luck 1985 and Daniel Ogden 2009).

But Paul's audience in major cities like Rome and Corinth consisted to a large degree of Jews and god-fearers (see Chapter 5). The question to be asked then is what Jews and god-fearers in the Graeco-Roman Diaspora understood by the term 'God's spirit' or the 'Holy Spirit'. John Levison, in his 1997 monograph *The Spirit in First-Century Judaism*, discerns the following uses: the spirit as the breath of life, the Holy Spirit as the innate divine element in a person, or the Spirit of God as an invading angel. All three uses are based both on biblical antecedents as well Graeco-Roman concepts, ranging from human anthropology to one's personal *daimon* or even oracular ecstasy. In general, the use of the word spirit by Paul (mostly in connection with either the human spirit or the Spirit of God), in combination with his use of the word demon in a negative sense, is best understood in the specific context of Diaspora Judaism, rather than general Graeco-Roman culture. There is also a more particular use of the term 'Holy Spirit' that is connected to Messianic and eschatological expectations. First, Levison notes that 'Holy Spirit' normally refers to the divine but innate spirit of a person, with the exception of Isa. 63.10-14. Here the Holy Spirit is the Spirit of the Lord, leading his people. Second, Levison concludes that the idea of the Spirit of the Lord *resting* on a person is not very common either. In the Hebrew Bible, it occurs only in Isaiah, where it is related to the anointing of an eschatological leader (61.1), from the house of David (11.2).

In addition, I note that the idea in the early churches that *all* believers receive the Spirit and the spiritual gifts, like visions and prophecies, fits with the *eschatological* prophecy in Joel 2.28-9. After repentance and conversion, the day of the Lord will come and God will rescue his people and restore his covenant with them for eternity:

Then afterward I will pour out my Spirit on all flesh; your sons and your daughters shall prophesy, your old men shall dream dreams and your young men shall see visions. Even on the male and female slaves, in those days, I will pour out my Spirit.

The spiritual experiences in the letters of Paul are therefore best understood in the context of Messianic hopes among Jews, activated by a belief that these hopes are now being fulfilled.

The Gifts of the Spirit

As we saw in Chapter 6, Paul's letters to Rome and Corinth were not directed to his ardent followers alone. He had never visited Rome, and some people in Corinth preferred the leadership of Peter or Apollos over that of Paul. When reading Paul's letters, a careful distinction should be made between the points that Paul argues already and those that he seems to share with his broader audience. 1 Cor. 12 through 14 contains an argument over the question whether all should be speaking in tongues, or whether the practice should be forbidden – perhaps especially in the case of women. In his answer, Paul advocates the idea that everyone receives different spiritual gifts, which should be brought together in order to benefit the entire community (12.4-11):

Now there are different gifts (*charismata*), but it is the same *Spirit*; and there are different tasks (*diakoniai*), but it is the same *Lord* (Jesus); and there are different activities (*energemata*), but it is the same *God* who activates everything in everyone.

And to each individual the manifestation of the Spirit is given in order to benefit together: To one person is given (1) a word of wisdom through the Spirit, and to another (2) a word of knowledge from the same Spirit. To the next person is given (3) faith through the same Spirit, and to another (4) gifts of healings in the one Spirit. To another (5) activities of power are given, to yet another (6) the discernment of spirits, to the next person (7) different types of tongues and to another (8) the interpretation of tongues. But the one and the same Spirit activates all these things, distributing specific gifts to each individual as he intends to.

It is striking that a large part of his audience saw such experiences not as experiences restricted to a specific class of prophets or the like, but rather as a general experience of Jesus' followers. Indeed, it seems to have been a *norm* that every follower of Jesus would receive this spirit. One can speculate that this is the impact of a text like Joel 2.28-9: 'I will pour out my Spirit on all flesh.' One of the questions some of the Corinthians may have had, then, is whether those who did not speak in tongues are truly spirit-filled people. Paul does not question the implied norm, but answers that through baptism, everyone becomes a member of the body of Christ, led by the Spirit and bound by love. Every member is needed for his or her own specific gifts, tasks or works. The understandable desire for spectacular spiritual gifts, however, should never obscure the humble but highest gift of all: love. Love lasts eternally, while spiritual gifts are meant only for the interim period.

Paul concludes with a practical arrangement in which the *charismata* function in a controlled setting (1 Cor. 14.26-33, 39-40):

What is it then, brothers (and sisters)? Whenever you come together, everyone has something: a psalm, a teaching, a revelation, a tongue, or an interpretation thereof; let everything happen constructively:

- If someone speaks in a tongue (two or three at the most, and each in turn) let someone give the interpretation; but if there is no interpreter then let him (or her) fall silent in the church and speak (privately) to himself (or herself) and to God.
- Let two or three prophets speak and let the others critically evaluate what they say. And when something is revealed to another person, while sitting (and listening), let the first (speaker) fall silent. For you can all prophesy in turn, in order that all may learn and all may be encouraged. For the spirits of the prophets are subject to the prophets, because God is not a God of disorder but of peace as in all the churches of the saints.
- ... (34-8) ...

Therefore my brothers (and sisters), be eager to prophesy, and forbid not to speak in tongues. But let everything happen in a fitting and orderly way.

It seems that the spiritual experiences are not entirely ecstatic; the Holy Spirit does not take over but rather inspires the believer. In the case of prophecies or revelations, a person's own intellect remains involved (14.6, 19). The words are the believer's own conscious interpretation of what the Spirit within him or her is revealing. This is different in the case of speaking in tongues, where the human spirit gives voice to the spiritual experiences without the intellect controlling it (14.14). Even then, however, the person can still pray consciously (14.13, 15) or stop speaking (14.28).

According to Bourguignon, altered states increase suggestibility, 'heightening the common faith of those who experience them jointly'. On the other hand, 'when states get out of hand, crisis results both for the individual and for the group'. Therefore, the 'key to a stable religion and a stable situation is the ability to utilize altered states under controlled, ritualized conditions' (Bourguignon 1973, 338). This is probably what happens in 1 Cor. 12–14, where Paul discusses the need for order in relation to the *charismata* like speaking in tongues and prophesying.

Contemporary speaking in tongues in community worship is a cross-cultural but predominantly charismatic Christian and Pentecostal phenomenon. In communal worship it is accompanied by a lowering of inhibitions and can facilitate other spiritual experiences such as the interpretation of tongues, prophesying and the revelation of diabolic possession among some of the members. Felicia Goodman (1973, 185) describes this type of *glossolalia* as 'an act of vocalization in trance', although other researches found that ecstasy is not required and people can stop speaking in tongues when requested. This accords well with the references to the practice in 2 Corinthians, although we cannot be sure that the experience of today's speakers in tongues is the same as that of the Corinthians, or of the Pentecost experience described in Acts

(Johnson 1998, ch. 4). For the analysis presented here it is not required that the phenomena are identical.

Of special interest are verses 14.34-5, which deal with the idea that women should be silent in the communal worship. This idea is so much at odds with the statement in 11.5, where women are assumed to prophesy, that some commentators suggest it is an early interpolation. Some textual witnesses solve the issue differently, by placing verses 34-5 after verse 40. The ban on women's speech is then an expression of fitting and orderly worship. A third option is to regard the ban as a quotation from a faction in the Corinthian community with whom Paul then disagrees in verse 39. Anthony Thiselton (2000, 1152–6), however, argues that Paul is speaking here of the critical evaluation of prophesying during which it is not fitting or helpful that a wife should question her husband. Whatever the correct interpretation may be, the entire passage is clearly a response to the fact that spiritual experiences in the community can be both constructive and disruptive and require a controlled setting. I also note that verse 33b (whether it concludes the section on prophecy or introduces the section on women) is an appeal to common practice among the *ekklesiai* with regard to such controls.

Paul's Own Spiritual Experiences

In several instances, Paul speaks about his own experiences. He claims to speak in tongues more than anyone in Corinth (1 Cor. 14.18) and to prophesy (implied in Chapters 13 and 14). He also claims to have had visions and revelations of the Lord, most likely including a heavenly journey without knowing whether he had left his body or not (2 Cor. 12.1-9), that he saw the risen Lord (1 Cor. 15.8), and that his Gospel for the nations was not revealed to him by humans but by Jesus Christ (Gal. 1.11-17, 2.2,7).

Colleen Shantz (2009) explains Paul's confusion about body and speech in his heavenly journey (2 Cor. 12.1-9) from a neurological perspective. She believes that the strong unitary awareness and feelings of transformation that often accompany the experience of ASC influenced the development of his theology (143):

> The neurocognitive phenomena of ecstatic religious experience generate a sense of shared identity. That experience creates in Paul the 'inner' resources that make the death of Jesus a transformative force in Paul's own life. In other words, Paul's own neural networks have been imprinted with his apprehension of the risen Jesus. In these cases, by placing experience before discourse, the resulting exegesis explains some of the unusual features of Paul's thought – especially his so-called Christ-mysticism – more satisfactorily than traditional theological readings can.

Spiritual Persons

Paul characterizes people as *pneumatikos*, *psychikos*, or *sarkinos* (1 Cor. 2.14–3.1), even if – as some commentators argue – he borrows the words from certain Corinthian believers. The words probably function as some kind of shorthand for what is leading a person: the spirit, the soul with its passions or the flesh with its lusts. Indeed, even a believer can still be *sarkinos* (Gal. 5.16, 6.1; compare Rom. 7.14), every time he or she submits to the lusts of the flesh or to the law (as the law seeks to control the flesh). Those who are spiritual receive the guidance of God's indwelling Spirit (1 Cor. 2.14), so that they are 'children of God' and their spirits join the Spirit in addressing God as 'Abba' (Rom. 8.14-16).

Paul's metaphor of the believer being subjected in marriage to either the flesh or the Spirit of the risen Lord (Rom. 7.1-4, 8.1-13), may well be based on a tripartite anthropology: in this text, the soul – although not explicitly mentioned – is subjected to the flesh or to the Spirit as a wife to her husband. In 1 Thess. 5.23, Paul speaks of the whole person as spirit, soul and body. These, I suggest, are not separate parts, but the three together make up the whole person (not unlike the school drawing of my youth, where the body was shown with the blood circulation transporting oxygen from the respiratory system throughout the body).

The importance of such a tripartite anthropology may not be immediately clear from a literary or historical perspective. Interesting, therefore, is the observation of anthropologist Thomas Csordas (1994, 39–40) with respect to the Catholic Charismatic Renewal, a movement that he studied for nearly 20 years:

> Essential to the Charismatic healing system is a concept of the person as a tripartite composition of body, mind, and spirit. Conceptualization of a tripartite person creates a decisive cultural difference between Charismatic healing and conventional psychotherapy and medicine, insofar as the latter are predicated on a concept of the person as a dualistic composite of body and mind. ... the spiritual is empirical in the sense that phenomena such as evil spirits, or the sense of divine presence, are experienced as real in their own domain, just as are viruses in the somatic and emotional traumas in the mental domains.

Corresponding to each component of the tripartite person is a type of healing: *physical healing* of bodily illness, *inner healing* of emotional illness and distress, and *deliverance* from the adverse effects of evil spirits.

I am not saying that Paul's anthropology is identical to that of a modern charismatic movement. Rather, I would like to stress that the way in which a person is conceptualized influences the experiences of people, as well as their interpretations of these experiences.

Unclean or Evil Spirits

Finally, I note that unlike the Gospels and Acts, the letters attributed to Paul seldom speak about unclean or evil spirits. With a few exceptions, the word spirit is used for the divine Spirit or the human spirit. Paul does, however, speak about gods and idols, or angels and demons from whom the believers turned away when they followed Jesus (1 Thess. 1.9; 1 Cor. 12.2). How Paul thinks about such beings becomes clear only in the discussion whether believers can eat meat from animals that were – quite commonly – slaughtered as sacrifice to certain pagan deities in 1 Cor. 8–10, from which I quote 8.4-6 and 10.18b-20:

> Now about the eating of meat sacrificed to idols: We know that there is no idol in the world and that there is no God except one. For even if there are beings that are called gods in heaven or on earth – as there are many gods and many lords –, still for us there is one God, the Father out of whom all things are, and we are in him; and one Lord, Jesus Christ, through whom all things are, and we are through him.
>
> … are not those who eat sacrifices in communion with the altar? What then do I say? That a sacrifice to an idol is anything, or that an idol is anything? (No,) but that the things that they sacrifice, are sacrificed to demons and not to God. And I do not want you to have communion with the demons.

For Paul there are no other deities but God alone. But there are demons. These are not gods, but lower-level beings. They can use idolatry to have communion with humans. Spirit-filled people do not have to fear them, quite possibly because a more powerful spirit dwells in them (cf. Lk. 11.24). Eating meat that was sacrificed will not give them power over believers. But they should be avoided and consciously participating in idolatry will defile the believer. If Paul believes that the indwelling of the Holy Spirit leaves no room for unclean spirits or demons, then we can ask from the perspective of anthropological psychology whether the function of spirit possession among the disempowered may have been transferred to the display of *charismata* from the religiously legitimate Holy Spirit.

How Did These Spiritual Experiences of the Outpouring of God's or Jesus' Spirit Originate and Spread?

The experience of the Spirit is assumed in all communities addressed in the undisputed Pauline letters, whether they were founded by Paul's mission (Thessaloniki and Philippi), by the mission of Barnabas, whom he assisted (the Galatian communities), or the communities that already existed before he arrived there (Corinth and Rome). For Paul, the proclamation of Jesus, the baptism of new members, the reception of the Spirit and the acceptance of the Gospel come hand-in-hand (cf. 2 Cor. 11.4). Already in perhaps the oldest New Testament document, 1 Thessalonians, the spiritual experience helped to establish the community (1.4-5): 'We know, God-beloved brothers (and sisters), your election, because our Gospel did not only come to you in words, but also in power and in Holy Spirit, and much proof.'

In other words, when the community of Thessaloniki was formed, they received the *charismata* of the Holy Spirit that proved the new faith and the election of the faithful. In order to function as such evidence, these experiences must have been new for these believers, they must have been profound and they must have been similar to what they heard had happened in other communities.

How is it possible that such a wide range of groups shared the same profound and innovative spiritual experiences? The psychologically plausible answer is to see these experiences at least in part as learned behaviour. An analogy is the phenomenon of *glossolalia* among Pentecostal churches in modern Christianity. The practice is spread through missionary activities and conversion, and is learned from other believers. Even if we acknowledge that the modern phenomenon is based on a particular interpretation of the New Testament description and not necessarily identical to first-century speaking in tongues, we are still dealing with a similar pattern of dissemination. The origins of the Pentecostal movement are well documented in Cecil Robeck's *Azusa Street Mission and Revival: The Birth of the Global Pentecostal Movement* (2006). In 1906, 35-year-old William Seymour came to the fast-growing migrant city of Los Angeles to serve a small mission church. Seymour, the son of former slaves, was raised in syncretistic Louisiana. He moved to Indianapolis, Cincinnati and Houston, where he took part in the Wesleyan Holiness Movement, learned the theory of 'baptism in the Holy Spirit', and heard about the first instances of speaking in tongues (attested since 1901). In his new church he spoke about his desire for baptism in the Holy Spirit, and was subsequently told that it disqualified him as pastor. Some of the church members, however, invited him to speak at their home prayer group. They came together each evening, fervently praying for revival, baptism in the Holy Spirit and the experience of speaking in tongues. After a month, one of the members started to speak in tongues. Several others followed, including pastor Seymour. In the midst of initial ridicule, the 18 April earthquake destroyed much of San Francisco and filled a number of people in Los Angeles with the idea that Judgment Day had arrived. The outpouring of the Holy Spirit was associated with the imminence of Christ's second coming. In this context, many Christians joined the congregation to experience the Holy Spirit, manifested in *glossolalia* and prophecy. The group baptized hundreds of 'new believers' each week and within six months several related congregations in and around Los Angeles had been established. The spread of the movement, at first, followed the existing network of trains and streetcars. By September 1906, evangelists were active in the major cities on the West Coast and, by December 1906, New York was reached and the first missionaries were sent to Africa. Within two years Canada, Mexico, Western Europe, Eastern Europe, the Middle East, West Africa and South Africa had been reached. Now, a hundred years later, the movement is to be measured in hundreds of millions.

It is important to note that similar growth factors apply in both cases. Pentecostalism grew fast among Christians with an eschatological outlook; the early movements of John and Jesus grew among Jews hoping for God's kingdom. The new movements did not destroy religious capital, but often enabled people who were already religious to develop their religious capital faster than they could have in their previous church or synagogue community. Both networks grew on the basis of existing social networks and transport networks; both spread at first to the bigger cities. It is probable that, in both cases, the spiritual experiences were induced by a desire to experience what others had experienced before them, by biblical precedent and by active and frequent prayers and fasting. In both cases, the spiritual experiences as well as the climate for prophecy contributed to the rapid and authoritative development and/or acceptance of certain theological concepts.

Donald Capps (2008, 10) describes as an example the wave of laughing among Tanzanian girls in 1962. An extraordinary outbreak of contagious laughter, crying and agitation forced a boarding school to close within seven weeks. The girls sent home were 'agents' for the further spread of the epidemic. Within ten days several villages and schools were affected. The contagion even crossed the border with Uganda. Over a period of a good two years fourteen schools were closed. Those affected were primarily girls and women of lower social classes. Boys were also affected, but men were not. Capps assumes that the outbreak was a symptom of stress-induced conversion disorder, influenced by socio-economic and cultural factors. I also note that the specific expression it found was innovative and contagious.

The First Pentecost

If the shared spiritual experiences were 'learned' from those who had the experience previously, the most economic assumption is that these experiences originated in the same community of believers that in 1 Cor. 15 is described as having had the resurrection experiences in the period after the crucifixion of Jesus (which begs the question of how these experiences relate to one another). Although it is impossible to verify to what extent the story in the book of Acts represents historic events, I do note that from a psychological and an anthropological point of view, a story like that of Acts 2 would fit with what we see in the letters of Paul: the experience was profound, new and foundational. The closest that Paul comes to the language of Acts 2 and Joel 2 is in 2 Cor. 12.13: 'For indeed in one Spirit we were all baptized into one body, – whether Jew or Greek, or slave or free, – and we have all been given to drink one Spirit.' Let us assume, therefore, that there was a community in Jerusalem that came together in spiritual activities, such as fasting and praying, and that experienced something that was interpreted as the presence of the Holy Spirit and resembled what we find some 20 years later in the letters of Paul. What then was their expectation as they prayed and perhaps fasted? From a psychological and an anthropological point of view, we are looking for an expectation that both induced the spiritual experience that followed and at the same time provided for its interpretation. I see two alternatives that could be explored further.

- The group already expected the outpouring of the Holy Spirit because it saw Jesus' crucifixion as the inauguration of the *eschaton* as described by Joel 2. This would explain perfectly what followed, but it does not square very well with the indications in the Gospels that the disciples had been surprised and confused by the death of Jesus. It requires an eschatological scenario shared between Jesus and his followers, in which the crucifixion was already foreseen.
- Alternatively, the group accepted the death of Jesus as the death of a prophet such as Elijah and expected to receive his spirit, in the same way that Elisha received 'a double portion' of Elijah's spirit in 2 Kgs 2.9, 15. Note that in this story Elisha takes the initiative to ask for this and that it is granted to him in a sort of ascension scene. This reception of the Spirit by the Twelve would have marked their 'great commission', the resumption of the work of John the Baptist and Jesus. Scot McKnight (2009) argues that Jesus' choice of the Twelve reflects an eschatological scheme that included leadership roles for the Twelve in the *eschaton*. Perhaps it was first expected that the Twelve would receive this spirit. When, however, others in the group, men and women, adults and children, servants and freeborn people, received the spirit, this needed to be interpreted. Perhaps texts like Joel 2.28-9 or Zech. 12.10 came to mind, thus reinforcing the eschatological element that was already present in the preaching of John and Jesus (see Chapter 11). The crucifixion and the subsequent spiritual experiences, as well as the Scriptures used to interpret them, all interacted to both confirm and direct their eschatological outlook.

The first alternative would explain the idea that God's Spirit had been poured out, but not necessarily how this Spirit could be the Spirit of Jesus. In the second alternative the transfer of Jesus' Spirit to his pupil(s) is combined with the outpouring of God's Holy Spirit. This alternative is a better explanation of what follows, but it is only plausible if his pupils already associated the Spirit of Jesus with the Holy Spirit of God.

How Can Jesus Have Been Associated With the Holy Spirit?

Jesus did not receive John's spirit. The key thing to observe is that Jesus did not succeed John after his death, but rather started his mission while John was still alive. There is an interesting story about John and Jesus in Lk. 7. After John, who is imprisoned, hears about Jesus' healings, he sends out messengers to Jesus to ask whether Jesus 'is the one who would come'. Surprisingly, Jesus gives a rather defensive answer. Paraphrasing texts like Isa. 61.1-2, Jesus points to his healings as proof of his Messianic status. It seems that John expected the Coming One as someone who would behave differently from the way Jesus did. It seems unlikely that John would have been offended by healings. It rather seems that the real reason for John's concern is stated in the passage that follows. While John lived a sober life, Jesus was known as a glutton and a drinker. But the story has so many embarrassing aspects that it most likely contains at least some historical data: Jesus and John shared certain eschatological notions, but Jesus was not John's appointed successor. John had a problem with Jesus' life style and therefore had doubts whether Jesus and his friends, all (former) disciples of John, truly acted in line with John's mission.

Did Jesus really quote Isaiah to justify his role and even position himself as part of an eschatological scenario? Most scholars would rather ascribe the application of such prophecies to the early church, rather than to Jesus. In Lk. 4.18-19 the prophecy from Isaiah is quoted in full. It starts with 'The Spirit of the Lord is on me'. Is it possible that already in Jesus' lifetime, his healings and exorcisms were associated with the Holy Spirit, both by Jesus' followers and by himself? Before answering that question, it is important to try to understand Jesus' healings from an anthropological and a psychological point of view.

The Psychological Dimension

Many modern scholars take seriously the claim that Jesus had a reputation as a healer and an exorcist and that some of his healings are historic (as argued in detail in John Meier 1994). Some scholars consider it helpful to look at sickness as both a physical *disease* as well as a socially constructed *illness*, like exclusion (e.g. Pilch 2000, 13–14; Crossan 1991, 336–7). Perhaps in contrast to the specialization that we see in modern medicine, traditional healers tend to look at both the disease and the illness, applying both physical and mental methods to help their patients.

The evangelists' Jesus, however, hardly uses physical means (with the exception of the use of spittle on the deaf man in Mk 7.33 and on the blind man in Mk 8.23). Jesus, therefore, seems to cure mainly through mental processes. In his 2008 *Jesus the Village Psychiatrist*, psychologist Donald Capps makes a persuasive case to see these diseases and possessions through the lens of stress-related conversion disorders. Capps notes that some physical ailments are due to psychological factors or causes. He reconstructs village life in first-century Palestine as being full of 'tensions between city and village, between family and family, between parents and children, and between siblings', that would 'manifest themselves in anxieties'. Such anxieties may cause 'somatoform disorders', the term used in the American psychiatric manual (DSM-IV), including, for example, paralysis, blindness, epilepsy and hysteria (which earlier generations might have regarded as demon-possession). According to Freud, these are *conversion disorders*, in the sense that an unacceptable idea in the mind is converted into a bodily symptom. In a sense, the symptom benefits the patient, in regulating (or suppressing) the cause for anxiety. On the basis of DSM-IV and those healings that Meier evaluated as likely to go back to Jesus, Capps discusses how each patient can be understood as having a conversion disorder, reasoning both from the symptoms in the Gospel narrative as well as Jesus' communication with the person.

In a way, Capps's approach resembles Robert Leslie's 1965 efforts to interpret Jesus' ministry through the 'logotherapy' of Viktor Frankl, who designed a type of psychotherapy that aimed to include the strengths of religion in the treatment of patients. According to Frankl (1969, 2nd edn 1988), people are not only driven by Freud's pleasure principle or Adler's power drive, but also by the 'will' to live a meaningful life. He sees illnesses as caused by somatic, psychic and noetic (or spiritual) causes. *Logos*, as in logotherapy, stands both for 'meaning' and for 'spirit' (18).

I appreciate the way that these psychological insights help us to understand the potential mechanics of the illnesses behind some of the Gospel narratives. Of course one can argue that it would be rather coincidental that all these illnesses were caused by mental rather than physical processes. On the other hand, however, Jesus gained his reputation because of the people he did heal, not because of those he did not heal. And I do note that the overall number of healings that are described in some detail in the Gospel narratives is not very high, while it is acknowledged that Jesus did not always succeed (Mk 6.5), perhaps not in most cases (Lk. 4.27). Less persuasive, however, is the idea that Jesus healed his patients through some sort of modern psychiatry. I cannot see how he would have acquired these skills or why an untrained 'psychiatrist' would succeed in a single encounter where modern psychoanalysis often takes years.

The Anthropological Dimension

Illnesses caused by evil spirits are far more prevalent in the Gospel narratives than in the New Testament epistles or the Hebrew Bible. Furthermore, Jesus can 'rebuke' the fever in Peter's mother-in-law as if it is an evil spirit (Lk. 4.39) and call a crippled woman 'bound by Satan' (Lk. 13.10-17). This is perhaps attributable to the Aramaic background of these narratives. Palestine stands both in the Hellenistic and in the Aramaic world. In the first century, one of the oldest and largest Diaspora communities was found in Mesopotamia. This was the birth ground of the great and influential Rabbi Hillel, who flourished before Jesus' ministry. It was also the place that would later see the birth of the Babylonian Talmud, the greatest monument of rabbinical Judaism. Living prior to the invention of the microscope, Babylonian healers saw all kinds of illnesses as caused by spirits and gods (JoAnn Scurlock 2006), a view that finds its way into a Jewish novel such as *Tobit* (ch. 6). But there is nothing primitive about the Assyro-Babylonian medical tradition, as Scurlock and Anderson (2005, 12) write:

> All this may sound very strange to modern ears, but the fact is that attributing diseases to spirits is considerably closer to the modern theory of infection by organisms invisible to the naked eye attacking the body from without than is the Hippocratic notion of imbalance of humors.

> ... It is no exaggeration to say that the skill of ancient Mesopotamians in diagnosis and therapy was only surpassed in the late nineteenth century C.E., a startling tribute to the potential of the human mind to reason, if armed with an observation-based approach and an attitude of 'use whatever works.'

Whereas Greek medicine separated spirit possession from diseases caused by bodily imbalances, the Aramaic culture assumed that a host of normal diseases could be caused by spirits, without any of the signs that we normally associate with demon-possession. Babylonian and Assyrian texts contain sophisticated lists of symptoms, causes and tested treatments, addressing both the bodily, psychological and spiritual wellbeing of their patients until about the third century CE.

Like Donald Capps, Stevan Davies believes that conversion disorders may stand behind Jesus' healings, but he considers the anthropological dimension in his 1995 *Jesus the Healer: Possession, Trance and the Origins of Christianity*. Davies makes the observation that Pneumatology was 'an explanatory paradigm for altered states of consciousness' and Christology often for Pneumatology. 'Psychology can help us understand those states' and 'Anthropology can provide explanations for the social relationships among persons who experience' these states. He concludes that 'the ability of minds to experience dissociation' is the key to understanding a 'comprehensive causal system whereby reported New Testament events hold together and lead from one to the other, from Jesus' baptism to healing, to exorcism, to group formation, ..., to Pentecost' and to the New Testament texts. He argues that Jesus believed he received John's prophetic spirit at baptism. He does not see Jesus as a trained 'shaman' (Craffert's term), but as a 'medium' selected because of his spontaneous spirit-possession experience. A medium heals 'primarily through the ASC of possession'. Davies proposes 'that Jesus presented himself as one whose alter-persona was the spirit of God'. 'The spirit of God alleviated conversion disorders by forgiveness and the spirit of God alleviated radical negative dissociation by casting out demons'. He argues that his speech induced altered states of consciousness, both within himself as well as with his followers.

I greatly benefited from the ideas in Davies's book. It is in the details, however, that I am left with questions. If all prophets and also John the Baptist were thought to have been bearers of the Holy Spirit, why then was only Jesus' Spirit equated to the Holy Spirit? Why was no one healed by the Spirit of God in John the Baptist? If his followers experienced altered states of consciousness during Jesus' ministry, why then did they remember the days after the crucifixion as the period in which the spiritual experiences originated? In fact, we do see instances in the Gospels in which the evil spirit takes control of the 'patients'. But we never read that the Holy Spirit induces altered states of consciousness, trance or speaking in tongues within Jesus' 'patients'.

In a 2002 monograph, *The Jewish Context of Jesus' Miracles*, Eric Eve makes the case that the Gospel stories about Jesus' healings, exorcisms and nature miracles are not out of step with other Jewish miracle stories, except for the role of Jesus as a miracle-worker. He uses Werner Kahl's (1994) distinction between *bearers*, *petitioners* and *mediators* of numinous power. Consistently, in Jewish miracles, Moses, Elijah and other human figures are portrayed as petitioners or mediators, whereas God is the bearer of numinous power. In the Gospel narratives, however, the spirit-endowed Jesus is quite consistently described as a bearer of numinous power. Whether this goes back to Jesus or not, his earliest followers saw him differently from the way Davies sees him. In other words, we cannot simply use general anthropological and Jewish-cultural categories to understand the unique impact Jesus had on his followers. Something more is going on than standard psychology and anthropology.

The Eschatological Dimension

Craig Evans (2009) places the exorcisms and healings performed by Jesus in the context of contemporary Jewish expectations of the kingly rule of God. He suggests that the *Testament of Levi* 18.11b-12 can be compared to Mk 3.27: 'The Spirit of holiness shall be upon him. And Beliar shall be bound by him, and he shall grant authority to his children to trample over the wicked spirits.' A text close to the story about the temptation of Jesus is the *Testament of Naphtali* 8.4: 'The devil will flee from you, wild animals will be afraid of you; and the Lord will love you and the angels will stand by you.' Furthermore, Evans sees similarities between Dan. 7.22 ('the time has arrived') and the *targum* of Isa. 40.9 and 52.7 ('the kingdom of your God is revealed') and the rallying cry of John and Jesus, 'The time is fulfilled, the kingdom of God has come!' Many scholars regard the saying in Mt. 12.28/ Lk. 11.20 as authentic (the Jesus Seminar rates it as 'probably Jesus'), in which Jesus claims that he (as the bearer of numinous power) exorcises through the finger of God, or Holy Spirit. Evans points to the expression 'finger of God' in the mouth of Pharaoh's magicians in the Exodus story (8.15). In this new exodus, Jesus is leading the children out of the kingdom of Satan. As in the *Testament of Zebulon* 9.8: 'the Lord himself will arise over you, the light of righteousness, with healing and compassion in his wings. He himself will ransom every captive of the sons of men from Beliar, and every spirit of error will be trampled down.' He also points to the *Testament of Moses*, dated to circa 30 CE: 'And then his kingdom will appear in his whole creation. And then the Devil will have an end, and sorro[w] will be led away with him.' As part of his mission, Jesus sends out his followers to expel the evil spirits and heal the sick (Mk 6.7-13 and Mt. 10.7-8/Lk. 9.1-2). Evans notes that some of Jesus' healings are similar to his exorcisms: the fever is rebuked in Lk. 4.39 and the crippled woman in Lk. 13.10-17 was 'bound by Satan'.

Although we cannot be certain about the exact eschatological expectations of Jesus and his contemporaries, we did see in Chapter 8 above that Jesus and his disciples will have shared John's eschatological convictions and prophetic understanding of texts like Isaiah and Malachi. Therefore, it is not impossible that the understanding that Lk. 4.18 and 11.20 places on the lips of Jesus somehow does reflect Jesus' own understanding of his healings in the light of Isa. 61. As Graham Twelftree (1999, 346–8) puts it:

> ... there was a problem of accounting for Jesus' self-consciousness in view of the great variety of Messianic expectations and for miracles not generally being expected of Messiahs. I suggested that the answer is probably to be found in the coincidence of two factors for Jesus: on the one hand, Jesus was conscious of being empowered by God's Spirit (cf. e.g. Mt. 12.28/Lk. 11.20); on the other hand, he appears to have been aware that his miraculous activities had echoes in some of the Isaianic expectations of the Messianic age.

A Combination of Psychology, Anthropology and Eschatology

We do not need to assume years of psychotherapy or ritually induced trance to explain Jesus' healings. The most powerful element in the healing of people with disabling anxieties was the fact that some people ascribed their illnesses to the work of the devil, and were convinced that the evil spirits would flee in the face of God's kingly rule as proclaimed by Jesus. The charisma of Jesus, as one who proclaimed God's forgiveness and fatherly care, and who spoke authoritatively against their illness or evil spirit, may have given many the impulse needed to overcome their psychosomatic illness. It is important to note that the healings are only reported after John was arrested and Jesus decided to continue his mission. I think it is very plausible that the first persons to be healed were healed rather coincidentally in response to Jesus' actions. We can easily imagine that Jesus would address a man in the synagogue who interrupted his teaching with 'possessed' language (Mk 1.22), or that he would sit and pray with Peter's mother-in-law as she was unwell with fever (Mk 1.31). Perhaps Mk 1.32-7 catches something of the initial surprise among Jesus' friends and townsmen, as well as the effect on Jesus, who is described as leaving the house in the middle of the night without telling anyone, in order to seek God's will in what he had just experienced.

Here, too, we may have an instance of learned behaviour, both on the side of Jesus as well as on that of the sufferers, which may have led to a self-reinforcing process. Because Jesus proclaimed God's kingly rule, people associated the healings with Jesus' role in God's eschatological plan. Thus more people came, now with a firmer expectation to be healed. Likewise, the experience may have enhanced Jesus' own experience of God's presence in him. He may have started to speak with more authority and to address the demons in people directly. He placed himself in God's fatherly presence and presented a loving God to the patient, because he believed that the Spirit of God worked and spoke through him. This probably made some of the followers of John, including Jesus himself, wonder what his role was in God's plan.

Texts such as Isa. 35 may well have been part of the eschatological expectations of John's movement: 'the desert shall rejoice' (35.1). 'Here is your God. He will come with vengeance ... He will come and save you' (35.4). 'The eyes of the blind shall be opened, and the ears of the deaf unstopped; then the lame shall leap like a deer, and the tongue of the speechless sing for joy' (35.5-6). 'And the ransomed of the Lord shall return, and come to Zion with singing; ... they shall obtain joy and gladness' (35.10). When such healings actually happened through Jesus' own hands and words, a text such as Isa. 61 may well have influenced Jesus' understanding. The healings confirmed that it was God's plan that he should proclaim the kingdom, and that it was God's Spirit that guided him and gave him the powers to release people from Satan's bonds (61.1). They also changed his understanding with regard to the phase of God's eschatological plan that he was in, as the year of the Lord's favour and vengeance had now come (61.2). The passage in Isaiah goes on beyond the quotation in Lk. 4. Whereas John had lived an ascetic lifestyle in expectation of and preparation for the coming reign of God, Jesus must now give the broken-hearted people 'a garland instead of ashes, the oil of gladness instead of mourning' (61.3). This would give a plausible and efficient explanation for the controversy with John in Lk. 7.

We do not need to assume that the healings immediately led Jesus to a detailed eschatological scenario with respect to his own role. But within the eschatological context of John's movement the healings may well have provided the impulse for Jesus to start seeing his own ministry as part of a larger divine plan. Furthermore, as Jesus chose the Twelve to continue his preaching and healing activities, they needed to receive his spirit, something that they experienced after his death. At the same time, his followers saw that the healings authenticated Jesus' words as the words of the Holy Spirit. Herein lies perhaps the origin of the equation of Jesus' Spirit with the Spirit of God, rather than the idea that Jesus was possessed by God's spirit. Because Jesus did *not* display signs of trance or ecstasy but spoke in his own consciousness, some of his closest followers retrospectively started to see God's Spirit as Jesus' own spirit. This was decidedly different in the spiritual experiences of his followers after Easter. They experienced the spiritual *charismata* in a way that resembles possession by an outside spirit, leading to visions, prophecies and speaking in tongues. Many of them felt overpowered by Jesus' spirit, again suggesting that Jesus' own consciousness had been identical to God's Holy Spirit. None of these experiences are reported about the followers of Jesus prior to his crucifixion. In retrospect, then, it may have seemed to them that he needed to give up his life in order to release the Holy Spirit to his followers. Or, as Paul put it in 1 Cor. 15.42-6:

> So it is with the resurrection of the dead:
> It is sown in perishability, but raised in imperishability.
> It is sown in shame, but raised in glory.
> It is sown in weakness, but raised in power.

It is sown a soul-body, but raised a spiritual body.

...

The first man, Adam, became a living soul, the last Adam a life-giving spirit.

Conclusion

Anthropology or anthropological psychology is an essential tool in theorizing about the spiritual experiences of Jesus and his early followers, which seem so far removed from modern culture. But as anthropology focuses on existing cultural patterns, it falls short in explaining the religious innovations of both Jesus and his early followers. It is in the combination with Jewish eschatology that a plausible and efficient theory emerges that can explain the impact of Jesus on the post-Easter spiritual experiences of his followers.

Chapter 10

COPING WITH DEATH

Some of the aspects of the historical Jesus and his earliest followers are undisputed, such as the fact that they were religious people who had to cope with the death of some of their leaders. It seems that John the Baptist, Jesus, Stephen, James, James the brother of Jesus, Peter and Paul were lynched or executed in a period of about three decades, while trying to obey God.

How do religious people cope with loss under such circumstances? How does it influence feelings of security or insecurity for the survivors? How do they see God's role? Do they maintain faith in God's providence and care? Such questions are the subject of the psychology of religion, and in particular the psychology of religious coping. Kenneth Pargament summarizes and analyses a large number of empirical studies in his 1997 *The Psychology of Religion and Coping: Theory, Research, Practice* (an update of the field is given in Pargament, Ano and Wachholtz 2005).

'In Accordance with the Scriptures'

The starting point for this chapter is 1 Cor. 15.3, where Paul discusses the 'tradition' of the earliest followers of Jesus, which he in turn received and passed on to the Corinthians:

> For among the first things I handed on to you is what I in turn had received:
>
> 'Christ died for our sins
> - in accordance with the scriptures.
>
> He was buried and he was raised on the third day
> - in accordance with the scriptures. ...'

This tradition apparently goes back to Jesus' first followers, including the Twelve and his brother James (15.5-7). It shows us the outcome of their coping process: Jesus' death was both meaningful and part of God's plan. It also shows us something of the process of coping: the followers of Jesus turned to God and the 'scriptures' to come to terms with Jesus' death. Anthony Thiselton (2000) emphasizes the plural of the word 'scriptures' and refers to texts such as Isa. 53, Psalm 22, Deut. 18 and Lam. 1. The death of God's servant is not a single isolated prophecy that was fulfilled, but, literally, a crucial step in God's master plan. Paul makes the same point in Rom. 4.25 and 2 Cor. 5.21. The sinless Jesus was 'made sin' in order to make his followers justified. Paul contrasts this with the story of Adam's fall in Rom. 5.18-19. Having said that, some specific elements are to be found only in Isa. 53, which in a way continues the songs of the servant who is the bearer of God's Spirit (Isa. 61.1 and 42.1). The righteous servant suffers, dies and is buried to make his sinful people righteous, in accordance with God's will. But having given his life as a sin-offering, he shall see the light and his days will be prolonged.

Of course, it can be argued that Jesus' followers came to this conclusion because of the resurrection experiences. But such experiences only testify to Jesus being alive and vindicated by God. They do not make his death part of God's plan and beneficial for his followers. In this chapter, therefore, I wish to focus solely on coping with the death of the leader and ask the question whether the way that Jesus coped with the death of John the Baptist may have had an impact on the way that his followers attached meaning to his death.

The Psychology of Religion and Coping

Kenneth Pargament (1997, 90 and 32) defines coping as 'a search for significance in times of stress' and religion as 'a search for significance in ways related to the sacred'. Significance is searched for by certain means and to certain ends. Education, for instance, can be a means to attain a meaningful career. Pargament argues that all people seek significance and construct events in terms of their significance. In coping with stressful events, they translate their existing 'orienting system' (including their religion) into specific methods of coping that are compelling to them personally in the context of their culture. In coping, they seek significance through the mechanisms of conservation or transformation. If in a stressful situation a 'significant object' (like health, status, self-esteem, family or faith) is at risk, 'the first response is to try to hold on to it' (108). If that is not possible, either the means or the ends will have to change, or both. This is illustrated as follows (111):

	Conversation of Ends	Transformation of Ends
Conversation of Means	**Preservation**	**Re-Valuation**
Transformation of Means	**Reconstruction**	**Re-Creation**

Four methods of coping.

Religious Coping

In religious coping, people can try to *Preserve* significance through the means that they are familiar with. They can persevere in their religious way of life despite external pressures. They can intensify their religious commitment and enforce or create physical or psychological boundaries between the outside world and their own religious beliefs or community. They can seek spiritual support in devotional activities, or personal support through interacting with fellow believers.

People can also try to conserve the ends of their religious orientation through different means, or *Reconstruction*. This includes penitence or purification, switching to a new religious group or to a different faith or religious reframing. Pargament discusses in some more detail the religious reframing of, firstly, the event, secondly, the individual and, thirdly, the sacred. With regard to reframing an event, Pargament remarks (223):

> A religious reframing of the event says that what seems to be so terrible is not in fact so terrible. Though the event may hurt or threaten, there is another and more important dimension to it. Beneath the surface of the situation, we can find God working his will; we can find a spiritual companion who makes the trauma more manageable; and we can find opportunities and challenges for spiritual growth. By redefining the negative situation more positively, the relationship between God, oneself, and the world remains in balance; the benevolence of the divine, the fairness of the world and the basic worth and security of the individual can be conserved.

At the expense of their own worth, people can also reconstruct significance through reframing the person. God did not abandon his people, but they have turned their backs on him. When pure evil seems to occur, it is the limited human ability to understand that conceals its deeper purpose. When a prayer for healing fails to result in health, it is not God who is powerless or absent, but the human lack of faith or the sins of the patient prevent healing. In turn, the sufferer can be stimulated to try even harder to please God. As a result, the depreciation of self-worth can be more than compensated for with feelings of grace when, despite human shortcomings, God does bestow some kind of blessing, comfort or experience. Thirdly, people can reconstruct significance through reframing the sacred. God has indeed turned angry towards his people, he may – after all – have limited powers, or Satan may be found to be more powerful than previously thought.

Reframing leads to a new orientation system (231–2):

> It is important to note that once a reconstruction occurs, the new orienting system becomes the filter for viewing and dealing with life events. The reframed event, person, or God becomes a part of the individual's new worldview; experiences that come after are now *framed* rather than *reframed* through this changed perspective.

> ... once a reconstruction takes place, the focus shifts from rebuilding the orienting system to sustaining it. It is a shift from reconstruction to preservation.

... Just as the failed effort to preserve significance is often followed by reconstruction, the reconstructive effort is often followed by the attempt to preserve the new path.

People can also cope through a transformation of ends. This may be limited to a *Re-Valuation* within the existing religious framework. Even though some life events are so disruptive that they can 'throw an entire set of values in disarray', religion can often assist the sufferer in finding a new set of priorities or goals to pursue. People seek God's will to find new meaning in life, as they go from adolescence to adulthood, when they marry or divorce, when they expect their first child, or when they experience a burn-out. Religions offer rites of passage that can help the believer go through such a transition. Often a revaluation will be followed by a reconstruction to align the new ends with the means. 'Having discovered a new purpose in living, life must be reshaped to fit with the new mission' (239).

Finally, the most extreme form of coping is radical change of both means and ends through which significance is *Re-Created*. Pargament discusses two forms: conversion and forgiveness. In a retrospective study, two-thirds of young converts to a charismatic Christian denomination reported personal problems three to five years before their conversion, as opposed to one-fifth of the control group. They are also more likely to report a major life event prior to their conversion, or chronic feelings of depression, loneliness and unsatisfactory parental relationships. For a conversion to occur, usual forms of coping must have been found wanting, underscoring both the limits of one's power and the inadequacy of that person's often self-centred ends. Conversion is then an act of letting go and allowing the sacred to be incorporated into the identity of the individual (253):

'God entered my life and I became a new person.' ... Through the conversion experience, the individual has gone beyond exclusive self-preoccupation to an identification with something larger than the self, the sacred.

Pargament notes that there may be some bias in the self-reporting of converts who may want to stress the difference in their lives pre- and post-conversion, but for those who are in such a situation, conversion may be a radical coping strategy. He also notes that conversion is not only towards a specific spiritual power, but also towards a specific religious group. Sometimes it may take a universal form, beyond identification with specific existing religions (256):

The spiritual encounters of great figures from Moses and Muhammad, to the Buddha and Joseph Smith were followed not by lives of religious retreat and isolation, but by a return to the world to serve others and share their message of revelation.

... Universal converts hope to re-create not only the self in the image of God but the larger social whole. Social change, for them, becomes a form of religious expression and a mark of personal identity. Thus, we can find religious prophets speaking out against injustice, Mahatma Ghandi and Martin Luther King Jr. promoting nonviolent resistance to social and political oppression.

The second example is religious forgiving as an act of Re-Creation. This is the case when people come from a situation in which anger, fear, resentment and hatred are mechanisms to cope with past mistreatment. Such coping mechanism can be used to try to conserve what is left of significance, to overcome paralysis and to avoid future mistreatment. These mechanisms also explain why life is not any better and communicate the person's plight to others. But the same mechanisms also condemn the sufferer to the past and 'beneath the surface of resentment and hatred are reminders of the individual's great shame' (261). Religion can lend significance to forgiveness and provide a set of models to facilitate the process. Through forgiveness the individual can act in the image of God and restore community. In religious narratives the believer finds ways to express anger, to decide how to let go, to accept the humanity of the offender, and to receive strength in the act of forgiving.

A Doomsday Cult

Pargament (150–3) gives an interesting example of a 'Doomsday Cult', a group of people expecting to survive the imminent destruction of the world with the help of 'Guardians' from outer space. When the date had passed without anything happening, many group members remained strongly committed. While this may seem utterly irrational on first sight, it becomes more understandable from the perspectives of these members. Many had joined the cult after rather problematic life histories in which more traditional coping methods had been of little help. The involvement with the cult was already a form of finding some kind of significance: 'hope for the future, feelings of worth and importance, a sense of meaning in life, or feelings of spiritual connectedness.' Many had given up work and family, sold their meagre possessions, and moved house in order to be ready for the spaceship arriving at the predicted date. When the spaceship did not arrive, their entire social and religious capital was invested in the group, and there were few other methods of coping available other than through their religious group. They did not have to cope with the fact that the earth was *not* destroyed, but with the associated threatening loss of the significance they had found in the group. In order to conserve significance, the group turned to reframing: they had misinterpreted the plan or the destruction had been postponed, or averted because of the group's faithful activities. They also engaged in proselytizing: 'if more and more people can be persuaded that the system of beliefs is correct, then clearly it must, after all, be correct.'

Three Styles of Religious Coping

Research shows that many people turn to religion in coping with adversity, depending on factors like the nature of the situation, whether it came by surprise, the cultural and social context, the (non-)availability of other means of coping, and people's personal faith. As Pargament puts it (147):

> To the extent that religion becomes a larger and more integrated part of the orienting system, it takes on a greater role in coping. To the extent that religion becomes less prominent in the orienting system, more disconnected from other resources, and less relevant to the range of life experiences, it recedes in importance in coping.

Pargament discerns three types of religious orientations, each with its own combination of means to and ends of significance (63):

Religious orientation			
	Intrinsic	*Extrinsic*	*Quest*
Means	Highly embedded in life Guide for living Convincing	Peripheral Lightly held Passively accepted Compartmentalized Sporadic	Active struggle Open to question Flexible Complex Differentiated
Ends	Spiritual Unification Compassion Unselfish	Safety Comfort Status Sociability Self-justification Self-gain at other's expense	Meaning Truth Self-development Compassion

Related to these religious orientations are three styles of religious coping (181): self-direction, deferring and collaboration:

- People with a high self-esteem and a higher sense of personal control, but with a low score on religiousness, often opt for self-direction, even if they regularly attend church or synagogue. In other words, they try to solve their own problems. Their religious orientation can often be characterized as 'Quest'.
- People with a lower sense of personal control and a high level of extrinsic religiousness tend to defer their problem to God. A deferring style is correlated with doctrinal orthodoxy and extrinsic religiousness.
- Finally, people with a greater self-esteem and sense of personal control, combined with a high level of intrinsic religiousness and a more relational form of religion, tend to choose a collaborative approach in coping. They communicate with God, look for understanding and guidance, and suggest approaches in prayer.

Mystical Experiences under Stress

People can have mystical experiences in periods without stress, and especially intrinsically religious people have ways and beliefs that facilitate the regular experience of God, for example through prayer, meditation, fasting, music, worship, and so on. Stressful situations do not necessarily lead to mystical experiences, as there is a host of coping strategies available. But under some conditions stressful situations are likely to lead to mystical experiences (155):

> The sense of the holy comes to the foreground for most people when they are disturbed, when issues of greatest significance are confronted and challenged in ways that push people beyond their personal and social resources. Beyond this threshold religious approaches to problems become particularly compelling to many people.

Pargament discusses the research of Ralph Hood (1977, 1978), who 'proposed that mystical religious experiences … are triggered by an incongruity between the individual and the situation'. This does not only happen in situations of unanticipated stress, but also 'when a stressful situation is anticipated and, instead, an unstressful one is encountered'. Hood points to an experiment in which high school students were asked to spend a solitary night in the woods. On some nights the weather was beautiful, on others it was bad. Mystical experiences were reported most often by those who had to cope with unexpected bad weather, and by those who anticipated a stressful night but who instead encountered lovely weather conditions.

Jesus' Coping

In the Gospel of Mark, there are several so-called 'passion predictions' that are remarkably similar to the passage from 1 Cor. 15.3 quoted at the start of this chapter. They are found in Mk 8.31, 9.12, 9.30-1 and 10.33-4, spoken after the death of John and before Jesus' arrival in Jerusalem: the Son of Man will suffer, be killed and rise again after three days.

Historical-critical scholars have good reason to see here a retrospective of the early church and a literary theme of Mark. Mark emphasizes the lack of understanding of the disciples to a point where it becomes illogical: if Jesus had foretold to them that clearly what would happen in Jerusalem, then why did not one of them expect it to happen on Easter morning, and why – in Luke – did they initially not believe the women? Having said that, it is also unlikely that Jesus would not have spoken with his friends about the risks of dying at the hands of the authorities. They would have been extremely naïve if they had not reckoned with the possibility that what had happened to John could also happen to Jesus. And it would be no exaggeration, for in the end, Jesus did die at the hands of the authorities. This type of reasoning does not require us to believe that Jesus was certain of his death. Just like Martin Luther King Jr (Ling 2002, 283), one does not have to receive a revelation in order to proceed in the face of a threatening death. But it does allow us to ask the question whether the way in which Jesus coped with John's death may have contributed to the conviction of his earliest followers that Jesus' death was beneficial and in accordance with God's will.

Jesus and Religious Coping

Jesus was no stranger to suffering and loss. In Chapter 7, I discuss the probable loss of his father and some of his siblings in the light of Attachment Theory. I also argue that Jesus was securely attached to God and turned to him in times of need. In Chapter 8, I argue that Jesus, as a disciple of John, shared a belief in John's message about God's rule and John's interaction with Jewish Scriptures. After John's arrest by Herod, Jesus continued his mission, which would not have been without risks. While Jesus celebrated the reign of God, he encountered rejection by John, by his mother and brothers, and by the elders of his synagogue.

If Jesus was a securely attached and intrinsic religious person with a high self-esteem, he would fit Pargament's third category and would most likely have used a collaborative approach to make sense of his experience of rejection, the violent death of his mentor John the Baptist, and the danger to his own life. The Gospel narratives portray him as one who would regularly seek lonely places to spend time in prayer. The question now is whether he conserved the ends and means of significance or whether these were somehow transformed in these crucial months.

Coping with John's Arrest and Rejection of Jesus' Lifestyle

The ideas that Jesus, as a disciple of John, may have shared with John's movement include the following (see Chapter 8): John expected God's intervention and reign; he urged people to convert to live in accordance with God's will, to be purified in anticipation of that kingdom, and believed that God, or his agent, would come to purify with spirit and fire.

According to Mk 1.14, Jesus started his ministry after John's arrest. To what extent this is due to Mark's composition is difficult to say, but it is probably correct that Jesus' ministry gained in intensity and importance after John's arrest. At this point in time, Jesus uses his preaching (the means) to urge the people to convert so that the day of God would come as a blessing (the end). In Chapter 9, I suggest that his view of the mission was somewhat changed in the light of the healings that occurred, leading Jesus to adopt the idea that the Kingdom had in part already come when evil spirits fled before the Holy Spirit in Jesus. His task shifted to helping people to enter that kingdom and celebrate it. This is a form of Re-Valuation of Ends. It was followed by a Reconstruction of Means, as predicted by Pargament. For this insight allowed Jesus to depart from John's ascetic lifestyle and celebrate the year of God's favour (Isa. 61.2).

When people disagreed with his lifestyle (Lk. 5.33), including John himself or some of his other followers (Lk. 7.19), Jesus had to cope with rejection. They did not join him in celebration of God's rule, they stayed out of the kingdom (see also the parable of the banquet and the marriage feast). In the continuation of the narrative in Lk. 7, Jesus expresses his anger with John and the 'generation' as a whole (7.28-35, NRSV):

> I tell you, among those born of women no one is greater than John, yet the least in the kingdom of God, is greater than he.
> ...
> To what then will I compare the people of this generation, and what are they like? They are like children sitting in the marketplace and calling to one another,
> 'We played the flute for you, and you did not dance,
> we wailed for you, and you did not weep.'
>
> For John the Baptist has come eating no bread and drinking no wine, and you say, 'He has a demon';
> the Son of Man has come eating and drinking, and you say, 'Look a glutton and a drunkard, a friend of tax collectors and sinners!'

I believe that another Q passage may confirm this interpretation (Lk. 16.16/ Mt. 11.12):

> The Law and the Prophets [are] until John; from then on the good news of God's reign is proclaimed [*Matthew:* From the days of John the Baptist until now, the Kingdom of the Heavens breaks through with force], and everybody is forcibly against it.

Coping with John's Death

John did not join Jesus' celebration of God's reign and died before the day of God's judgement came. When he was arrested, John may still have been waiting for God's intervention in his lifetime (Lk. 7.19). If Jesus shared this hope, the death of John must have been a stressor, as it challenged his expectation of God. Furthermore, the Gospel narrative of John's death because of a rash promise to a young girl (Mk 6.14-28) underscores the pointlessness of his death. Whether the gossips were correct is immaterial; John's followers had to cope with the embarrassingly useless death of their leader. In Mt. 14.13, the narrator perceptively links the news of John's death to Jesus' desire to withdraw from the crowds and go to a deserted place to be on his own and pray (14.23).

Perhaps it is possible to see in the contradicting statements with regard to John and Elijah something of a reframing of the event. According to Jn 1.19, John the Baptist explicitly denied the role of Elijah. But many did expect an Elijah figure 'before the great and terrible day of the LORD comes' (Mal. 4.5). This traditional expectation is also the subject of Mk 9.11-13 (NRSV):

Then they asked him, 'Why do the scribes say that Elijah must come first?'
He said to them, 'Elijah is indeed coming first to restore all things. How then is it
written about the Son of Man, that he is to go through many sufferings and be treated
with contempt? But I tell you that Elijah has come, and they did to him whatever they
pleased, as it is written about him.'

This text is often attributed to the early church, just like the other passion
predictions. But this requires an explanation. As Adela Yarbro Collins (2007)
comments, the idea of Elijah as the forerunner of the Messiah is not a Jewish
idea but a Christian one. Many Jews expected him to come back to inaugurate
the general resurrection of the dead. Why would the early followers invent the
idea that John fulfilled the role of Elijah if his life did not match the prophecy?
It would be more logical if the belief that John fulfilled an Elijah-role preceded
his death (just like Jesus could be seen by some to be an Elijah-like figure
in Mk 6.15). In John's case, there are even signals that he saw himself in
that light: he clothed himself like Elijah, lived by desert streams and led a
restoration movement.

Confronted with John's death, those followers who had seen him fulfilling
the role of Elijah had to reframe their religious orienting system. Some of them
concluded they had misinterpreted God's plan with John: he was not Elijah
and someone else would fulfil that role. Post-Easter Christians reframed the
story differently: Elijah would not come to restore all things and inaugurate
the general resurrection on the day of the Lord, but rather prepare the way
for the Lord and baptize/anoint Jesus as the Messiah (cf. 1 Kgs 19.15-16). But
how did Jesus reframe his understanding of God's plan with John?

If we disregard the Messianic elements in Mk 9.11-13, we are left with
a final sentence that is difficult to explain: 'Elijah has come, and they did
whatever they pleased, *as it is written about him*.' But nowhere is it written
that Elijah would be 'dealt with as they pleased'. The idea is known, however,
from early Christian reflection on the deaths of Jesus (Justin Martyr, *Dialogue*
136) and James (Eusebius/Hegesippus) on the basis of a Greek text of Isa.
3.10: 'Let us take away the righteous man, for he is troublesome to us.' The
suffering of the righteous man at the hands of the powerful is a theme in the
righteous servant sections in Isaiah. If the same were to be applied to the
prediction about Elijah in Mal. 4.5-6, the following scenario unfolds: John
did come in the role of Elijah to 'turn the hearts of parents to their children
and the hearts of children to their parents, so that I will not come and strike
the land with a curse'. But many did not listen. They killed John, so that the
threat of the curse on the land was not averted.

I am not claiming that the above passage in Mark necessarily goes back to
Jesus. But I do argue that Jesus and his friends had to reframe the event of
John's death or the divine plan behind it. As parallels show, the idea of the
suffering servant of God in Isaiah lends itself to such reframing. As Isaiah was
already part of the group's religious orientation system, it is likely that the
concept of the suffering servant was readily available to Jesus.

Coping with the Threats to Jesus' Own Life

The death of John also demonstrated the risks to the life of the group members and to Jesus in particular. In Q 10.3 he tells his envoys, 'I send you like sheep in the midst of wolves'. The idea that prophets are persecuted and killed is expressed in Q 6.22-3 and Q 11.47. It is expanded into a scheme in Q 11.49-51. Wisdom keeps sending the people prophets and sages. Some of them are killed so that the blood of all the prophets will be required from 'this generation'. In Q 13.34-5 Jesus laments Jerusalem 'who kills the prophets and stones those sent to her'. Some have seen in his journey to Syria (Mk 7.24), the Decapolis (7.31), and the Golan (Bethsaida in 8.22 and Caesarea Philippi in 8.27) a flight out of Herod's territory and into relative anonymity. Edersheim (1886, 2.56) reads Jesus' appeal to the story of David and Abjathar as based on the similarity between David's flight from Saul and Jesus' flight from Herod, which he places at the time of Jesus' journey to Syria. Such a flight is certainly not the theme of Mark's narrative and would need to be read in(to) the sources behind the Gospel. On the other hand, however, given the circumstances it would have been wise for Jesus to avoid the larger cities and villages, and to keep on moving or find a place outside Herod's reach. In Q 9.58 Jesus says, 'Foxes have holes, and birds of the sky have nests; but the son of man does not have anywhere he can lay his head.' In Lk. 13.31 he is warned, 'Get away from here, for Herod wants to kill you.'

We do not have to assume that all such sayings were reflections of the early church on the death of Jesus. It is highly likely that such feelings were present in the period after John's death. The question, then, is how did Jesus cope with such a constant threat to both his life and his belief system? I will look at this question in two ways. First, I will investigate whether the narrative turning point of Jesus' ministry can be read as a coping experience. Second, I will look at the way in which the theme of the persecuted prophets may have led to the idea that Jesus was God's final envoy.

In Mark, and even more in Luke, the transfiguration story seems to function as a turning point in the narrative. Having reached the northernmost limits of his journeys on a mountain in Caesarea Philippi, a mystical experience sets Jesus and his friends back on the road south, to Jerusalem. In Mark, the transfiguration stands at the same 'level' as the baptism story at the beginning and the crucifixion at the end (Marcus 2009, 635). The story of the otherworldly encounter with Moses and Elijah is set between the question and answer of the roles and suffering of Jesus and John in God's plan: 'Who do you say that I am?' Luke enforces the idea of a turning point: he adds that Moses and Elijah came to speak with Jesus about his 'exodus' that he would accomplish in Jerusalem. Following the episode, in Lk. 9.51, the journey towards the end is begun with the words: 'when the days were being fulfilled for his assumption, he hardened his face to go forward to Jerusalem.'

I do not claim that these narratives describe history; they were written and shaped retrospectively (but note that Wilkins 2009 argues for the historicity of Peter's declaration of Jesus' identity). But I am tempted to think that this episode retains traces of Jesus' struggle. Jesus is coping through interaction with his friends, the traditions of his people and God. It is not impossible that within such a period of stress, Jesus – alone or with his best friends – had a mystical experience; either because they employed the known religious means to seek God's presence, and/or because they were surprised by conditions of grace in a particularly stressful period (which is a way of reading the transfiguration story). At some point in time, Jesus accepted the threat to his life, and went to Jerusalem. The difference with John is clear: before his arrest, John had no reason to expect he would die a violent death; but Jesus had to resume his mission accepting the possibility that it would lead to his death. From a coping perspective, the experience that may lie behind the transfiguration story must have been extraordinary to produce this result. I think that Pargament would call this a conversion. Not in the sense that Jesus changed religion, but in the sense that he let go of fear and anger and embraced his mission towards Jerusalem. This would most likely have been a Re-Creation of Significance, in which both the ends and the means to attain significance are changed.

Through this process, Jesus may have come to understand his own role as a 'final envoy' (I borrow the term from M. De Jonge 1998) who, at the risk of losing his life, would call his people one last time to return to God. The scenario that he would suffer and die was simply the application prospectively rather than retrospectively of Isaiah's suffering servant. Note, for example, how the scenario in Q 11.49-51 is extended with a final envoy in the parable of the tenants (Mk 12.1-8 and parallels, Thomas 65.1-7). After a number of servants (prophets such as John the Baptist), the owner of the vineyard (God in Isa. 5.1-7) sends his son in the hope that his tenants will listen to the son. But when he too is killed, the owner will bring judgement on the tenants. Scholars have found difficulty in accepting the idea that Jesus would think of himself as the 'son' of God. But we do not have to assume that Jesus spoke of a pre-existing only-begotten Son of God. We have already seen that Jesus occupies a different place from that occupied by the prophets before him. They proclaimed the coming of God's reign, but Jesus' healings inaugurated it. He could celebrate God's presence as a son and as the bearer of God's Holy Spirit.

But if Jesus accepted the risk that his loving father would let him die, how then did he preserve the idea of God's benevolence towards him? Again Isaiah's suffering servant holds the key. The righteous servant in Isa. 53 did not suffer because God had turned against him, but because he took upon himself the suffering and the sins of his people. His death would be the ultimate sin-offering that would purify many. And as he would give his life, God would grant him light and longevity in the general resurrection of the dead.

The Impact on Jesus' Earliest Followers

The impact on Jesus' followers may have been threefold. First the confusion: if Jesus was struggling to cope with John's death and the risks to his own life, he could not present his friends with a complete and unchanging eschatological scenario. Rather he should be seen as trying different kinds of understanding before finally embracing his recreated mission. And even then, he would have been open to various possibilities: the people of Jerusalem might respond to his call and receive God's blessing, or they might turn against him and enter a period of tribulations. This would help to understand why on the one hand there is a significant amount of material in the Gospels in which Jesus prepares his friends for such a trying period without him, and why on the other hand the disciples (or Jesus) do not seem to know beforehand what will happen during that fateful Pesach in Jerusalem.

Second, the process of coping: as Jesus was their leader, his followers may have learnt from him how to cope with the stress of the last part of Jesus' mission, as well as with Jesus' own death and stressful situations after Easter. In such situations they too would seek God's presence, spend the night in prayer, and search the Scriptures (even if only in an oral form). This helps to explain how they could come to understand, for example, the death of Jesus as part of God's plan, or how James, Paul or Peter found the strength to proceed in life-threatening situations. The picture in Acts of his friends and family coming together to fast and pray makes perfect sense in the light of this analysis. The impulse to continue his mission makes sense in the light of what Jesus did after John's arrest and the eventuality for which he may have prepared them. The prayer to receive his Spirit to fulfil that mission is consistent with the central role of the Holy Spirit in Jesus' ministry, the example of Elisha (2 Kgs 2.9), and the theme in Isaiah (44.3, 32.15).

Third, the content of their coping resolution: if Jesus did indeed share the idea of Isaiah's suffering servant with his friends while coping with John's death and his own fears, this explains how the group as a whole could come to the conclusion that Jesus' death was willed by God as an offering for the sins of his people, that he was buried and that he nevertheless lives in God's light (53.9-12).

Conclusion

This chapter demonstrates that we need not assume that Jesus came to his baptism with an eschatological scenario that would lead inevitably to his death, or that Jesus' followers created *ex nihilo* an eschatological scenario to make sense of their leader's unexpected death. Theorizing about Jesus' coping with John's death and the risks to his own life helps us to explain the extraordinary conclusions they reached in the tradition that we find in 1 Cor. 15.3.

Chapter 11

THE ROLE OF CHRIST THE LORD

Throughout the New Testament the name of Jesus is linked with the words *christos* and *kurios* or even substituted by these. The title Christ refers to Jewish expectations regarding an eschatological anointed king or priest. It is so often used for Jesus that it has in fact become his name to his followers as well as to outsiders (Acts 11.26). The title Lord is often used for God himself.

The debate about Jesus' psychology in the nineteenth century was focused to a large extent on the question of whether Jesus saw himself as the Messiah or as divine. Rather than answering that question with 'yes' or 'no', I would want to demonstrate the usefulness of another psychological theory, role theory, in designing a plausible theory about the impact that Jesus may have had on the Christological convictions of some of his earliest followers.

Role Theory

The pioneering work on role theory in the specific context of the psychology of religion is Hjalmar Sundén's *Religionen och Rollerna* (1959, translated into German as *Die Religion und die Rollen*, 1966). He explains his ideas to a larger public under the title *Gott erfahren* (1975, Swedish original 1961). Indeed, religious *experience* in relation to religious traditions and religious learning is the subject of his *Religionspsychologie* (1982, Swedish original 1977). Several scholars have taken his work further, such as Thorvald Källstad, Owe Wikström, Nils Holm and Jan van der Lans (*Journal for the Scientific Study of Religion* 26, 1987). After his death in 1993, his work has found new expression in articles by various scholars under the title *Sundén's Role Theory – an Impetus to Contemporary Psychology of Religion* (ed. Holm and Belzen 1995).

For Sundén, every sensual perception is interpreted through mental processes. Religious tradition is a precondition for interpreting reality in religious terms. Religious traditions contain many narratives and roles that the believer can approach directly (from memory) or indirectly (by listening or reading). The roles include those of various people interacting with God, such as Moses, David, Jesus or Paul. A central concept is role-taking, more specifically, taking the role of God. Just as children can take the role of their parents, in anticipating their parents' reaction to what they are doing (even though the parent is not actually present), so can a believer anticipate God's reactions from the repertoire of traditional narratives available to him or her. People can interpret their own situations in terms of specific stories about these persons. As such they enter into the roles of Abraham or Peter while simultaneously taking up the role of God. This is not at all comparable to the delusion of someone who thinks he is Napoleon or Jesus. In fact, several narratives and roles can be 'active' in a person's interpretation of his or her circumstances. Especially when subsequent developments fit with the way God is anticipated to respond in one or more of these roles, the believer interacts with God. In this way, those who have learned a religious tradition become predisposed to experience God's presence, will and activity in their particular circumstances.

Especially in coping situations, role theory can help to explain not only how people come to (re)interpret their situation or orienting system (see Chapter 10), but also how they come to 'try' certain responses in order to interact with God. Thus an iterative process can take place in which various traditional roles are taken up in order to understand God's unfolding will. This has been shown in psychobiographical studies of John Wesley (Thorvald Källstad 1974) and John Henry Newman (Donald Capps 2001).

The Coming Messiah and Lord

The oldest New Testament writing is Paul's first letter to Thessaloniki, written in 50 or 51 CE. In this letter, Jesus is called 'Lord Jesus Christ' (1.1 and 1.3). Jesus is the Son of God, raised from the dead, who will come from the heavens to deliver his followers from the coming wrath (1.10), when Paul expects to stand before him in his *parousia* 'with all his saints' (2.19, 3.13, 5.23). The word *parousia* (presence or arrival) was also used in Hellenistic Greek as a technical term for the arrival of a ruler or a god, in Judaism for the arrival of God or the Messiah. Upon his arrival he will receive his subjects or servants to meet out punishment and reward. This is clearly the image that Paul is thinking of. For Paul, Jesus is the royal Messiah and Lord who will descend from heaven on the Lord's day when the dead will be brought to life and each will appear before the throne of the Lord. Paul claims that it is Jesus himself who revealed this scenario to his followers (4.13-17):

> We do not want you to be ignorant, brothers and sisters, regarding those who 'sleep', lest you would grieve (for them), as indeed the others do who have no hope. For as we believe that Jesus died and rose again, even so will God bring the ones who have fallen asleep in Jesus with him.

> For this we tell you with a word from the Lord, that we who are alive and who remain until the *parousia* of the Lord, will certainly not precede those who have fallen asleep:

- The Lord himself will descend from heaven upon a command, spoken with the voice of an archangel and God's trumpet, and the deceased in Christ will firstly rise again.
- Then we who are alive and who remain will be caught up together with them in the clouds to meet the Lord in the air. And so we will be forever with the Lord.

Therefore, encourage each other with these words.

In contrast to Rome or Corinth, Thessaloniki around 50 CE is Pauline territory. Paul had recently founded the community. We therefore need to verify from other letters whether the ideas presented here indeed precede Paul as he claims they do.

First, in 1 Cor. 11.23-7, Paul describes the 'tradition' he received regarding the supper of the Lord. There, too, he claims to use the words of the Lord:

For I received from the Lord, what I also passed on to you:

The Lord Jesus, in the night that he was handed over,
took bread and, having said grace, broke it.

And he said:
    'This is my body for you.
    Do this for my remembrance.'

Similarly also the cup after supper, saying:
    'This cup is the new covenant in my blood.
    'Do this, as often as you drink, for my remembrance.'

For as often as you eat this bread and drink the cup,
you declare the death of the Lord until he comes.

So whoever eats the bread or drinks the cup of the Lord unworthily
will be guilty of (abusing) the body and the blood of the Lord.

Paul emphasizes that the death of Jesus is closely linked to his return. The element of remembrance invites comparison with Passover (Exod. 12.14) and the sacrifice of the paschal lamb (explicitly so in 1 Cor. 5.7). Paul reminds the Corinthians of the words of Jesus to stress the importance of the meal so he can call upon all the Corinthian believers to celebrate it in a worthy way. The words themselves seem to be undisputed in Corinth. That this includes the concept of the coming of the Lord is confirmed by Paul's use of the Aramaic *Maranatha*, 'Our Lord, come!', at the end of the letter (16.22). Combined with the use of Peter's Aramaic name *Cephas*, in 1.12, we are left with the impression that the view of Jesus as the coming Lord has roots in the earliest Palestinian movement.

Another point regards Paul's initial opposition to the idea of a crucified Messiah (1 Cor. 1.18, 23), which then became his central message in Corinth (1 f 2.2). For Paul, this was a foolish and scandalous idea. As a 'zealous' Jew, Paul knew that a crucified man was accursed by God (Gal. 3.13, quoting Deut. 21.23). The Gospel of a Messiah who was crucified and raised from the dead is the scandalous faith Paul tried to destroy in the 30s CE (Gal. 1.13 and 23). Only his own experience of the risen Lord near Damascus forced him to let go of his firm convictions (Gal. 1.11-17, Rom. 1.4) and accept the faith of his opponents.

Finally, in his letter to Rome, a city that he had not yet visited with believers who 'were apostles before him' (16.7), Paul feels free to refer to Jesus as a descendant of David and hence a royal Messiah (1.1-4):

> Paul, a servant of Christ Jesus, called to be an envoy, set apart for the good news of God regarding his son, which he announced before through his prophets in the Holy Scriptures:
>
> > The one who has come from the seed of David, with respect to (his) flesh.
> >
> > The one who, by the resurrection of the dead, was powerfully demonstrated to be God's son, with respect to (his) Spirit of holiness:
> >
> > Jesus Christ our Lord!

It seems reasonable, therefore, to assume that there was a pre-Pauline belief that identified Jesus as the royal Messiah as well as the Lord who would descend from heaven on the day of the Lord when the dead would be resurrected, and who would pass judgement and deliver his people. This description in 1 Thessalonians and Romans is not found in this form in any Jewish Scripture, but is a combination of prophecies such as Zech. 9.14 ('the Lord will appear over them, ... the Lord God will sound the trumpet'), Zech. 14.5b ('Then the Lord my God will come, and all the holy ones with him'), Dan. 7.13-14 ('I saw one like a son of man, coming with the clouds of heaven, ... To him was given dominion and glory and kingship'), and Isa. 11.1-2 (about a descendant of David and bearer of the Lord's spirit). All these elements individually fit within the range of Jewish expectations regarding the Messiah, but that does not explain why these early followers of Jesus shared this specific combination of ideas, and why they identified the crucified Jesus as this heavenly Messiah and Lord. In this chapter, I will put forward the theory that (1) the concept of the coming One was already part of the beliefs of Jesus and his friends, (2) other people identified Jesus as the royal Messiah, and (3) Jesus engaged with the various roles that he found in familiar prophecies and narratives during his final journey to Jerusalem, such that his followers, even if only in hindsight, could conclude that he did indeed seem to fit the part.

1. John, Jesus and Their Followers Expected a Coming One

The first reason why Jesus' earliest followers in Rome, Corinth and Thessaloniki (including people who were apostles before Paul) expected their Lord to descend from heaven and judge the living and the resurrected dead, is probably because the belief in a Coming One and a day of judgement was already part of the beliefs of John the Baptist and his followers.

John the Baptist

As discussed in Chapter 8, Robert Webb (1991) demonstrates that the movement of John anticipated the rule of God and the coming of his agent who would purify his people. In anticipation, John provided a purification rite as an alternative to temple rituals, which he probably saw as corrupted and in need of cleansing. In Chapter 10, I argue that John took the role of Elijah in Mal. 4.5, who was generally believed to return before the general resurrection of the dead, and who would call the children of Israel to return to their ancestral covenant with God. If this is correct, then the application of Mal. 3.1 to John the Baptist may not have originated in the early church, but rather in the movement of John himself. Indeed the entire passage (Mal. 3.1-7, NRSV) would then have been part of the beliefs of John's movement:

> See, I am sending my messenger to prepare the way before me, and the Lord whom you seek will suddenly come to his temple. The messenger (angel) of the covenant in whom you delight – indeed, he is coming, says the Lord of hosts. But who can endure the day of his coming, and who can stand when he appears?
> For he is like a refiner's fire and like fuller's soap; he will sit as a refiner and purifier of silver, and he will purify the descendants of Levi and refine them like gold and silver, until they present offerings to the Lord in righteousness. Then the offering of Judah and Jerusalem will be pleasing to the Lord as in the days of old and as in former years.
> Then I will draw near to you for judgment; I will be swift to bear witness against the sorcerers, against the adulterers, against those who swear falsely, against those who oppress the hired workers in their wages, the widow and the orphan, against those who thrust aside the alien, and do not fear me, says the Lord of hosts.
> For I the Lord do not change; therefore you, O children of Jacob, have not perished. Ever since the days of your ancestors you have turned aside from my statutes and have not kept them. Return to, and I will return to you, says the Lord of hosts. But you say, 'How shall we return?'

Jesus

There are several parables in which Jesus speaks about the coming of a king, or master, who will sit with his servants to apportion punishment and reward (e.g. Mt. 25.31-46, Lk. 19.11-17). If it is accepted that Jesus shared the beliefs of the movement he had joined, we do not need to suppose that such teaching originated in the early church, nor that Jesus saw himself as the Coming One, but merely that the early church believed that Jesus referred to himself when he spoke about the Coming One.

There are two passages that particularly resemble Paul's statement in 1 Thess.: Mt. 16.27-8 and Mt. 24.30-1. E.P. Sanders (1993, 181) printed the three passages next to each other to highlight their common elements:

1 Thessalonians 4.15-17	Matthew 24.30-31	Matthew 16.27-28
We who are alive, who are left until the *appearance of the Lord*, will not precede those who have fallen asleep. For *the Lord* himself will *come down* from *heaven* with a command, with the voice of an *archangel*, and *with a trumpet* of God; and the dead in Christ will rise first, then *we who are alive* … at the very same time will be *snatched up* with them in the clouds to greet the Lord in the air.	The sign of the *Son of Man will appear* in heaven, and then all the tribes of earth shall mourn, and they shall see the *Son of Man coming* on clouds of *heaven* with power and great glory. And he will send his *angels with a trumpet* of great voice, and they will *gather* his elect from the four winds, from one side of heaven to the other.	*The Son of Man* is about to come in the glory of his father with his *angels*, and then he will repay to each according to his or her deeds. Truly, I say unto you, there are some of those standing here who *will not taste death*, until they see the Son of Man coming in his kingdom.

The Jesus Seminar voted that both passages in Matthew do not go back to Jesus, as they are prophecies applied retrospectively. Sanders, however, claims (182):

> Scholars who try to 'test' sayings of Jesus for authenticity will see that this tradition passes with flying colours. First, the predicted event did not actually happen; therefore the prophecy is not a fake. … Secondly, the tradition is attested in more than one source.

Again, that does not have to mean that Jesus believed that he himself was the Son of Man who would come on clouds of heaven. Like John, he may simply have expected the Lord (Mal. 3.1), coming with the sound of a trumpet (Zech. 9.14), perhaps in the form of a Son of Man who came with the clouds of heaven to reign on God's behalf (Dan. 7.13-14).

2. Some People Saw Jesus as the Royal Messiah, Son of David

The second reason why Jesus' earliest followers came to see him as the royal Messiah (which is not the same figure as the Lord who would come from heaven) lies in the fact that others saw him as such. Scholars such as Paula Frederiksen (*Jesus of Nazareth, King of the Jews*, 2000) have defended the theory that Jesus was crucified by the Romans, because sufficient people believed he could be the Messiah, which in turn could lead to serious security problems.

Michael J. Wilkins (2009) defends the historicity of Peter's declaration in Caesarea Philippi: 'You are the Messiah' (Mk 8.29). Whether Wilkins is correct or not, Jesus himself is not likely to have proclaimed himself to be the royal Messiah. First of all, he expected a heavenly Lord, not a human king. Secondly, the confusion in the Gospels on this issue is best explained if he did not proclaim himself to be the Messiah. On the other hand, however, it is also unlikely that he clearly dismissed the title when outsiders or his own disciples called him thus. If he had made absolutely clear that he was not the Messiah, it would be rather odd that the movement that included his friends and family would have started to call him Jesus Christ.

3. Jesus Took Various Roles During His Last Pesach in Jerusalem

E.P. Sanders (1993, 253–64) argues that Jesus, not unlike several biblical prophets and contemporary Messianic pretenders, performed three symbolic acts in his last week: he rode into Jerusalem on an ass, thus fulfilling Zechariah's prophecy in order to proclaim himself king, he turned over the tables of the traders in the temple as a sign of its impending destruction, and he celebrated a last supper as a symbol of the future kingdom of God.

Again the Jesus Seminar is less convinced: the story of Jesus' entry 'was conceived under the influence of Zech. 9.9'. But the fellows did agree that Jesus spoke 'some words against the temple or temple practices', and that it is possible 'that Jesus may have performed some symbolic acts during table fellowship with his followers'. They were, however, sceptical that the evangelists preserved his words, and rather saw the hand of the evangelists who cited and paraphrased Scriptures to provide Jesus with words. As a rule, the Seminar does not attribute echoes from prophetic Scriptures to Jesus, nor any Messianic claims, and hardly any pronouncement about himself in the first person.

I believe role theory can suggest a more dynamic view of Jesus' acts in his last week. With role theory, we can theorize about Jesus' interaction with various roles from Zechariah, Malachi and Isaiah, in order to find and do God's will. As discussed above and in previous chapters, it is likely that these prophets played an important role in the beliefs of the movement of John the Baptist, as well as in Jesus' coping with John's death and the threats to his own life.

Jesus' Entry into Jerusalem

Brent Kinman (2009) defends the historicity of Jesus' entry into Jerusalem. A key consideration is the fact that Jesus was crucified as a Messianic pretender and 'king of the Jews'. Craig Evans (2002) argues that its connection with the prophecy in Zech. 9.9 goes back to Jesus, despite the fact that the oldest version, Mk 11.1-11, does not mention the prophecy. Evans notes that references to the book of Zechariah abound in the passion narratives and that some texts are directly relevant for the temple incident (Zech. 14.20-1) and the

Last Supper (Zech. 9.11). Like Sanders, Evans believes that Jesus consciously enacted Zechariah's prophecy.

Yet there is a problem in seeing the entry as a fully preconceived, symbolic action that proclaimed Jesus' kingship. If anything, it seems that Jesus expected someone to come down from the heavens, not a human king who would expel the Romans through normal military means. If the action was symbolic, it cannot have signified Jesus' own present role but only the role of the future Son of Man. Second, the Gospel of John (12.12-16) confirms the opinion of the Jesus Seminar that the disciples did indeed apply Zech. 9.9 retrospectively. Furthermore, the evangelist claims that not Jesus but the *disciples* were the actors of the symbolism:

> The next day the great crowd that had come for the the feast heard that Jesus was coming into Jerusalem. They took branches from the palm-trees and went out to meet him and cried out: 'Hosanna', 'Blessed is the Coming One in the name of the Lord' (Psalm 118.25-26), and 'the King of Israel'.
>
> And finding a donkey, Jesus sat on it as it has been written: 'Fear not, daughter of Sion, behold your king comes, sitting on the foal of an ass.
>
> At first his disciples did not understand all this. But when Jesus was glorified, then they remembered: these things had been written about him, and *they* had done them to him. [emphasis mine]

In John's version, there was no preconceived idea of entering Jerusalem on a donkey to proclaim Jesus as king. Rather, Jesus simply mounted a donkey when he was found one. As discussed in Chapter 10, Jesus may well have come to Jerusalem to urge the people one last time to return to God before the day of judgement, while accepting the likelihood that he would suffer and die as John had, in case he too would be rejected by the authorities. From the perspective of role theory and coping, Jesus is likely to have been sharply attuned to any development that would reveal God's will with him during this crucial journey. This may have reached a high point when he approached Jerusalem, came over the last hill and saw the temple mount with its high-rising sanctuary. As the crowds of pilgrims grew thicker, many sung the traditional *Hallel* for the festivals, including Psalm 118.25-6, 'Hosanna, ... Blessed is the one who comes in the name of the Lord'. As argued in Chapter 10, Jesus most likely saw himself as the final envoy of the Coming Lord, but some people may have approached him as if he were a royal Messiah. After he had mounted the donkey, some may have seen a parallel with the anointing of Salomo (1 Kgs 1.29-40). Whether Jesus chose to respond in line with the prophecy in Zechariah when he 'found' the ass, or whether the fact that he was already sitting on the ass brought Zech. 9 to mind, is important but not crucial. If Zech. 9.14 ('The Lord will appear ... with the trumpet') was on Jesus' mind during his final journey, it is quite likely that Zech. 9.9 was evoked in this joyous and responsive crowd. The 'down-to-earth' entry of the king in Zech. 9.9 precedes the 'appearance' of the Lord in 9.14. In taking the role of that specific king, Jesus felt confirmed in his role as God's final envoy announcing the coming of the Lord, while at the same time it may have expanded that role to include elements of the royal Messiah.

His followers, after Easter, could interpret Jesus' role-taking as a clue to his true identity, not only as the crowd's royal Messiah but also as the Lord, coming to his temple.

The 'Cleansing' of the Temple

Few scholars dispute the historicity of the temple incident (Klyne Snodgrass 2009). For Sanders, the temple incident is not so much a 'cleansing' of the temple as it is a symbolic action pointing to its imminent destruction. He connects it to the charge against Jesus and early Christians that they posed a threat to the temple. But again, it is hard to see the temple incident as a symbolic action. Jesus did not cleanse anything, let alone destroy anything. He is reported only to have shouted at some traders and turned over some tables in an area that was probably not even part of the original temple of Salomon. Furthermore, and again according to John, his own disciples did not remember the incident as a symbolic act of destruction or cultic reform, but seem to have been rather surprised at his 'zeal' for God's house (Jn 2.17).

From the perspective of role theory, a different interpretation is more plausible. After a hopeful entry, Jesus would most likely have been looking for signs of conversion. But entering the temple, he may have been struck by its business as usual and the profaneness of commerce around the temple. If there is one thing historical about the story with the fig tree, it would be the realization that Jerusalem would not show the fruits of conversion anytime soon. In line with his mission and the scenario in Mal. 3.1-7, he took the role of God who would come to purify his temple, burning the evildoers like stubble (4.1) and he anticipated God's judgement (4.5b). Malachi does not explicitly speak of the destruction of Jerusalem, but familiar texts like Isaiah (5.4), Daniel (9.26), and Zechariah (12.2, 14.2) do. Indeed, the harassment of the traders may have been prompted by Zech. 14.20-1, where it is promised that there will 'no longer be traders in the house of the Lord'. (Note, however, that the word for traders is also translated as Canaanites.)

The temple incident, then, may have been a brief moment of divine anger and human fear. Jesus would not only have been angry because the temple was used for commercial purposes, but also because it signalled the failure of Jesus' mission, which activated the fear of his now inevitable death and the fearful coming of the Lord. The inevitability of his death, however, did not follow from the act itself (which may have been fairly insignificant at the time, else he would have been arrested sooner), but it had become clear to him that it was God's will that he would die like John the Baptist. In the unfolding scenario, the role of Isaiah's suffering servant would now have become more compelling again.

The Last Supper

The *status questionis* with regard to the last supper is well described by I. Howard Marshall (2009). There is considerable dispute about the historicity of the last supper. Given the confusion already in the Gospel narratives, it is not surprising that there is no consensus on the circumstances of the meal: Was it a Passover celebration? What was the day of the week? Who was present? But the tradition itself is well attested, both in the Gospels as well as in Paul's letter to the Corinthians. Even John's account does not really contradict the synoptic account if the 'post-resurrection' elements are stripped away (Van Os 2009). Furthermore, the fact that early Christians celebrated meals is beyond dispute, and the most efficient explanation would be that it goes back to Jesus. Those who do not take the last supper as historical do recognize that Jesus celebrated meals with his followers and thought that these meals were significant. Their problem is not that Jesus ate a meal together with his friends shortly before his arrest, but the idea that Jesus foresaw his death and believed it to be beneficial to his followers in a cultic sense and in accordance with the will of God. But if those beliefs do not go back to Jesus, how then could these words that were linked to such an important element in the life of the community be accepted as 'traditional' in a community like Corinth? On the other hand, the idea that Jesus substantially said what Paul and the Synoptics report is not without difficulty either. For how then did Jesus obtain these ideas, and how is it possible that the composed and purposeful Jesus during the meal breaks down afterwards in Gethsemane?

I suggest that role theory can help to design an explanation, for in the words of the last supper Jesus takes up the role of the Paschal lamb. Whether or not Jesus' last supper was a Passover meal is of less importance; he was in Jerusalem for the festival of Passover and the Passover story has some important links with the prophetic roles with which Jesus interacted during this week.

In Exod. 12, the Paschal lamb is slaughtered to protect the Israelites from the Lord, who would come to pass judgement and kill all the first-born sons. Only the families who ate the lamb during the night and smeared its blood on their doorposts would be passed over, and they would be taken to the Promised Land. Henceforth, they would celebrate the Passover in remembrance of their deliverance. Likewise, in Mal. 3 and 4, it is the Lord who will burn the sinners, but deliver the righteous and Jesus expected this to happen soon, now that both John and he himself had been rejected. In Isa. 53, the suffering servant is struck down by God and slaughtered like a lamb to turn sinners into righteous people. Thus, Malachi's Coming Lord would pass over them when he would come to bring judgement over Jerusalem and punish the evildoers. By taking the role of the lamb, Jesus expected God to arrange for his slaughter and his friends to belong to the righteous who would be saved. If it is historical that Jesus understood that Judas would turn him in, this would, oddly enough, have confirmed to him that God is in control and fulfilling his plan. Having realized this, it would have made sense to Jesus to prepare his friends for his death and he may have chosen the elements of the meal to make his point in a symbolic way. His body would be broken, but his blood would mark the covenant between the Lord and his justified people.

For those who object that a Jewish Jesus could not have spoken about 'drinking blood', I note two things. First, Jesus is not reported as saying that they have to eat his flesh and drink his blood, but that they should remember him when they eat the bread and drink the cup. In fact, 1 Cor. 11 is hardly a description of a symbolic act or the institution of a new rite (contrary to Mk 14). Jesus makes a remark during the meal about the bread, and *after supper* he offers a toast with the request to remember him. Thus understood, it is not at odds with the celebration in the Didache where the 'words of the institution' are not spoken at all, but which ends with the exclamation *Maranatha!* (10.6). Second, in 1 Cor. 11 Jesus does not say that the cup is his 'blood of the covenant' (Mk 14.24), but that it is the 'new covenant in my blood'. In the symbolic context of the Passover festival the bread 'is' his body, because he takes the role of the lamb in Isa. 53, but the cup with *wine* is the celebration of the covenant.

I believe that the author of Mark 'updated' the tradition before him. For Mk 14.25 fits perfectly after 1 Cor.: 'Truly I tell you: I will not drink anymore from the fruit of the vine until that day when I will drink it anew in the kingdom of God.' Read from the perspective I have been developing thus far, Jesus would have expected that the Lord (or Daniel's Son of Man) would come and with him the general resurrection. In accordance with Isa. 53.10-11, Jesus expected to see the light again and live joyously in God's kingdom.

Then, according to Mk 14.26, they went out to the Mount of Olives and Jesus explicitly quoted Zech. 13.7 to tell his friends that God would strike their shepherd down (in the *Targum* their king and prince), and that they would be scattered (compare Jn 16.32). Most scholars ascribe this statement to the early church, but I am not so certain. The point is that the shepherd in this passage is the worthless shepherd of Zech. 11.15-17, who 'does not care for the perishing or seek the wandering'. It is somewhat unlikely that the early church would want to cast Jesus in this role. But it would fit with a coping crisis prior to Jesus' 'conversion' on the mountain in the north (see Chapter 10). If Jesus had felt he had left his flock out of fear for his life, he could have perceived himself as a bad shepherd. Now that his final mission had failed and he expected to be crushed by God, this idea may have come to the fore again. In his final months or days, the prophecy in Zech. 12.10–13.1 may have provided Jesus with a link between the royal Messiah and Isaiah's suffering servant. It seems that 'the house of David and the inhabitants of Jerusalem' mourn a son (of David?) 'whom they have pierced'. But his death proves to be to their benefit (13.1), 'On that day a fountain shall be opened for the house of David and the inhabitants of Jerusalem, to cleanse them from sin and impurity.'

The interpretation of Jesus' last supper in the light of role theory makes the agony in Gethsemane understandable. Jesus was not having second thoughts about God's plan, but had all the time been searching to do God's will. For a sane religious person, the process of role-taking never yields a certainty beyond doubt; it remains an interactive process in which the believer keeps looking for guidance and confirmation. Believing now that the most troubling scenario was God's will for him, Jesus turned to his heavenly Father for confirmation and for strength to face the ordeal. As the author of Heb. 5.7-9 puts it:

> In the days of his flesh, he offered prayers and supplications
> to the One who was able to save him from death
> with loud cries and tears.
> And being heard in his devotion – even as a son,
> he learned obedience from what he suffered.
> And having come to his end, he became the cause of salvation
> for all those who obey him.

Conclusion

Jesus made a significant contribution to the belief of early Jesus followers that their Messiah had died in order to ascend to heaven, from where he would return as their Lord on the last day, at the sound of the trumpet, to pass judgement over the living and the resurrected dead. But the relation between the royal Messiah and the coming Lord is not straightforward.

Role theory allows us to come to a psychologically plausible scenario regarding Jesus' beliefs and self-awareness in his final week. Especially towards the end of his life, he may have considered the question of whether his own mission as God's final envoy could be described as that of a royal Messiah who would die like Isaiah's suffering servant to purify his people, as a son of David did in Zech. 12.

Jesus also taught his disciples to expect the Coming of the Lord ('Maranatha'), but until the very end Jesus did not identify himself as the Coming Lord who would descend from heaven. That role was to be fulfilled by God himself (Malachi, Zechariah), possibly in the form of a Son of Man (Daniel). But he did take the role of his Lord and his followers may have understood this retrospectively as an expression of his true identity.

After Easter, a significant number of his followers identified Jesus as both the royal Messiah and the Coming Lord. The specific understanding of these two roles may well go back to Jesus. Even the idea that Jesus fulfilled the role of the royal Messiah may plausibly be traced to his last months or days. But role theory does not help to explain why his followers combined the two roles in one person, in Jesus – a question that I will consider in Capter 12.

Chapter 12

CONCLUSIONS AND REFLECTIONS

This study can perhaps be best characterized as an essay, or a series of essays, on the basis of a new research framework. As such, the findings here are tentative and subject to further proofing. Nevertheless, following the order of the chapters, some conclusions can be drawn:

1. With James Charlesworth, I conclude that 'historical research raises questions that have been charted by the psychologists of religion' and that 'those devoted to Jesus research need not only sociology ... but also psychobiography'.
2. A psychobiography of Jesus can only be hypothetical, as there is simply not enough data about Jesus. Psychoanalytical reconstructions of Jesus' personality and behaviour on the basis of reconstructed childhood experiences are probably unhelpful in historical research.
3. All we have are the literary remains of some of his early followers. But the framework of psychobiography and psychohistory of groups provides us with various psychological, sociological and demographic methods that can be used to propose and test hypotheses that help to explain these literary remains. Jesus himself cannot be observed and is therefore not the *object* of theorizing but part of the theory itself. Methodologically, then, such a 'Theoretical Jesus' is part of a larger theory to explain what can be observed: the literary remains of his followers.

Before proceeding with theorizing about Jesus, we first need to assess how these followers relate to Jesus, and how their traditions about him were formed and conserved:

4. The study of ancient demographics can help to clarify the presence of first-generation believers and their descendants (e.g. the list of resurrection witnesses mentioned in 1 Cor. 15.5-8). Thus it can be argued that throughout the first century, there were a significant number of people who had known Jesus, or whose parents or grandparents belonged to the first generation of believers.
5. The study of conversions and new religious movements can help to understand the dynamics of the movement, as demonstrated by Rodney

Stark. Working with a spreadsheet model to develop and test various assumptions, I argue that the Diaspora communities started out as a movement among migrant Jews, and were both more Jewish and less 'Pauline' than is often thought. I also argue that the interaction between Diaspora communities and the believers in Palestine was significant and even more so when large numbers of Jews were forced out of Palestine during the Jewish War (66–70 CE).

6. Despite the presence of first-generation believers among Pauline audiences and the communities that received and copied the first-century Gospels, we need to take into account both the conserving and creative forces in social memory.

Based on the findings in the first five chapters, I conclude that it is likely that Jesus did indeed have an impact on the beliefs and traditions of his followers. In order to demonstrate the usefulness of psychological methods to explore this issue, I used a three-step approach:

• First, I have isolated in the undisputed letters of Paul certain beliefs that are likely to be pre-Pauline and shared by many first-generation believers. This regards likely points that are not argued but are already shared with his audiences, especially in cities that were influenced by other apostles and 'men of James' such as Rome, Corinth and Galatia. Beliefs that cannot be explained easily on the basis of contemporary Jewish or Hellenistic thinking could conceivably go back to Jesus.

• Second, I have selected various empirically tested theories that are central in the contemporary psychology of religion and likely to be helpful in theorizing about the relationship between these beliefs and Jesus, given the rather secure facts that he was a religious man, who joined the movement of John the Baptist, earned a reputation as a healer and an exorcist, had to cope with the death of John and the associated risks to his own life, but who nevertheless went to Jerusalem for what was to be his final Passover.

• Third, I have used each theory in combination with a critical reading of the relevant traditions about Jesus (foremost in Q and Mark) to come to a psychologically plausible theory of how Jesus could have contributed to these beliefs.

The remaining five chapters each concern an essay about Jesus' impact with regard to a specific belief and a specific theory.

7. The veneration of God as a Father most likely goes back to the religious experience of Jesus. Using Attachment Theory in the context of religion, I argue that various sayings of Jesus about God as his Father and certain stories about Jesus suggest that Jesus was a securely attached religious Jew from a religious home, who turned to God in times of distress and who transferred his trust in God as his caregiver to his followers.

8. The fact that both the disciples of Jesus and his brothers are mentioned in Paul's letters as part of a movement that professed belief in a Messiah can fruitfully be assessed on the basis of Rational Choice Theory. In combination with the likelihood that both Jesus and his friends were followers of John the Baptist, it is plausible that there was a considerable overlap in religious and social capital between the family of Jesus and his friends, as well as with the movement of John the Baptist. It is therefore likely that Jesus shared key beliefs with the movement of John, as well as the way John may have applied prophecies from books such as Malachi and Isaiah to his own situation. Such beliefs included the expectation that the Lord would soon come to establish his kingdom and purify his people.

9. The ease with which Paul can equate the Spirit of Jesus with the Holy Spirit of God that empowered the believers and provided the communities with *charismata* was explored with the help of anthropological psychology. Combining psychology, anthropology and John's eschatology we can understand how Jesus believed that his healings and exorcisms confirmed Isaiah's prophecies about the signs of God's Kingdom and the presence of God's Holy Spirit within him. The wish of his disciples to continue his mission and receive his Spirit may explain the subsequent spiritual experiences that spread across the Jewish Diaspora.

10. The idea that Jesus' death was in accordance with God's will and beneficial for his followers can be understood in the light of the psychology of religion and coping. Jesus had to cope with the death of John and the associated threats to his own life. Appropriating the concept of the suffering servant from Isa. 53, who would die for the sins of his people and would live in God's light, may have been a way to preserve significance of and the belief in a benevolent God.

11. The veneration of Jesus, as both the royal Messiah and the coming Lord, is mostly assigned to the creativity of the early church. But the early and general acceptance of these beliefs suggests they have roots in the life of Jesus. Like John, Jesus did believe in the Coming of the Lord (Malachi, Zechariah) or a heavenly figure like 'a son of man' (Daniel). Furthermore, Jesus was probably crucified because the Romans had reasons to believe that people saw him as a Messianic pretender. Role theory in the context of religion provides a framework in which we can explore how the struggles of Jesus in his last days may have led to certain acts that seem symbolic: the entry into Jerusalem, the cleansing of the temple and last supper. Role theory helps to understand how the specific scenarios of the Coming Lord and the suffering Messiah came about in the life of Jesus. It cannot fully explain, however, why the two roles were combined together in the person of Jesus.

Jesus and Christological Innovation

On the basis of the conclusions presented above, it is now possible to reconsider the question about the extent to which the beliefs found in Paul's letters originated with Jesus and the extent to which they were the result of innovation after Easter.

From the perspective of psychology, some key beliefs may well go back to Jesus: He saw God as a benevolent Father and rightful King. The Lord – in some way identical to the heavenly 'one like a son of man' – would descend from heaven to judge the living and the dead as either righteous or sinner. When people were healed and evil spirits fled before him, Jesus saw this as the graceful inauguration of God's Kingdom and believed that God's Holy Spirit worked these miracles through him. He proclaimed God's benevolence and fatherly love. Following the death of John, Jesus may have considered his execution as well as the threats to his own life in the light of Isaiah's suffering servant, whose death for the sins of his people would make them righteous. Nevertheless, the servant, too, would be rewarded in the resurrection of the dead. Despite his fears, Jesus embraced his mission, and went to Jerusalem as God's final envoy to call the people one last time before the coming of the Lord. Other people saw Jesus as the royal Messiah who would restore the earthly kingdom of David and Jesus may have come to consider the death of the royal son of David in Zechariah in the light of Isaiah's prophecy, again to the benefit of his people.

If it is accepted that the above elements can be plausibly traced to Jesus, then the question remains whether the remaining (pre-Pauline) elements discussed in this study can more plausibly be traced to his earliest followers than to Jesus. These elements are at least the following two: (1) Jesus is not only the royal Messiah but also the coming Lord, and (2) the Spirit of Jesus is the Holy Spirit that filled the believers. One other potentially pre-Pauline element that I did not discuss is contained in the Christ-hymn in Phil. 2.6-11, the divine pre-existence of Christ Jesus. I will briefly discuss how each of these three elements may have originated in the community of Jesus' followers after Easter.

Jesus is the Coming Lord

If my conclusions are correct that Jesus died the death of Isaiah's suffering servant and Zechariah's son of David, while expecting the Lord God himself to descend and pass judgement on the living and the dead, his grieving followers reckoned not with the possibility of Jesus' individual resurrection, but with the general resurrection following on the appearance of the Lord God himself.

When we accept the resurrection experiences in 1 Cor. 15.5-8, as many scholars do, as actual experiences of his followers, then these are nearly sufficient for the Christological innovation that Jesus was raised as the Lord

(YHWH) who would appear. I say *nearly* sufficient, for this logical response to the resurrection experiences creates an enormous dissonance with previously held beliefs, especially with the belief in the One God, who is distinct from what he created. If we accept that Jesus' followers had learned to turn to the Scriptures in similar ways as John the Baptist and Jesus had done before them, then perhaps the prophecy about the Son of Man in Dan. 7 may have been instrumental in bridging the two sides and reducing the dissonance. On the one hand, the Son of Man in Daniel is a celestial being who will descend from heaven (as the Lord/YHWH would in Malachi and Zechariah), on the other hand, he is like a human being who will be king over the people like the Davidic royal Messiah. Furthermore, it would explain why the Lord did not come down immediately after the death of Jesus: as the Son of Man, he would first have to ascend to God's throne to receive his kingship. In this way Daniel's Son of Man may have proven a powerful means for Jesus' followers to deal with the resurrection experiences that several of his followers reported. In Daniel, the Son of Man is not the Lord/YHWH himself, but in combination with Malachi and Zechariah he carries the name and identity of the Lord/ YHWH.

The Spirit of Jesus Is God's Holy Spirit

If the resurrection experiences proved to Jesus' followers that there would be an 'interim' between the resurrection of Jesus and the general resurrection of the dead, and between the death of Jesus and the Day of Judgement, then the mission of John and Jesus should continue: people were still to be called to return to God, and to accept the righteousness and purification provided by Jesus' sacrifice, before the *parousia* of the Lord. If, then, the Twelve were to continue the mission, they may have prayed for the Spirit of Jesus, just as Elisha wanted two portions of Elijah's spirit (see Chapter 9). The spiritual experiences, as argued in Chapter 9, would have convinced them of the power of the Spirit that they received and passed on to new groups of Jesus' followers that they founded during their missionary activities. If the Holy Spirit was the Spirit who was active in Jesus' healings and exorcisms, and if Jesus is the Lord/ YHWH, then the Holy Spirit is Jesus' Spirit and the Spirit of God.

Jesus is the Pre-existing Son of God

A number of scholars believe that the so-called *Carmen Christi* (R.P. Martin 1967/1983/1997) in Phil. 2.6-11 was an existing hymn that Paul quoted in his letter. In this hymn, the entire drama of Jesus as the suffering servant and glorious Lord is summarized, with one extra element: Jesus is the pre-existing Son of God:

Being already in the form of God,
he thought it no prize
to be the same as God,

but he emptied himself,
taking the form of a servant,
becoming in the likeness of men.

And in his shape found like a man
he humbled himself
becoming obedient until death

(– even to death on a cross.)

Therefore indeed did God super-exalt him,
and grant him the name above all other name.

So that in the name of Jesus
every knee should bend
of those in the heavens, on the earth and beneath the earth;
and that every tongue should confess:

'Jesus Christ is Lord,
to the glory of God the Father.'

The idea that God sent his Son is also present in Rom. 8.3 and Gal. 4.4; that he deprived himself may be inferred from 2 Cor. 8.9. Whether the hymn in Philippians is pre-Pauline or not is, I believe, less important than the fact that for a Jewish group the idea of a pre-existing Jesus was inevitable, once he was identified as the Lord/YHWH. Because Jews are monotheists, and because God is eternal, Jesus could only be included in the divine identity if he had been so from eternity. There is no further impulse needed for this concept.

Important in this theory of Christological innovation, then, is that the observed remains of early Christianity can be explained without assuming the passing of generations and the dominance of Gentile believers. It also does not require us to assume that most traditions about Jesus are completely disconnected from what he said or did. Integrating psychological methods in our research allows us to develop a good explanation that is both plausible and economical.

Status

I am aware that my results put my work in the corner of those New Testament scholars who are targeted in *Redescribing Christian Origins*, edited by Cameron and Miller (2004, 501–2):

In fact, we are persuaded that we can explain the data of the dominant paradigm itself, better, by starting with the Jesus schools of Q and *Thomas* than the way New Testament scholars have traditionally approached the matter: (1) by presupposing at the inauguration of the Christian era a dramatic event, a kerygmatic conviction and a linear development; and (2) by assuming that there was an essential bond that existed and a continuous development that led from the historical Jesus to the Gospel story of his appearance, death, and resurrection, and from there to the Jerusalem church in Acts and the apostle Paul.

The keywords here are 'presupposing' and 'assuming'. I have made my analysis not on the basis of the narrative in the book of Acts, or Eusebius, but through a critical (and 'un-Pauline') reading of Paul's letters, the oldest preserved documents of the movement. They are not a hypothetical document, like Q, nor a relatively late collection like Thomas (although I readily acknowledge the value of Q and Thomas for our research).

But what is more important: they are contemporary documents that shaped a worldwide movement and for that reason alone the origins of the innovative ideas in those letters deserve to be explained. Through the use of relevant insights from demography, sociology, anthropology and psychology, I developed what I consider now to be a likely scenario. If that scenario is somewhat compatible with the work of many 'traditional' New Testament scholars, so be it. But the scenario presented here is not a presupposition or an assumption. It is a theory constructed within the context of scientific enquiry: the theoretical basis, the data and the assessment of probabilities are here to verify, discuss and improve.

Perhaps I should re-emphasize the status of my findings. I have not tried to find a core of facts that we can know for certain about Jesus. All I have done is use psychological methods to design a theory about some of the observable remains of Jesus' earliest followers that are difficult to explain solely from the perspective of the early church. I have also not tried to produce the most plausible construction of the historical Jesus, but rather a theoretical Jesus that helps to explain the remains of his earliest followers better than current historical Jesus studies do, in terms of explanatory force, plausibility and theoretical economy (in that order). Whether I have succeeded is up to the reader to decide. Furthermore, as with any theory, this is only a simple step in the process of theorizing about Jesus and his earliest followers. The sooner this theory can be improved, the better.

Further Research

Undertaking a work of this scope is frustrating in the sense that one can merely touch upon so many passages that have been discussed in far more depth by other scholars. All I could do in this work is to argue that psychological insights should have a place in those in-depth discussions. I could suggest numerous topics that deserve such an interdisciplinary monograph, like, for instance, the description of the Eucharist in Paul, Mark and the *Didache*.

Some readers may wonder why I have not included a chapter on the resurrection experiences, a topic that has been approached previously from a psychological perspective (such as Jack Kent's *The Psychological Origins of the Resurrection Myth*, 1999). The methodological answer to that is that the nature of such experiences will change nothing with regard to the theory I have set out above. A more personal answer is that the theological consequences related to this question are far more profound than to any of the questions dealt with in this study. Paul, for example, only came to accept the foolish and scandalous beliefs of his opponents (I Cor. 1.23) because he had personally 'seen' this crucified and cursed criminal in God's glory (Rom. 1.4; Gal. 1.16). Furthermore, it is not an easy task. We should recognize that the experiences of the women, Peter, James, the Twelve, the '500' and Paul may have occurred in different psychological settings, while at the same time the earlier experiences would have influenced the later. I would like to see first some consensus on what it is that the resurrection experiences explain before theorizing about their nature.

On the basis of the insights into the growth and composition of the movement (Part Two), I believe a psycho-historical approach (see Chapter 3) that uses the psychology of religion could prove useful for theorizing about the first-century movement and such themes as the development of baptism and the Eucharist, the mission to the Gentiles, Paul's understanding of the function of the Law versus that of the Jerusalem leadership, the Apocalypse, the emergence of Christianity as a new race, and the development of dogmas such as the virgin birth and the Trinity. In combination with Social Memory theory, this could also help to improve the methods of historical criticism of the Gospels.

This study can be seen as a preliminary attempt at integrating the framework of psychobiography and the findings and insights of the psychology of religion with the historical study of Jesus and his earliest followers. What is needed now is for these essays to be evaluated by others, both in terms of their usefulness in explaining early Christianity as well as with regard to the implications this approach may have for the way in which the New Testament authors and the historical Jesus are studied. If my work proves to be of any use, there is much more to be done.

BIBLIOGRAPHY

Adamson, T. (1898). *Studies of the Mind in Christ*. T&T Clark.

Alexander, I. (2005). 'Erikson and Psychobiography, Psychobiography and Erikson.' In W.T. Schultz (ed.), *Handbook of Psychobiography* (pp. 265–84). Oxford University Press.

Alexander, I.E. (1990). *Personology: Method and Content in Personality Assessment and Psychobiography*. Duke University Press.

Alexander, L. (1998). 'Ancient Book Production and the Circulation of the Gospels.' In R. Bauckham (ed.), *The Gospels for All Christians: Rethinking the Gospel Audiences* (pp. 71–112). Wm.B. Eerdmans.

Anderson, P.N. (2006). *The Fourth Gospel and the Quest for Jesus: Modern Foundations Reconsidered*. Library of New Testament Studies (vol. 321). T&T Clark.

Anderson, R.D. (1999). *Inside the Mind of Joseph Smith: Psychobiography and the Book of Mormon*. Signature Books.

Arnal, W.E. (2001). *Jesus and the Village Scribes: Galilean Conflicts and the Setting of Q*. Fortress Press.

—— (2005). *The Symbolic Jesus: Historical Scholarship, Judaism and the Construction of Contemporary Identity*. Equinox.

Ashton, J. (2000). *The Religion of Paul the Apostle*. Yale University Press.

—— (2003). 'The Religious Experience of Jesus,' 2002–2003 James Lecture, Harvard Divinity School. *Harvard Divinity Bulletin* 32(1): pp. 17–20.

Aune, D.E. (1987). *The New Testament in Its Literary Environment*. Library of Early Christianity. The Westminster Press.

Bagnall, R.S. and Frier, B.W. (1994). *The Demography of Roman Egypt*. Cambridge Studies in Population, Economy and Society in Past Times. Cambridge University Press.

Baldensperger, W. (1888/1892). *Das Selbstbewußtsein Jesu im Lichte der messianischen Hoffnungen seiner Zeit*, Straßburg.

Barnett, P. (1999). *Jesus and the Rise of Early Christianity: A History of New Testament Times*. InterVarsity Press.

—— (2005). *The Birth of Christianity: The First Twenty Years*. Wm.B. Eerdmans.

Barton, S.C. (1998). 'Can We Identify the Gospel Audiences? In R. Bauckham (ed.), *The Gospels for All Christians: Rethinking the Gospel Audiences* (pp. 173–94). Wm.B. Eerdmans.

Bauckham, R. (1990). *Jude and the Relatives of Jesus in the Early Church*. T&T Clark.

—— (1998). 'For Whom Were Gospels Written?' In R. Bauckham (ed.), *The Gospels for All Christians: Rethinking the Gospel Audiences*. Wm.B. Eerdmans.

—— (1998). 'John for Readers of Mark.' In R. Bauckham (ed.), *The Gospels for All Christians: Rethinking the Gospel Audiences*. Wm.B. Eerdmans.

—— (1999). *James: Wisdom of James, Disciple of Jesus the Sage*. Routledge.

—— (2002). *Gospel Women: Studies of the Named Women in the Gospels*. Wm.B. Eerdmans.

—— (2006). 'James and the Jerusalem Community.' In O. Skarsaune and R. Hvalvik (eds), *Jewish Believers in Jesus: The Early Centuries* (pp. 55–95). Hendrickson Publishers.

—— (2006). *Jesus and the Eyewitnesses: The Gospels as Eyewitness Testimony*. Wm.B. Eerdmans.

—— (2008). *Jesus and the God of Israel: 'God Crucified' and Other Studies on the New Testament's Christology of Divine Identity*. Paternoster. (The essay *God Crucified* was originally published in 1998.)

Beck, R. (2006). 'The Religious Market of the Roman Empire: Rodney Stark and Christianity's Pagan Competition.' In L.E. Vaage (ed.), *Religious Rivalries in the Early Roman Empire and the Rise of Christianity* (vol. 18, pp. 213–32). Studies in Christianity and Judaism. Wilfrid Laurier University Press.

Beit-Hallahmi, B. and Argyle, M. (1997). *The Psychology of Religious Behaviour, Belief and Experience*. Routledge.

Berger, K. (1991/1995, English translation 2003). *Historische Psychologie des Neuen Testaments*. Verlag Katholisches Bibelwerk GmbH.

Birgegrad, A. and P. Granqvist (2000). 'Religiosity, Adult Attachment, and "Why Singles" are More Religious.' *International Journal for the Psychology of Religion* 10(2): pp. 111–23.

—— (2004). 'The Correspondence between Attachment to Parents and God: Three Experiments Using Subliminal Separation Cues.' *Personality and Social Psychology Bulletin* 30: pp. 1122–35.

Black, M. (1946/1954/1967). *An Aramaic Approach to the Gospels and Acts*. Oxford University Press.

Blasi, A.J., Turcotte, P.-A. and Duhaime, J. (eds). (2002). *Handbook of Early Christianity: Social Science Approaches*. AltaMira Press.

Bockmuehl, M. (2003; German original 2000). *Jewish Law in Gentile Churches: Halakhah and the Beginning of Christian Public Ethics*. T&T Clark.

Bockmuehl, M. and Hagner, D.A. (eds). (2005). *The Written Gospel*. Cambridge University Press.

Boisen, A.T. (1936). *The Exploration of the Inner World: A Study of Mental Disorder and Religious Experience*. Chicago.

—— (1952). 'What Did Jesus Think of Himself?' *Journal of Bible and Religion* 20(1): pp. 7–12.

—— (1960). *Out of the Depths: An Autobiographical Study of Mental Disorder and Religious Experience*. New York.

Borg, M.J. (1987). *Jesus, a New Vision: Spirit, Culture, and the Life of Discipleship*. Harper & Row.

Borgen, P. (1998). *Early Christianity and Hellenistic Judaism*. T&T Clark.

Boritt, G.S. (ed.), (1988). *The Historian's Lincoln: Pseudohistory, Psychohistory, and History*. University of Illinois Press.

Bornkamm, G. and Hammer, P.L. (trans.). (1969). *Early Christian Experience*. The New Testament Library. SCM Press Ltd.

Bourguignon, E. (1973). 'Introduction: A Framework for the Comparative Study of Altered States of Consciousness.' In E. Bourguignon (ed.), *Religion, Altered States of Consciousness, and Social change* (pp. 3–35). Ohio State University Press.

—— (1979). *Psychological Anthropology: An Introduction to Human Nature and Cultural Differences*. Holt, Rinehart and Winston.

Bousset, W. (1892). *Jesu Predigt in ihrem Gegensatz zum Judentum. Ein religiongeschichtlicher Vergleich*. Göttingen.

Bowie, E. (2001). 'Literature and Sophistic.' In A.K. Bowman, P. Garnsey and D. Rathbone (eds), *The Cambridge Ancient History: Second edition: Volume XI: The High Empire, A.D. 70–192* (vol. 11, pp. 898–921). Cambridge University Press.

Bowie, F. (2000/2006). *The Anthropology of Religion: An Introduction*. Blackwell Publishing.

Bowlby, J. (1969/1982). *Attachment*. Attachment and Loss, vol. 1. Basic Books.

—— (1973). *Separation: Anxiety and Anger*. Attachment and Loss, vol. 2. Basic Books.

—— (1980). *Loss: Sadness and Depression*. Attachment and Loss, vol. 3. Basic Books.

—— (1990). *Charles Darwin: A New Life.* W.W. Norton & Company.

Bremmer, J. (2010). *The Rise of Christianity through the Eyes of Gibbon, Harnack and Rodney Stark.* Groningen: Faculteit Godgeleerdheid en Godsdienstwetenschap.

Brown, S.L., Nesse, R.M., House, J.S. and Utz, R.L. (2004). 'Religion and Emotional Compensation: Results from a Prospective Study of Widowhood.' *Personality and Social Psychology Bulletin* 30(9): pp. 1165–74.

Bultmann, R. (1926; repr. 1988). *Jesus.* UTB für Wissenschaft: Uni-Taschenbücher. J.C.B. Mohr (Paul Siebeck).

Burridge, R. A. (1992/2004). *What are the Gospels?: A Comparison with Graeco-Roman Biography.* Society for New Testament Studies: Monograph Series. Cambridge University Press.

—— (1997). 'The Gospels and Acts.' In S.E. Porter (ed.), *Handbook of Classical Rhetoric in the Hellenistic Period 330 B.C.–A.D. 400* (pp. 507–32). Brill.

—— (1997). 'Rhetoric in Practice: Biography.' In S.E. Porter (ed.), *Handbook of Classical Rhetoric in the Hellenistic Period 330 B.C.–A.D. 400* (pp. 371–92). Brill.

—— (1998). 'About People, by People, for People: Gospel Genre and Audiences.' In R. Bauckham (ed.), *The Gospels for All Christians: Rethinking the Gospel Audiences* (pp. 71–112). Wm.B. Eerdmans.

Byrskog, S. (2000). *Story as History, History as Story: The Gospel Tradition in the Context of Ancient Oral History.* Mohr Siebeck.

Callan, T. (2007). 'Psychological Perspectives on the Life of Paul.' In W.G. Rollins and D.A. Kille (eds), *Psychological Insights into the Bible: Texts and Readings* (pp. 127–36). Wm.B. Eerdmans.

Cameron, R. and Miller, M.P. (2004). 'Introduction: Ancient Myths and Modern Theories of Christian Origins.' In R. Cameron and M.P. Miller (eds), *Redescribing Christian Origins* (pp. 1–30). Society of Biblical Literature: Symposium Series (vol. 28). Society of Biblical Literature.

Capps, D. (2000). *Jesus: A Psychological Biography.* Chalice Press.

—— (2001). 'Sundén's Role-Taking Theory – The Case of John Henry Newman and His Mentors.' In J.A. Belzen (ed.), *Psychohistory in Psychology of Religion: Interdisciplinary Studies* (pp. 41–64). International Series in the Psychology of Religion (vol. 12). Rodopi.

—— (2004). 'A Psychobiography of Jesus.' In J.H. Ellens and W.G. Rollins (eds), *From Christ to Jesus* (vol. 4, pp. 59–70). Psychology and the Bible: A New Way to Read the Scriptures, vol. 4. Praeger Publishers.

—— (2004). 'Beyond Schweitzer and the Psychiatrists: Jesus as Fictive Personality.' In J.H. Ellens and W.G. Rollins (eds), *From Christ to Jesus* (vol. 4, pp. 89–124). Psychology and the Bible: A New Way to Read the Scriptures, vol. 4. Praeger Publishers.

—— (2004). 'Erik Erikson's Psychological Portrait of Jesus: Jesus as Numinous Presence.' In J.H. Ellens and W.G. Rollins (eds), *From Christ to Jesus* (vol. 4, pp. 163–208). Psychology and the Bible: A New Way to Read the Scriptures, vol. 4. Praeger Publishers.

—— (2008). *Jesus the Village Psychiatrist.* Westminster John Knox Press.

Capps, D., Capps, W.H. and Bradford, M.G. (eds), (1977). *Encounter with Erikson: Historical Interpretation and Religious Biography.* American Academy of Religion: AAR/ UC - IRS: Joint Series on Formative Contemporary Thinkers. Scholars Press.

Carlson, S.C. (2005). *The Gospel Hoax: Morton Smith's Invention of Secret Mark.* Baylor University Press.

Casey, M. (1991). *From Jewish Prophet to Gentile God: The Origins and Development of New Testament Christology.* James Clarke & Co.

—— (1998). *Aramaic Sources of Mark's Gospel.* Society for New Testament Studies Monograph Studies (vol. 102). Cambridge University Press.

—— (2002). *An Aramaic Approach to Q: Sources for the Gospels of Matthew and Luke.* Society for New Testament Studies Monograph Studies (vol. 122). Cambridge University Press.

Cassidy, J. and Shaver, P.R. (eds). (1999/2008). *Handbook of Attachment: Theory, Research, and Clinical Applications*. The Guilford Press.

Castelli, E.A. (1998). 'Gender, Theory, and The Rise of Christianity: A Response to Rodney Stark.' *Journal of Early Christian Studies* 6.2.

Charlesworth, J.H. (2004). 'Psychobiography: A New and Challenging Methodology in Jesus Research.' In J.H. Ellens and W.G. Rollins (eds), *From Christ to Jesus* (vol. 4, pp. 21–58). Psychology and the Bible: A New Way to Read the Scriptures, vol. 4. Praeger Publishers.

Childs, H. (2000). *The Myth of the Historical Jesus and the Evolution of Consciousness*. Society of Biblical Literature: Dissertation Series. Society of Biblical Literature.

—— (2004). 'The Myth of History and the Evolution of Consciousness: A Jesus Scholar in Psychological Perspective.' In J.H. Ellens and W.G. Rollins (eds), *From Christ to Jesus* (vol. 4, pp. 277–304). Psychology and the Bible: A New Way to Read the Scriptures, vol. 4. Praeger Publishers.

Chilton, B. (2000). *Rabbi Jesus: An Intimate Biography*. Doubleday.

—— (2006). 'Recovering Jesus' Mamzerut.' In J.H. Charlesworth (ed.), *Jesus and Archaeology* (pp. 84–110). Wm.B. Eerdmans..

Chilton, B. and Evans, C.A. (eds), (1999). *Authenticating the Activities of Jesus*. Brill.

Clarke, G. (2001). 'The Origins and Spread of Christianity.' In A.K. Bowman, E. Champlin and A. Lintott (eds), *The Cambridge Ancient History: Second Edition: Volume X: The Augustan Empire, 43 B.C.–A.D. 69* (vol. 10, pp. 848–72). Cambridge University Press.

Coale, A.J., and P. Demeny (1966/1983). *Regional Model Life Tables and Stable Populations*. Academic Press.

Collins, A.Y. (2007). *Mark: A Commentary*. Hermeneia – A Critical and Historical Commentary on the Bible. Fortress Press.

Coltrera, J.T. (ed.) (1981). *Lives, Events and Other Players: Directions in Psychobiography*. Downstate Psychoanalytical Institute Twenty-fifth Anniversary Series, vol. 4. Jason Aronson.

Conant, R.D. (1996). 'Memories of the Death and Life of Spouse: The Role of Images and *Sense of Presence* in Grief.' In D. Klass, P. R. Silverman and S. L. Nickman (eds), *Continuing Bonds: New Understandings of Grief* (pp. 179–96). Series in Death Education, Aging and Health Care. Routledge.

Cotter, W. (1999). *Miracles in Greco-Roman Antiquity: A Sourcebook for the Study of New Testament Miracle Stories*. The Context of Early Christianity. Routledge.

Craffert, P.F. (2008). *The Life of a Galilean Shaman: Jesus of Nazareth in Anthropological-Historical Perspective*. Matrix: The Bible in Mediterranean Perspective (vol. 3). Cascade Books.

Crossan, J.D. (1991). *The Historical Jesus: The Life of a Mediterranean Jewish Peasant*. HarperSanFrancisco.

—— (1998). *The Birth of Christianity: Discovering what Happened in the Years Immediately after the Execution of Jesus*. HarperSanFrancisco.

Crossan, J.D. and Reed, J. L. (2001). *Excavating Jesus: Beneath the Stones, Behind the Texts*. HarperSanFrancisco.

Crossley, J.G. (2004). *The Date of Mark's Gospel: Insight from the Law in Earliest Christianity*. Journal for the Study of the New Testament Supplement Series (vol. 266). T&T Clark.

—— (2006). *Why Christianity Happened: A Sociohistorical Account of Christian Origins (26–50 CE)*. Westminster John Knox Press.

Csordas, T.J. (1994). *The Sacred Self: A Cultural Phenomenology of Charismatic Healing*. University of California Press.

Czachesz, I. (2003). 'The Gospels and Cognitive Science.' In A.A. MacDonald, M.W. Twomey and G. J. Reinink (eds), *Learned Antiquity: Scholarship and Society in the Near East, the Greco-Roman World, and the Early Medieval West* (pp. 25–36). Peeters.

—— (2007). 'The Transmission of Early Christian Thought: Toward a Cognitive Psychological Model.' *Studies in Religion/Sciences Religieuses* 36(1): pp. 65–83.

D'Aquili, E.G. and Newberg, A.B. (1999). *The Mystical Mind: Probing the Biology of Religious Experience.* Theology and the Sciences. Fortress Press.

Daly, L.J. (1993). 'Psychohistory and St. Augustine's Conversion Process.' In E. Ferguson (ed.), *Conversion, Catechumenate, and Baptism in the Early Church* (vol. 11, pp. 67–90). Studies in Early Christianity: A Collection of Scholarly Essays, vol. XI. Garland Publishing.

Davie, G. (2007). *The Sociology of Religion.* BSA New Horizons in Sociology. Sage Publications.

Davies, S.L. (1995). *Jesus the Healer: Possession, Trance, and the Origins of Christianity.* Continuum.

De Jonge, M. (1998). *God's Final Envoy: Early Christology and Jesus' Own View of his Mission.* Studying the Historical Jesus. Wm.B. Eerdmans.

DellaPergola, S. (1992). 'Introduction III: Nombres.' In Élie Barnavi (ed.), *Histoire Universelle des Juifs* (pp. xii–1). Hachette.

DeMause, L. (1982). *Foundations of Psychohistory.* Creative Roots.

Dickie, M.W. (2003). *Magic and Magicians in the Greco-Roman World.* Routledge.

Dixon, S.L. (1999). *Augustine: The Scattered and Gathered Self.* Chalice Press.

Dominian, J. (1998). *One like Us: A Psychological Interpretation of Jesus.* Darton, Longman and Todd.

Drake, H. (2005). 'Models of Christian Expansion.' In W. Harris (ed.), *The Spread of Christianity in the First Four Centuries: Essays in Explanation* (vol. 27, pp. 1–14). Columbia Studies in the Classical Tradition, vol. XXVII. Brill.

Drewermann, E. (1994). *Discovering the God Child Within: A Spiritual Psychology of the Infancy of Jesus.* The Crossroad Publishing Company.

Dunn, J.D. (1970). *Baptism in the Holy Spirit.* The Westminster Press.

—— (1975). *Jesus and the Spirit: A Study of the Religious and Charismatic Experience of Jesus and the First Christians as Reflected in the New Testament.* Wm.B. Eerdmans.

—— (1977/2005). *Unity and Diversity in the New Testament: An Inquiry into the Character of Earliest Christianity: Second edition.* SCM Press/Trinity Press International.

—— (2005). 'Q as Oral Tradition.' In M. Bockmuehl and D.A. Hagner (eds), *The Written Gospel* (pp. 45–69). Cambridge University Press.

Dunn, J.D.G. (1994). 'John the Baptist's Use of Scripture.' In C.A. Evans and W.R. Stegner (eds), *The Gospels and the Scriptures of Israel* (pp. 42–54). Journal for the Study of the New Testament Supplement Series (vol. 104) / Studies in Scripture in Early Judaism and Christianity (vol. 3). Sheffield Academic Press.

—— (2003). *Jesus Remembered.* Christianity in the Making, Volume 1. Wm.B. Eerdmans.

—— (2009). *Beginning in Jerusalem.* Christianity in the Making, Volume 2. Wm.B. Eerdmans.

Edersheim, A. (1888). *The Life and Times of Jesus The Messiah* (2 vols). Oxford.

Edinger, E.F. (1987). *The Christian Archetype: A Jungian Commentary on the Life of Christ.* Studies in Jungian Psychology by Jungian Analysts. Inner City Books.

—— (1996), *The Aion Lectures: Exploring the Self in C. G. Jung's Aion.* Inner City Books.

Edwards, J.R. (2009). *The Hebrew Gospel & The Development of the Synoptic Tradition.* Wm.B. Eerdmans.

Ellens, J.H. (2007). 'Was Jesus Delusional?' In J.H. Ellens (ed.), *Text and Community: Essays in Memory of Bruce M. Metzger: Volume 2* (vol. 20, pp. 110–27). New Testament Monographs. Sheffield Phoenix Press.

Ellens, J.H. and Rollins, W.G. (2004). *Psychology and the Bible: A New Way to Read the Scriptures* (4 vols). Praeger Publishers.

Ellis, E.E. (2002). *The Making of the New Testament Documents.* Brill.

Elms, A.C. (1988). 'Freud as Leonardo: Why the First Psychobiography Went Wrong.' In D.P. McAdams and R.L. Ochberg (eds), *Psychobiography and Life Narratives*. Duke University Press.

—— (1994). *Uncovering Lives: The Uneasy Alliance of Biography and Psychology*. Oxford University Press.

—— (2005). 'Freud as Leonardo: Why the First Psychobiography Went Wrong.' In W.T. Schultz (ed.), *Handbook of Psychobiography* (pp. 210–22). Oxford University Press.

—— (2005). 'If the Glove Fits: The Art of Theoretical Choice in Psychobiography.' In W.T. Schultz (ed.), *Handbook of Psychobiography* (pp. 84–95). Oxford University Press.

Epp, E.J. (2005). *Junia: The First Woman Apostle*. Augsburg Fortress.

Erikson, E.H. (1958/1993). *Young Man Luther: A Study in Psychoanalysis and History*. W.W. Norton & Company.

—— (1968/1994). *Identity: Youth and Crisis*. (Austen Riggs Monograph, no. 7). W.W. Norton & Company.

—— (1969/1993). *Gandhi's Truth: On the Origins of Militant Nonviolence*. W.W. Norton & Company.

Esler, P.F. (2000). 'The Mediterranean Context of Early Christianity.' In P.F. Esler (ed.), *The Early Christian World* (pp. 3–25). Routledge.

Evans, C.A. (1999). 'Jesus and Zechariah's Messianic Hope.' In B. Chilton and C.A. Evans (eds), *Authenticating the Activities of Jesus* (pp. 373–88). Brill.

—— (2009). 'Exorcisms and the Kingdom: Inaugurating the Kingdom of God and Defeating the Kingdom of Satan.' In D.L. Bock and R.L. Webb (eds), *Key Events in the Life of the Historical Jesus: A Collaborative Exploration of Context and Coherence* (pp. 151–79). Wissenschaftliche Untersuchungen zum Neuen Testament (vol. 247). Mohr Siebeck.

Eve, E. (2002). *The Jewish Context of Jesus' Miracles*. Journal for the Study of the New Testament Supplement Series. Sheffield Academic Press.

—— (2005). 'Meier, Miracle and Multiple Attestation.' *Journal for the Study of the Historical Jesus: Volume 3.1* (pp. 23–45). Sage Publications.

Everson, S. (1995). 'Psychology.' In J. Barnes (ed.), *The Cambridge Companion to Aristotle* (pp. 168–94). Cambridge Companions. Cambridge University Press.

Fee, G.D. (1994). *God's Empowering Presence: The Holy Spirit in the Letters of Paul*. Hendrickson Publishers.

—— (2007). *Pauline Christology: An Exegetical-Theological Study*. Hendrickson Publishers.

Feeney, J.A. (1999). 'Adult Romantic Attachment and Couple Relationships.' In J. Cassidy and P.R. Shaver (eds), *Handbook of Attachment: Theory, Research, and Clinical Applications* (pp. 355–77). The Guilford Press.

Fiensy, D.A. (1995). 'The Composition of the Jerusalem Church.' In R. Bauckham (ed.), *The Book of Acts inIits Palestinian Setting* (vol. 4, pp. 213–36). Carlisle/Wm.B. Eerdmans/ The Paternoster Press.

Finn, T.M. (2000). 'Mission and Expansion.' In P.F. Esler (ed.), *The Early Christian World* (pp. 295–315). Routledge.

Fitzmyer, J.A. (2007). *The One Who Is to Come*. Wm.B. Eerdmans.

Fletcher, M.S. (2007). 'On Conversion.' In W.G. Rollins and D.A. Kille (eds), *Psychological Insights into the Bible: Texts and Readings* (pp. 226–7). Wm.B. Eerdmans.

Fletcher, S. (1912). *The Psychology of The New Testament*. Hodder and Stoughton.

Flusser, D. (1988). *Judaism and the Origins of Christianity*. The Magnes Press.

Fowler, J.W. (1981). *Stages of Faith: The Psychology of Human Development and the Quest for Meaning*. HarperSanFrancisco.

Fraley, R.C. and Shaver, P.R. (1999). 'Loss and Bereavement: Attachment Theory and Recent Controversies Concerning "Grief Work" and the Nature of Detachment.' In J. Cassidy and P.R. Shaver (eds), *Handbook of Attachment: Theory, Research, and Clinical Applications* (pp. 735–59). The Guilford Press.

Frankl, V.E. (1969/1988). *The Will to Meaning: Foundations and Applications of Logotherapy.* Meridian.

Fredriksen, P. (1988/2000). *Jesus of Nazareth, King of the Jews: A Jewish Life and the Emergence of Christianity.* Macmillan.

Freud, S. (1900). *Die Traumdeutung.* Franz Deuticke.

Freud, S., Tyson, A. (trans.), Strachey, J. (ed.), Gay, P. (introduction by). (1989; German original 1910). *Leonardo da Vinci and a Memory of his Childhood: The Standard Edition.* W.W. Norton & Company.

Freyne, S. (2000). 'The Galilean World of Jesus.' In P.F. Esler (ed.), *The Early Christian World* (pp. 113–35). Routledge.

—— (2004). *Jesus, a Jewish Galilean: A New Reading of the Jesus-story.* T&T Clark.

Friedman, L.J. (1999). *Identity's Architect: A Biography of Erik H. Erikson.* Harvard University Press.

Frier, B.W. (2000). Demography. In A.K. Bowman, P. Garnsey and D. Rathbone (eds), *The Cambridge Ancient History: Second Edition: Volume XI: The High Empire, A.D. 70–192* (pp. 787–816). Cambridge University Press.

Funk, R.W. and Hoover, R.W. (1993). *The Five Gospels: The Search for the Authentic Words of Jesus.* Polebridge Press.

Funk, R.W. and the Jesus Seminar (1999). *The Gospel of Jesus: According to the Jesus Seminar.* Polebridge Press.

Gamble, H.Y. (1995). *Books and Readers in the Early Church: A History of Early Christian Texts.* Yale University Press.

Garber, D.G., Jr. (2004). 'Traumatizing Ezekiel, the Exilic Prophet.' In J.H. Ellens and W.G. Rollins (eds), *From Genesis to Apocalyptic Vision* (vol. 2, pp. 215–36). Psychology and the Bible: A New Way to Read the Scriptures, vol. 2. Praeger Publishers.

Gerhardsson, B. and Sharpe, E.J. (trans.). (1998). *Memory and Manuscript: Oral Tradition and Written Transmission in Rabbinic Judaism and Early Christianity: With Tradition and Transmission in Early Christianity.* The Biblical Resource Series. Wm.B. Eerdmans.

Goodacre, M. (2002). *The Case against Q: Studies in Markan Priority and the Synoptic Problem.* Trinity Press International.

Goodacre, M. and Perrin, N. (eds). (2004). *Questioning Q: A Multidimensional Critique.* InterVarsity Press.

Goodman, F.D. (1973). 'Apostolics of Yucatán: A Case Study of a Religious Movement.' In E. Bourguignon (ed.), *Religion, Altered States of Consciousness, and Social Change* (pp. 178–218). Ohio State University Press.

Grafton, A. and Williams, M. (2006). *Christianity and the Transformation of the Book: Origen, Eusebius and the Library of Caesarea.* The Belknap Press of the Harvard University Press.

Granqvist, P. (1998). 'Religiousness and Perceived Childhood Attachment: On the Question of Compensation or Correspondence.' *Journal for the Scientific Study of Religion* 37: pp. 350–67).

—— (2002). *Attachment and Religion: An Integrative Developmental Framework.* Acta Universitatis Upsaliensis.

Granqvist, P. and Hagekull, B. (1999). 'Religiousness and Perceived Childhood Attachment: Profiling Socialized Correspondence and Emotional Compensation.' *Journal for the Scientific Study of Religion* 38: pp. 254–73.

Granqvist, P. and Kirkpatrick, L.A. (2000). 'Religious Conversion and Perceived Childhood Attachment: A Meta-analysis.' *International Journal for the Psychology of Religion* 14: pp. 223–50.

Grant, M. (1995). *Greek and Roman Historians: Information and Misinformation.* Routledge.

Haley, J. (1986). *The Power Tactics of Jesus Christ: And Other Essays: Second Edition.* Crown House Publishing Limited.

Hall, D.R. (1998). *The Gospel Framework: Fiction or Fact?* Paternoster Press.

Hall, G.S. (1917/1923). *Jesus the Christ, in the Light of Psychology.* D. Appleton.

Halperin, D.J. (1993). *Seeking Ezekiel: Text and Psychology.* The Pennsylvania State University Press.

—— (2007). 'Seeking Ezekiel.' In W.G. Rollins and D.A. Kille (eds), *Psychological Insights into the Bible: Texts and Readings* (pp. 118–26). Wm.B. Eerdmans.

Halpern, B. (2001). *David's Secret Demons: Messiah, Murderer, Traitor, King.* The Bible in Its World. Wm.B. Eerdmans.

Harland, P.A. (2003). *Associations, Synagogues, and Congregations: Claiming a Place in Ancient Mediterranean Society.* Augsburg Fortress Press.

Harlow, M. and Laurence, R. (2002). *Growing Up and Growing Old in Ancient Rome: A Life Course Approach.* Routledge.

Harris, W. (ed.). (2005). *The Spread of Christianity in the First Four Centuries: Essays in Explanation.* Columbia Studies in the Classical Tradition, vol. 27. Brill.

Hellerman, J.H. (2001). *The Ancient Church as Family.* Augsburg Fortress.

Hengel, M. (1995). *Studies in Early Christology.* T&T Clark.

—— (2005). 'Eye-witness Memory and the Writing of the Gospels.' In M. Bockmuehl and D.A. Hagner (eds), *The Written Gospel* (pp. 70–96). Cambridge University Press.

Hengel, M., Bowden, J. (trans.). (2000). *The Four Gospels and the One Gospel of Jesus Christ: An Investigation of the Collection and Origin of the Canonical Gospels.* Trinity Press International.

Hitchcock, A.W. (1908). *The Psychology of Jesus: A Study of the Development of his Self-Consciousness.* The Pilgrim Press.

Hogan, N. and DeSantis, L. (1996). 'Basic Constructs of a Theory of Adolescent Sibling Bereavement.' In D. Klass, P.R. Silverman and S.L. Nickman (eds), *Continuing Bonds: New Understandings of Grief* (pp. 235–54). Series in Death Education, Aging and Health Care. Routledge.

Holm, N.G. and Belzen, J.A. (eds). (1995). *Sundén's Role Theory – an Impetus to Contemporary Psychology of Religion.* Religionsvetenskapliga skrifter (vol. 27). Åbo Akademi.

Holtzman, H. (1863). *Die Synoptische Evangelien. Ihr Ursprung und geschichtlicher Charakter*, Leipzig.

Hopkins, K. (1998). 'Christian Number and Its Implications.' *Journal of Early Christian Studies* 6(2).

Hood, R.W. Jr. (ed.). (1995). *Handbook of Religious Experience.* Religious Education Press.

Hood, R.W. Jr., Spilka, B., Hunsberger, B. and Gorsuch, R. (1996). *The Psychology of Religion: An Empirical Approach: Second Edition.* The Guilford Press.

Horrell, D.G. (1989/1994). *Sociology and the Jesus Movement.* Continuum.

—— (1996). *Archaeology, History, and Society in Galilee: The Social Context of Jesus and the Rabbis.* Trinity Press International.

—— (2000). 'Early Jewish Christianity.' In P. F. Esler (ed.), *The Early Christian World* (pp. 136–67). Routledge.

Horsley, R.A. (2005). 'Jesus Movements and the Renewal of Israel.' In R.A. Horsley (ed.), *Christian Origins* (vol. 1, pp. 22–46). A People's History of Christianity. Fortress Press.

Hübner, S.R. and. Ratzan, D.M. (eds). (2009). *Growing Up Fatherless in Antiquity.* Cambridge University Press.

Hurtado, L.W. (2003). *Lord Jesus Christ: Devotion to Jesus in Earliest Christianity.* Wm.B. Eerdmans.

—— (2005). *How on Earth Did Jesus Become a God? Historical Questions about Earliest Devotion to Jesus.* Wm.B. Eerdmans.

Hvalvik, R. (2007). 'Jewish Believers and Jewish Influence in the Roman Church until the Early Second Century.' In O. Skarsaune and R. Hvalvik (eds), *Jewish Believers in Jesus: The Early Centuries* (pp. 179–216). Hendrickson Publishers.

—— (2007). 'Named Jewish Believers Connected with the Pauline Mission.' In O. Skarsaune and R. Hvalvik (eds), *Jewish Believers in Jesus: The Early Centuries* (pp. 154–78). Hendrickson Publishers.

James, W. (1902). *The Varieties of Religious Experience: A Study in Human Nature*. Simon & Schuster.

Janowitz, N. (2001). *Magic in the Roman World: Pagans, Jews and Christians*. Religion in the First Christian Centuries. Routledge.

Jeffery, P. (2006). *The Secret Gospel of Mark Unveiled: Imagined Rituals of Sex, Death, and Madness in a Biblical Forgery*. Yale University Press.

Jeremias, J. (1969; German original 1962). *Jerusalem in the Time of Jesus*. SCM Press.

Jobling, D. (2004). 'An Adequate Psychological Approach to the Book of Ezekiel.' In J.H. Ellens and W.G. Rollins (eds), *From Genesis to Apocalyptic Vision* (vol. 2, pp. 203–14). Psychology and the Bible: A New Way to Read the Scriptures, vol. 2. Praeger Publishers.

Johnson, L.T. (1998). *Religious Experience in Earliest Christianity: A Missing Dimension in New Testament Studies*. Fortress Press.

Jones, F.S. (1995). *An Ancient Jewish Christian Source on the History of Christianity: Pseudo-Clementine Recognitions 1.27-71*. Texts and Translations (vol. 37), Christian Apocrypha Series 2. Society of Biblical Literature/Scholars Press.

Jung, C.G. (1959/1969; German original 1951). *Aion: Researches into the Phenomenology of the Self*. Bollingen Series, vol. 20. Princeton University Press.

Kahl, W. (1994). *New Testament Miracle Stories in their Religious-Historical Setting: A Religionsgeschichtliche Comparison from a Structural Perspective*. FRLANT (vol. 163). Vandenhoeck & Ruprecht.

Källstad, T. (1974). *John Wesley and the Bible: A Psychological Study*. Acta Universitatis Upsaliensis Psychologia Religionum (vol. 1). Uppsala.

Kasher, A. (2007). *King Herod: A Persecuted Persecutor: A Case Study in Psychohistory and Psychobiography*. Studia Judaica: Forschungen zur Wissenschaft des Judentums, vol. 36. Walter de Gruyter.

Kee, H.C. (1980). *Christian Origins in Sociological Perspective: Methods and Resources*. The Westminster Press.

Kent, J.A. (1999). *The Psychological Origins of the Resurrection Myth*. Open Gate Press.

Kille, D.A. (2001). *Psychological Biblical Criticism*. Guides to Biblical Scholarship: Old Testament Series. Fortress Press.

Kinman, B. (2009). 'Jesus' Royal Entry into Jerusalem.' In D.L. Bock and R.L. Webb (eds), *Key Events in the Life of the Historical Jesus: A Collaborative Exploration of Context and Coherence* (pp. 383–428). Wissenschaftliche Untersuchungen zum Neuen Testament (vol. 247). Mohr Siebeck.

Kirkpatrick, L.A. (1999). 'Attachment and Religious Representations and Behavior.' In J. Cassidy and P.R. Shaver (eds), *Handbook of Attachment: Theory, Research, and Clinical Applications* (pp. 803–22). The Guilford Press.

—— (2005). *Attachment, Evolution, and the Psychology of Religion*. The Guilford Press.

Klass, D., Silverman, P.R. and Nickman, S.L. (eds). (1996). *Continuing Bonds: New Understandings of Grief*. Series in Death Education, Aging and Health Care. Routledge.

Klauck, H.-J. (2000). *Magic and Paganism in Early Christianity: The World of the Acts of the Apostles*. T&T Clark.

Kloppenborg Verbin, J.S. (2000). *Excavating Q: The History and Setting of the Sayings Gospel*. T&T Clark.

Klutz, T. (2000). 'Paul and the Development of Gentile Christianity.' In P.F. Esler (ed.), *The Early Christian World* (pp. 168–97). Routledge.

Klutz, T.E. (1998). 'The Rhetoric of Science in The Rise of Christianity: A Response to Rodney Stark's Sociological Account of Christianization.' *Journal of Early Christian Studies* 6(2).

Knohl, I. (2009). *Messiahs and Resurrection in 'The Gabriel Revelation.'* The Kogod Library of Judaic Studies. Continuum.

Knohl, I. and Maisel, D. (trans.). (2000). *The Messiah before Jesus: The Suffering Servant of the Dead Sea Scrolls.* University of California Press.

Lambek, M. (1989). 'From Disease to Discourse: Remarks on the Conceptualization of Trance and Spirit Possession.' In C.A. Ward (ed.), *Altered States of Consciousness and Mental Health: A Cross-cultural Perspective* (vol. 12, pp. 36–62). Cross-cultural Research and Methodology Series, vol. 12. Sage Publications, Inc.

Lambers-Petry, D. (2003). 'Verwandte Jesu als Referenzpersonen für das Judenchristentum.' In P.J. Tomson and D. Lambers-Petry (eds), *The Image of the Judaeo-Christians in Ancient Jewish and Christian Literature* (vol. 158, pp. 32–52). Wissenschaftliche Untersuchungen zum Neuen Testament. Mohr Siebeck.

Lampe, P., Steinhauser, M. (trans.). (2003; German original 1989). *From Paul to Valentinus: Christians at Rome in the First Two Centuries.* Fortress Press.

Lang, B. (2004). 'A Romantic Psychologist Reads the Bible: Eugen Drewermann.' In J.H. Ellens and W.G. Rollins (eds), *From Freud to Kohut* (vol. 1, pp. 209–24). Psychology and the Bible: A New Way to Read the Scriptures, vol. 1. Praeger Publishers.

Le Donne, A. (2009). *The Historiographical Jesus: Memory, Typology, and the Son of David.* Baylor University Press.

Leslie, R.C. (1965). *Jesus and Logotherapy.* Abingdon Press.

Levinskaya, I. (1996). *The Book of Acts in Its Diaspora Setting.* The Book of Acts in Its First Century Setting. Wm.B. Eerdmans The Paternoster Press.

Levinson, D.J. (1978). *The Seasons of a Man's Life.* Ballantine Books.

Levison, J.R. (1997). *The Spirit in First-Century Judaism.* Brill.

Lewis, I.M. (1971/1989/2003). *Ecstatic Religion: A Study of Shamanism and Spirit Possession.* Routledge.

—— (1986/1996). *Religion in Context: Cults and Charisma.* Cambridge University Press.

Lietaert Peerbolte, L. (2003). *Paul the Missionary.* Contributions to Biblical Exegesis and Theology. Peeters.

Ling, P.J. (2002). *Martin Luther King, Jr.* Routledge Historical Biographies. Routledge.

Lofland, J. and Stark, R. (1965). 'Becoming a World-Saver: A Theory of Conversion to a Deviant Perspective.' *American Sociological Review* 30: pp. 862–75.

Longenecker, R.N. (1970). *The Christology of Early Jewish Christianity.* Regent College Publishing.

—— (2001). 'Prayer in the Pauline Letters.' In R.N. Longenecker (ed.), *Into God's Presence: Prayer in the New Testament* (pp. 203–27). McMaster New Testament Studies. Wm.B. Eerdmans.

Luce, T. (1997). *The Greek Historians.* Routledge.

Luck, G. (ed. and trans.). (1985). *Arcana Mundi: Magic and the Occult in the Greek and Roman Worlds.* The Johns Hopkins University Press.

Mack, B.L. (1995). *Who Wrote the New Testament?: The Making of the Christian Myth.* HarperSanFrancisco.

—— (2001). *The Christian Myth: Origins, Logic, and Legacy.* Continuum.

MacMullen, R. (1984). *Christianizing the Roman Empire (A.D. 100–400).* Yale University Press.

Malina, B.J. (1998). *Social Science Commentary on the Gospel of John.* Fortress Press.

—— (1999). 'Assessing the Historicity of Jesus' Walking on the Sea: Insights from Cross-culture Social Psychology.' In B. Chilton and C.A. Evans (eds), *Authenticating the Activities of Jesus* (pp. 351–72). Brill.

—— (2001). *The New Testament World: Insights from Cultural Anthropology* (3rd edn.) Westminster John Knox Press.

—— (2002). 'Social-scientific Methods in Historical Jesus Research.' In W. Stegemann, B.J. Malina and G. Theissen (eds), *The Social Setting of Jesus and the Gospels* (pp. 3–26).

Fortress Press.

Malina, B.J. and Neyrey, J.H. (1996). *Portraits of Paul: An Archaeology of Ancient Personality.* Westminster John Knox Press.

Malina, B.J. and Pilch, J.J. (2006). *Social Science Commentary on the Letters of Paul.* Fortress Press.

Malina, B.J. and Rohrbaugh, R.L. (1992). *Social Science Commentary on the Synoptic Gospels.* Fortress Press.

Marcus, J. (1999). 'The Beelzebul Controversy and the Eschatologies of Jesus.' In B. Chilton and C.A. Evans (eds), *Authenticating the Activities of Jesus* (pp. 247–78). Brill.

—— (2000). *Mark 1–8.* The Anchor Bible (vol. 27). Doubleday.

—— (2009). *Mark 8–16.* The Anchor Yale Bible (vol. 27A). Yale University Press.

Markus, R. (1980). 'The Problem of Self-definition: From Sect to Church.' In E. Sanders (ed.), *The Shaping of Christianity in the Second and Third Centuries* (vol. 1, pp. 1–15). Jewish and Christian Self-definition: Volume One. Fortress Press.

Marshall, I.H. (2001). 'Jesus – Example and Teacher of Prayer in the Synoptic Gospels.' In R.N. Longenecker (ed.), *Into God's Presence: Prayer in the New Testament* (pp. 113–31). McMaster new Testament Studies. Wm.B. Eerdmans.

—— (2009). 'The Last Supper.' In D.L. Bock and R.L. Webb (eds), *Key Events in the Life of the Historical Jesus: A Collaborative Exploration of Context and Coherence* (pp. 481–588). Wissenschaftliche Untersuchungen zum Neuen Testament (vol. 247). Mohr Siebeck.

Marshall, M.J. (2005). 'Jesus: Glutton and Drunkard?' *Journal for the Study of the Historical Jesus* 3(1): pp. 47–60.

Martin, R.A. (1974). *Syntactical Evidence of Semitic Sources in Greek Documents.* Society of Biblical Literature.

—— (1987). *Syntax Criticism of the Synoptic Gospels.* Studies in Bible and Early Christianity, vol. 10. The Edwin Mellen Press.

—— (1989). *Syntax Criticism of Johannine Literature, The Catholic Epistles, and the Gospel Passion Accounts.* Studies in Bible and Early Christianity, vol. 18. The Edwin Mellen Press.

Martin, R.P. (1967/1983/1997). *Carmen Christi: Philippians ii. 5–11 in Recent Interpretation and in the Setting of Early Christian Worship.* Cambridge University Press.

Mazlish, B. (1971). 'What is Psycho-History?' In *Transactions of the Royal Historical Society* (Fifth Series) vol. 21 (pp. 79–99). Cambridge University Press.

McAdams, D.P. (2005). 'What Psychobiographers Might Learn from Personality Psychology.' In W.T. Schultz (ed.), *Handbook of Psychobiography* (pp. 64–83). Oxford University Press.

McAdams, D.P. and Ochberg, R.L. (eds) (1988). *Psychobiography and Life Narratives.* Duke University Press.

MacDonald, A., Allison, S., Beck, R. and Norsworthy, L. (2005). 'Attachment to God and Parents: Testing the Correspondence vs. Compensation Hypotheses.' *Journal of Psychology and Christianity* 24: pp. 21–8.

McKechnie, P. (2002). *The First Christian Centuries: Perspectives on the Early Church.* InterVarsity Press.

McKnight, S. (2002). *Turning to Jesus: The Sociology of Conversion in the Gospels.* Westminster John Knox Press.

—— (2005). *Jesus and his Death: Historiography, the Historical Jesus, and Atonement Theory.* Baylor University Press.

—— (2009). 'Jesus and the Twelve.' In D.L. Bock and R.L. Webb (eds), *Key Events in the Life of the Historical Jesus: A Collaborative Exploration of Context and Coherence* (pp. 181–214). Wissenschaftliche Untersuchungen zum Neuen Testament (vol. 247). Mohr Siebeck.

McMichaels, S.W. (1997). *Journey out of the Garden: St. Francis of Assisi and the Process of Individuation.* Paulist Press.

Megitt, J. (2007). 'Psychology and the Historical Jesus.' In F. Watts, *Jesus & Psychology* (pp. 16–26). Darton, Longman and Todd.

Meier, J.P. (1991). *A Marginal Jew: Rethinking the Historical Jesus: Volume I: The Roots of the Problem and the Person.* Doubleday.

—— (1994). *A Marginal Jew: Rethinking the Historical Jesus: Volume II: Mentor, Message, and Miracles.* Doubleday.

—— (2001). *A Marginal Jew: Rethinking the Historical Jesus: Volume III. Companions and Competitors.* Doubleday.

—— (2009). *A Marginal Jew: Rethinking the Historical Jesus: Volume IV: Law and Love.* Yale University Press.

Meissner, W.W. (1992). *Ignatius of Loyola: The Psychology of a Saint.* Yale University Press.

—— (2000). *The Cultic Origins of Christianity: The Dynamics of Religious Development.* The Liturgical Press.

Mellor, R. (1999). *The Roman Historians.* Routledge.

Merz, A. and Tieleman, T. (2008). 'The Letter of Mara Bar Sarapion: Some Comments on its Philosophical and Historical Context.' In A. Houtman, A. de Jong and M. Misset-van de Weg (eds), *Empsychoi Logoi – Religious Innovations in Antiquity: Studies in Honour of Pieter Willem van der Horst*, pp. 107–33. Brill.

Merz, A., Rensberger, D. and Tieleman, T. (eds). (Expected 2011). *Letter to His Son.* Mara Bar Serapion. Scripta Antiquitatis Posterioris ad Ethicam Religionemque pertinentia (SAPERE), vol. XVII. Tübingen, Germany: Mohr Siebeck.

Millard, A. (2000, 2001). *Reading and Writing in the Time of Jesus.* Sheffield Academic Press.

Miller, J.W. (1997). *Jesus at Thirty: A Psychological and Historical Portrait.* Fortress Press.

—— (2004). 'Jesus: A Psychological and Historical Portrait.' In J.H. Ellens and W.G. Rollins (eds), *From Christ to Jesus* (vol. 4, pp. 71–88). Psychology and the Bible: A New Way to Read the Scriptures, vol. 4. Praeger Publishers.

—— (2007). 'Jesus at Thirty.' In W.G. Rollins and D.A. Kille (eds), *Psychological Insights into the Bible: Texts and Readings* (pp. 149–55). Wm.B. Eerdmans.

Muir, S.C. (2006). '"Look How They Love One Another": Early Christian and Pagan Care for the Sick and Other Charity.' In L.E. Vaage (ed.), *Religious Rivalries in the Early Roman Empire and the Rise of Christianity* (vol. 18, pp. 213–32). Studies in Christianity and Judaism. Wilfrid Laurier University Press.

Neusner, J. (1969/1984). *A History of the Jews in Babylonia: I. The Parthian Period.* Brown Judaic Studies, vol. 62. Brill/Scholars Press.

—— (1994). *Introduction to Rabbinic Literature.* The Anchor Bible Reference Library. Doubleday.

Newberg, A.B. and Newberg, S.K. (2005). 'The Neuropsychology of Religious and Spiritual Experience.' In R.F. Paloutzian and C.L. Park (eds), *Handbook of the Psychology of Religion and Spirituality* (pp. 199–215). The Guilford Press.

Newman, C.C., Davila, J.R. and Lewis, G.S. (eds). (1999) *The Jewish Roots of Christological Monotheism: Papers from the St. Andrews Conference on the Historical Origins of the Worship of Jesus.* Supplements to the Journal for the Study of Judaism, vol. 63. Brill.

Nietzsche, F. (1895). *Der Antichrist. Versuch einer Kritik des Christenthums*, Leipzig.

Nock, A. (1933). *Conversion: The Old and the New in Religion from Alexander the Great to Augustine of Hippo.* The Johns Hopkins University Press.

Nodet, E. (2008; French original 2003). *The Historical Jesus? Necessity and Limits of an Inquiry.* T&T Clark.

Normand, C.L., Silverman, P.R. and Nickman, S.L. (1996). 'Bereaved Children's Changing Relationships with the Deceased.' In D. Klass, P.R. Silverman and S.L. Nickman (eds), *Continuing Bonds: New Understandings of Grief* (pp. 87–112). Series in Death Education, Aging and Health Care. Routledge.

Oakes, L. (1997). *Prophetic Charisma: The Psychology of Revolutionary Religious Personalities.* Syracuse University Press.

Ogden, D. (2002, 2009). *Magic, Witchcraft, and Ghosts in the Greek and Roman Worlds: A Sourcebook.* Oxford University Press.

Osiek, C., MacDonald, M.Y. and Tulloch, J.H. (2006). *A Woman's Place: House Churches in Earliest Christianity.* Fortress Press.

Paget, J.C. (2006). 'The Definition of the Terms Jewish Christian and Jewish Christianity in the History of Research.' In O. Skarsaune and R. Hvalvik (eds), *Jewish Believers in Jesus: The Early Centuries* (pp. 22–52). Hendrickson Publishers.

Palmer, M. (2001). *The Jesus Sutras: Rediscovering the Lost Scrolls of Taoist Christianity.* The Random House Publishing Group.

Paloutzian, R.F. (1996). *Inivitation to the Psychology of Religion: Second Edition.* Allyn and Bacon.

Paloutzian, R.F. and Park, C.L. (eds) (2005). *Handbook of the Psychology of Religion and Spirituality.* The Guilford Press.

Pargament, K.I. (1997). *The Psychology of Religion and Coping: Theory, Research, Practice.* The Guilford Press.

Pargament, K.I., Ano, G.G. and Wachholtz, A.B. (2005). 'The Religious Dimension of Coping: Advances in Theory, Research, and Practice.' In R.F. Paloutzian and C.L. Park (eds), *Handbook of the Psychology of Religion and Spirituality* (pp. 479–95). The Guilford Press.

Parkin, T. (1992). *Demography and Roman Society.* Ancient Society and History. The Johns Hopkins University Press.

Pelling, C. (2000). *Literary Texts and the Greek Historian.* Approaching the Ancient World. Routledge.

Pilch, J.J. (2000). *Healing in the New Testament: Insights from Medical and Mediterranean Anthropology.* Fortress Press.

—— (2004). *Visions and Healing in the Acts of the Apostles: How the Early Believers Experienced God.* Liturgical Press.

Pokorny, P. and Lefébure, M. (trans.). (1987; German original 1985). *The Genesis of Christology: Foundations for a Theology of the New Testament.* T&T Clark.

Porter, S.E. (2000). *The Criteria for Authenticity in Historical-Jesus Research: Previous Discussion and New Proposals.* Journal for the Study of the New Testament: Supplement Series. Sheffield Academic Press.

Potter, D.S. (1999). *Literary Texts and the Roman Historian.* Approaching the Ancient World. Routledge.

Powell, M.A. (1998). *Jesus as a Figure in History: How Modern Historians View the Man from Galilee.* Westminster John Knox Press.

Pratscher, W. (2003). Der Herrenbruder Jakobus bei Hegesipp. In P.J. Tomson and D. Lambers-Petry (eds), *The Image of the Judaeo-Christians in Ancient Jewish and Christian Literature* (vol. 158, pp. 147–61). Wissenschaftliche Untersuchungen zum Neuen Testament. Mohr Siebeck.

Pritz, R.A. (1988). *Nazarene Jewish-Christianity: From the End of the New Testament Period until Its Disappearance in the Fourth Century.* The Magnes Press.

Rambo, L.R. (1993). *Understanding Religious Conversion.* Yale University Press.

Redman, J.C.S. (2010). 'How Accurate Are Eyewitnesses? Bauckham and the Eyewitnesses in the Light of Psychological Research.' *Journal of Biblical Literature* 129(1).

Reed, J.L. (2000). *Archaeology and the Galilean Jesus: A Re-examination of the Evidence.* Trinity Press International.

—— (2010). 'Instability in Jesus' Galilee: A Demographic Perspective.' *Journal of Biblical Literature* 129(2): pp. 343–65.

Reimarus, H.S. (1766 unpublished; parts were published in 1774–8). *Fragmente eines Ungenannten.* Gotthold Ephraim Lessing.

Reinhardt, W. (1995). 'The Population Size of Jerusalem and the Numerical Growth of the Jerusalem Church.' In R. Bauckham (ed.), *The Book of Acts in its Palestinian Setting* (pp. 237–66). The Book of Acts in its First Century Setting: Volume 4. Wm.B. Eerdmans/The Paternoster Press.

Reinhartz, A. (2006). 'Rodney Stark and "The Mission to the Jews".' In L.E. Vaage (ed.), *Religious Rivalries in the Early Roman Empire and the Rise of Christianity* (vol. 18, pp. 197–212). Studies in Christianity and Judaism. Wilfrid Laurier University Press.

Rempel, M. (2002). *Nietzsche, Psychohistory, and the Birth of Christianity*. Contributions in Philosophy. Greenwood Press.

Reynolds, F.E. and Capps, D. (eds). (1976). *The Biographical Process: Studies in the History and Psychology of Religion*. Religion and Reason. Mouton & Co.

Richards, E.R. (2004). *Paul and First-Century Letter Writing: Secretaries, Composition and Collection*. InterVarsity Press.

Rives, J. (2005). 'Christian Expansion and Christian Ideology.' In W. Harris (ed.), *The Spread of Christianity in the First Four Centuries: Essays in Explanation* (vol. 27, pp. 15–42). Columbia Studies in the Classical Tradition, vol. 27. Brill.

Robeck, C.M. jr. (2006). *The Azusa Street Mission and Revival: The Birth of the Global Pentecostal Movement*. Thomas Nelson Inc.

Robinson, J.A. (1976). *Redating the New Testament*. Wipf and Stock Publishers repr.

Robinson, J.M., Hoffmann, P. and Kloppenborg, J.S. (eds). (2002). *The Sayings Gospel Q in Greek and English: With Parallels from the Gospels of Mark and Thomas*. Fortress Press.

Rodríguez, R. (2010). *Structuring Early Christian Memory: Jesus in Tradition, Performance, and Text*. Library of New Testament Studies, vol. 407. T&T Clark.

Roelofsma, P.H., Corveleyn, J.M. and Van Saane, J.W. (eds). (2003). *One Hundred Years of Psychology and Religion: Issues and Trends in a Century-long Quest*. VU University Press.

Rollins, W.G. (1999). *Soul and Psyche: The Bible in Psychological Perspective*. Minneapolis, USA: Fortress Press.

Rollins, W.G. and Kille, D.A. (eds). (2007). *Psychological Insights into the Bible: Texts and Readings*. Wm.B. Eerdmans.

Rubin, S.S. (1996). 'The Wounded Family: Bereaved Parents and the Impact of Adult Child Loss.' In D. Klass, P.R. Silverman and S.L. Nickman (eds), *Continuing Bonds: New Understandings of Grief* (pp. 217–32). Series in Death Education, Aging and Health Care. Routledge.

Runyan, W.M. (1982). *Life Histories and Psychobiography: Explorations in Theory and Method*. Oxford University Press.

—— (2005). 'Evolving Conceptions of Psychobiography and the Study of Lives: Encounters with Psychoanalysis, Personality Psychology, and Historical Science.' In W.T. Schultz (ed.), *Handbook of Psychobiography* (pp. 19–41). Oxford University Press.

—— (2005). 'How to Critically Evaluate Alternative Explanations of Life Events: The Case of Van Gogh's Ear.' In W.T. Schultz (ed.), *Handbook of Psychobiography* (pp. 96–103). Oxford University Press.

Runyan, W.M. (ed). (1988). *Psychology and Historical Interpretation*. Oxford University Press.

Saller, R. (1994). *Patriarchy, Property and Death in the Roman Family*. Cambridge University Press.

—— (2001). 'Family and Household.' In A.K. Bowman, P. Garnsey and D. Rathbone (eds), *The Cambridge Ancient History: Second Edition: Volume XI: The High Empire, A.D. 70–192* (pp. 855–74). Cambridge University Press.

—— (2001). 'Status and Patronage.' In A.K. Bowman, P. Garnsey and D. Rathbone (eds), *The Cambridge Ancient History: Second Edition: Volume XI: The High Empire, A.D. 70–192* (pp. 817–54). Cambridge University Press.

—— (2007). 'Household and Gender.' In W. Scheidel, I. Morris and R. Saller (eds), *The Cambridge Economic History of the Greco-Roman World* (pp. 87–112). Cambridge University Press.

Sanders, E. (1993). *The Historical Figure of Jesus*. Penguin Books.

Sanders, J. (1999). 'Did Early Christianity Succeed Because of Jewish Conversions?' *Social Compass* 46(4).

Saroglou, V., Kempeneers, A. and Seynhaeve, I. (2003). 'Need for Closure and Adult Attachment Dimensions as Predictors of Religion and Reading Interests.' In P.H. Roelofsma, J.M. Corveleyn and J.W. Van Saane (eds), *One Hundred Years of Psychology and Religion: Issues and Trends in a Century-long Quest* (pp. 139–54). VU University Press.

Schaberg, J. (2002). *The Resurrection of Mary Magdalene: Legends, Apocrypha, and the Christian Testament*. Continuum.

Scheidel, W. (2007). 'Demography.' In W. Scheidel, I. Morris and R. Saller (eds), *The Cambridge Economic History of the Greco-Roman World* (pp. 38–86). Cambridge University Press.

—— (2009). 'The Demographic Background.' In S.R. Hübner and D.M. Ratzan (eds), *Growing Up Fatherless in Antiquity* (pp. 31–40). Cambridge University Press.

Schmitt, J.J. (2004). 'Psychoanalyzing Ezekiel.' In J.H. Ellens and W.G. Rollins (eds), *From Genesis to Apocalyptic Vision* (vol. 2, pp. 141–84). Psychology and the Bible: A New Way to Read the Scriptures, vol. 2. Praeger Publishers.

Schultz, W.T. (2005). 'Introducing Psychobiography.' In W.T. Schultz (ed.), *Handbook of Psychobiography* (pp. 3–18). Oxford University Press.

Schultz, W.T. (ed.). (2005). *Handbook of Psychobiography*. Oxford University Press.

Schwartz, S. (2010). *Were the Jews a Mediterranean Society? Reciprocity and Solidarity in Ancient Judaism*. Princeton University Press.

Schweitzer, A. (1906/1913; English translation 1910). *Geschichte der Leben-Jesu-Forschung*.

Schweitzer, A., Joy, C.R. (trans.). (1948/1958). *The Psychiatric Study of Jesus: Exposition and Criticism*. The Beacon Press. (Original German version 1910).

Scurlock, J. (2006). *Magico-Medical Means of Treating Ghost-induced Illnesses in Ancient Mesopotamia*. Ancient Magic and Divination (vol. 3). Brill/Styx.

Scurlock, J. and Andersen, B.R. (2005). *Diagnoses in Assyrian and Babylonian Medicine: Ancient Sources, Translations, and Modern Medical Analyses*. University of Illinois Press.

Segal, A.F. (1990). *Paul the Convert: The Apostolate and Apostasy of Saul the Pharisee*. Yale University Press.

Shantz, C. (2009) *Paul in Ecstasy: The Neurobiology of the Apostle's Life and Thought*. Cambridge University Press.

Shaw, T.M. (2000). 'Sex and Sexual Renunciation.' In P.F. Esler (ed.), *The Early Christian World* (pp. 401–21). Routledge.

Shiner, W. (2003). *Proclaiming the Gospel: First-century Performance of Mark*. Trinity Press International.

Shuler, P.L. (1982). *A Genre for the Gospels: The Biographical Character of Matthew*. Fortress Press.

Skarsaune, O. (2002). *In the Shadow of the Temple: Jewish Influences on Early Christianity*. InterVarsity Press.

—— (2006). 'Jewish Believers in Jesus in Antiquity: Problems of Definition, Method, and Sources.' In O. Skarsaune and R. Hvalvik (eds), *Jewish Believers in Jesus: The Early Centuries* (pp. 3–21). Hendrickson Publishers.

Skarsaune, O. and Hvalvik, R. (eds). (2007). *Jewish Believers in Jesus: The Early Centuries*. Hendrickson Publishers.

Smith, M. (1973). *Clement of Alexandria and a Secret Gospel of Mark*. Harvard University Press.

—— (1978; repr. 1998). *Jesus the Magician: Charlatan or Son of God?* Seastone.

Snodgrass, K. (2005). 'The Gospel of Jesus.' In M. Bockmuehl and D.A. Hagner (eds), *The Written Gospel* (pp. 31–44). Cambridge University Press.

Snodgrass, K.R. (2009). 'The Temple Incident.' In D.L. Bock and R.L. Webb (eds), *Key Events in the Life of the Historical Jesus: A Collaborative Exploration of Context and Coherence* (pp. 429–80). Wissenschaftliche Untersuchungen zum Neuen Testament (vol. 247). Mohr Siebeck.

Snow, D. and Phillips, C.L. (1980). 'The Lofland-Stark Conversion Model.' *Social Problems*, vol. 27 (pp. 430–7).

Spence, S. (2004). *The Parting of the Ways: The Roman Church as a Case Study.* Interdisciplinary Studies in Ancient Culture and Religion. Peeters.

Stannard, D.E. (1980). *Shrinking History: On Freud and the Failure of Psychohistory.* Oxford University Press.

Stanton, G. (2002). *The Gospels and Jesus: Second edition.* Oxford Bible Series. Oxford University Press.

Starbuck, E.D. (1899). *The Psychology of Religion.* London.

Stark, R. (1997). *The Rise of Christianity: How the Obscure, Marginal Jesus Movement became the Dominant Religious Force in the Western World in a Few Centuries.* HarperSanFrancisco.

—— (2006). *Cities of God: The Real Story of how Christianity Became an Urban Movement and Conquered Rome.* HarperSanFrancisco.

Stark, R. and Finke, R. (2000). *Acts of Faith: Explaining the Human Side of Religion.* University of California Press.

Stark, R. and Neilson, R.L. (ed.). (2005). *The Rise of Mormonism.* Columbia University Press.

Stegemann, E.W., Stegemann, W. and Dean Jr., O. (trans.). (1999; German original 1995). *The Jesus Movement: A Social History of Its First Century.* Fortress Press.

Stegemann, W., Malina, B.J. and Theissen, G. (eds). (2002). *The Social Setting of Jesus and the Gospels.* Fortress Press.

Stuckenbruck, L.T. and North, W. (eds). (2004). *Early Christian and Jewish Monotheism.* Journal for the Study of the New Testament Supplements. T&T Clark.

Sundén, H. (1966; Swedish original 1959). *Die Religion und die Rollen: Eine psychologische Untersuchung der Frömmigkeit.* Alfred Töpelmann.

—— (1975; Swedish original 1961). *Gott erfahren: Das Rollenangebot der Religionen.* Gütersloher Verlagshaus Gerd Mohn.

—— (1982; Swedish original 1977). *Religionspsychologie: Probleme und Methoden.* Calwer Verlag.

Suomi, S.J. (1999). 'Attachment in Rhesus Monkeys.' In J. Cassidy and P.R. Shaver (eds), *Handbook of Attachment: Theory, Research, and Clinical Applications* (pp. 181–97). The Guilford Press.

Syreeni, K. (2004). 'Coping with the Death of Jesus: The Gospels and the Theory of Grief Work.' In J.H. Ellens and W.G. Rollins (eds), *From Gospel to Gnostics* (vol. 3, pp. 63–86). Psychology and the Bible: A New Way to Read the Scriptures, vol. 3. Praeger Publishers.

Szaluta, J. (1999). *Psychohistory: Theory and Practice.* American University Studies: Series XIX: General Literature, vol. 30. Peter Lang Publishing.

Thatcher, T. (2006). *Why John WROTE a Gospel: Jesus – Memory – History.* Westminster John Knox Press.

Theissen, G. (2001; German original 2000). *De godsdienst van de eerste christenen: Een theorie van het oerchristendom [Die Religion der ersten Christen].* Kampen/Averbode.

—— (2007). *Erleben und Verhalten der ersten Christen: Eine Psychologie des Urchristentums.* Gütersloher Verlagshaus.

—— (2007). 'Glossolalia: Language of the Unconscious.' In W.G. Rollins and D.A. Kille (eds), *Psychological Insights into the Bible: Texts and Readings* (pp. 219–25). Wm.B. Eerdmans.

Theissen, G., Merz, A. and Bowden, J. (trans.). (1998; German original 1996). *The Historical Jesus: A Comprehensive Guide [Der historische Jesus: Ein Lehrbuch].* Fortress Press.

Theissen, G., Winter, D. and Boring, M.E. (trans.). (2002; German original 1997). *The Quest for the Plausible Jesus: The Question of Criteria [Kriterienfrage in der Jesusforschung].* Westminster John Knox Press.

Thiselton, A.C. (2000). *The First Epistle to the Corinthians: A Commentary on the Greek Text.* The New International Greek Testament Commentary. Wm.B. Eerdmans/The Paternoster Press.

Thompson, M.B. (1998). 'The Holy Internet: Communication between Churches in the First Christan Generation.' In R. Bauckham (ed.), *The Gospels for All Christians: Rethinking the Gospel Audiences* (pp. 49–70). Wm.B. Eerdmans.

Tomson, P. (2003). 'The Wars against Rome, the Rise of Rabbinic Judaism and of Apostolic Gentile Christianity, and the Judaeo-Christians: Elements for a Synthesis.' In P.J. Tomson and D. Lambers-Petry (eds), *The Image of the Judaeo-Christians in Ancient Jewish and Christian Literature* (vol. 158, pp. 1–31). Wissenschaftliche Untersuchungen zum Neuen Testament. Mohr Siebeck.

Torres, J.O. (2008). *The Reluctant Prophet: A Psychobiography of Archbishop Oscar Romero.* Verlag Dr. Müller.

Trebilco, P. (2004). *The Early Christians in Ephesus from Paul to Ignatius.* Wissenschaftliche Untersuchungen zum Neuen Testament. Mohr Siebeck.

Tripolitis, A. (2002). *Religions of the Hellenistic-Roman Age.* Wm.B. Eerdmans.

Trumbower, J.A. (1994). 'The Role of Malachi in the Career of John the Baptist.' In C.A. Evans and W.R. Stegner (eds), *The Gospels and the Scriptures of Israel* (pp. 28–41). Journal for the Study of the New Testament Supplement Series (vol. 104)/Studies in Scripture in Early Judaism and Christianity (vol. 3). Sheffield Academic Press.

Tuckett, C.M. (1996). *Q and the History of Early Christianity: Studies on Q.* T&T Clark.

Turcan, R. and Nevill, A. (trans.). (1996; French original 1989, 1992). *The Cults of the Roman Empire.* Blackwell.

Twelftree, G.H. (1993). *Jesus the Exorcist: A Contribution to the Study of the Historical Jesus.* Hendrickson Publishers/J.C.B. Mohr (Paul Siebeck).

—— (1999). *Jesus the Miracle Worker: A Historical and Theological Study.* InterVarsity Press.

Tyson-Rawson, K. (1996). 'Relationship and Heritage. Manifestations of Ongoing Attachment Following Father Death.' In D. Klass, P.R. Silverman and S.L. Nickman (eds), *Continuing Bonds: New Understandings of Grief* (pp. 125–45). Series in Death Education, Aging and Health Care. Routledge.

Vaage, L.E. (2006). 'Why Christianity Succeeded (in) the Roman Empire.' In L.E. Vaage (ed.), *Religious Rivalries in the Early Roman Empire and the Rise of Christianity* (vol. 18, pp. 253–78). Studies in Christianity and Judaism. Wilfrid Laurier University Press.

Van Aarde, A. (2001). *Fatherless in Galilee: Jesus as Child of God.* Trinity Press International.

—— (2002). 'Jesus as Fatherless Child.' In W. Stegemann, B.J. Malina and G. Theissen (eds), *The Social Setting of Jesus and the Gospels* (pp. 65–84). Fortress Press.

Van Aarde, A.G. (2004). 'Social Identity, Status Envy, and Jesus as Fatherless Child.' In J. H. Ellens and W. G. Rollins (eds), *From Christ to Jesus* (vol. 4, pp. 223–46). Psychology and the Bible: A New Way to Read the Scriptures. Praeger Publishers.

Van IJzendoorn, M.H. and Sagi, A. (1999). 'Cross-Cultural Patterns of Attachment: Universal and Contextual Dimensions.' In J. Cassidy and P.R. Shaver (eds), *Handbook of Attachment: Theory, Research, and Clinical Applications* (pp. 713–34). The Guilford Press.

Van Os, B. (2007). 'Psychological Method and the Historical Jesus: The Contribution of Psychobiography.' In J.H. Ellens (ed.), *Text and Community: Essays in Memory of Bruce M. Metzger: Volume 2* (vol. 20, pp. 131–48). New Testament Monographs. Sheffield Phoenix Press.

—— (2008). 'The Jewish Recipients of Galatians.' In S.E. Porter (ed.). *Paul: Jew, Greek, and Roman* (pp. 51–64). Pauline Studies (vol. 5). Brill.

—— (2009). 'John's Last Supper and the Resurrection Dialogues.' In P.N. Anderson, F. Just and T. Thatcher (eds), *John, Jesus and History, Volume 2: Aspects of Historicity in the Fourth Gospel*. Early Christianity and Its Literature. Society of Biblical Literature.

Verhoef. E. (2005). 'The Church of Philippi in the First Six Centuries of our Era.' *HTS Teologiese Studies/Theological Studies*, vol. 61/1–2, pp. 565–92.

Vermes, G. (1981). *Jesus the Jew: A Historian's Reading of the Gospels*. Fortress Press.

—— (1993). *The Religion of Jesus the Jew*. Fortress Press.

Vines, M.E. (2002). *The Problem of Markan Genre: The Gospel of Mark and the Jewish Novel*. Society of Biblical Literature.

Ward, C.A. (1989). 'The Cross-cultural Study of Altered States of Consciousness and Mental Health.' In C.A. Ward (ed.), *Altered States of Consciousness and Mental Health: A Cross-cultural Perspective* (pp. 15–35). Cross-cultural Research and Methodology Series, vol. 12. Sage Publications.

—— (1989). 'Possession and Exorcism: Psychopathology and Psychotherapy in a Magico-religious Context.' In C.A. Ward (ed.), *Altered States of Consciousness and Mental Health: A Cross-cultural Perspective* (pp. 125–44). Cross-cultural Research and Methodology Series, vol. 12. Sage Publications.

Watts, F. (ed.). (2007). *Jesus & Psychology*. Darton, Longman and Todd.

Webb, R.L. (1991). *John the Baptizer and Prophet: A Socio-Historical Study*. Sheffield Academic Press.

——. (2009). 'Jesus' Baptism by John: Its Historicity and Significance.' In D.L. Bock and R.L. Webb (eds), *Key Events in the Life of the Historical Jesus: A Collaborative Exploration of Context and Coherence* (pp. 95–150). Wissenschaftliche Untersuchungen zum Neuen Testament (vol. 247). Mohr Siebeck.

Wenham, J. (1992). *Redating Matthew, Mark and Luke: A Fresh Assault on the Synoptic Problem*. InterVarsity Press.

White, L.M. (2004). *From Jesus to Christianity: How Four Generations of Visionaries and Storytellers Created the New Testament and Christian Faith*. HarperSanFrancisco.

Wilkins, M.J. (2009). 'Peter's Declaration Concerning Jesus' Identity in Caesarea Philippi.' In D.L. Bock and R.L. Webb (eds), *Key Events in the Life of the Historical Jesus: A Collaborative Exploration of Context and Coherence* (pp. 293–382). Wissenschaftliche Untersuchungen zum Neuen Testament (vol. 247). Mohr Siebeck.

Willitts, J. (2005). 'Presuppositions and Procedures in the Study of the "Historical Jesus": Or, Why I Decided not to be a "Historical Jesus" Scholar.' *Journal for the Study of the Historical Jesus: Volume 3.1* (pp. 61–108). Sage Publications.

Wilson, A. (1992). *Jesus: A Life*. W.W. Norton and Company.

Wolters, A. (2008) 'IOYNIAN (Romans 16:7) and the Hebrew Name Yehunni.' *Journal of Biblical Literature*. vol. 127/2.

Woolf, G. (2001). 'Literacy.' In A.K. Bowman, P. Garnsey and D. Rathbone (eds), *The Cambridge Ancient History: Second Edition: Volume XI: The High Empire, A.D. 70–192* (pp. 875–97). Cambridge University Press.

Wortham, R. (2006). 'Urbanization, Religious Pluralism, Cultural Continuity, and the Expansion of Gnostic Communities.' *Interdisciplinary Journal of Research on Religion*, vol. 2 (pp. 1–20).

Wrede, W. (1901). *Das Messiasgeheimnis in den Evangelien. Zugleich ein Beitrag zum Verständnis des Markusevangeliums*. Göttingen.

Wright, N. (1992). *The New Testament and the People of God*. Fortress Press.

—— (1996). *Jesus and the Victory of God:* Christian Origins and the Question of God. Fortress Press.

—— (2001). 'The Lord's Prayer as a Paradigm of Christian Prayer.' In R.N. Longenecker (ed.), *Into God's Presence: Prayer in the New Testament* (pp. 132–54). McMaster New Testament Studies. Wm.B. Eerdmans.

—— (2003). *The Resurrection of the Son of God.* Christian Origins and the Question of God. Fortress Press.

Wulff, D.M. (1997). *Psychology of Religion: Classic and Contemporary: Second Edition.* John Wiley & Sons.

Zetterholm, M. (2003). *The Formation of Christianity in Antioch: A Social-scientific Approach to the Separation between Judaism and Christianity.* Routledge.

Zetterholm, M. (ed.), (2007). *The Messiah in Early Judaism and Christianity.* Fortress Press.

INDEX OF BIBLICAL REFERENCES

INDEX OF AUTHORS